More praise for *Twelve by Twelve* by William Powers

"How much is enough? And what is really important? These are questions that William Powers runs into again and again in his time off the grid in the U.S. and overseas, but his humble and contemplative memoir handles them with freshness and honesty, recognizing that sometimes asking the questions is more important than finding the 'right' answers."

— Lester R. Brown, president of Earth Policy Institute and author of *Plan B 4.0: Mobilizing to Save Civilization*

"A true story of rediscovery of and reconnection with fundamental truths and values. Enchanting and heartwarming, *Twelve by Twelve* is a modern-day *Walden*."

— Dr. Thomas E. Lovejoy, president of the Heinz Center for Science, Economics, and the Environment

"A compassionate yet powerful personal odyssey into the heart of what it means to choose to live with less in a world gone mad for more. William Powers's *Twelve by Twelve* is not only a retreat of mind from which we all can draw sustenance as we gird ourselves to confront a world heading for catastrophe, it is also a template we can use to ask ourselves what, really, is important in our lives."

— Mira Kamdar, author of *Planet India*

Praise for *Blue Clay People* by William Powers

"A haunting account of one man's determination and the struggles of a people living in a deeply troubled country."　　　— *Booklist*

"William Powers is sensitive, reflective, and a fine stylist."

— *St. Louis Post-Dispatch*

"In this painful and joyful narrative, William Powers provides a vital stratum of truth about life and foreign aid in the worst parts of the underdeveloped world." — Robert D. Kaplan, author of *Balkan Ghosts*

"A masterful storyteller... Powers has a keen ear for dialogue and dialect, and his prose is lovely and lyrical.... [His] honesty about his own flaws places him in the congregation rather than the pulpit."

— *Providence Journal*

"Powers sketches scenes of transcendent beauty and grotesque violence, and writes with disarming honesty."

— *Publishers Weekly*, starred review

"Few authors sustain a tone of outraged hopefulness through a whole book. Dickens could, as could any number of gloomy Russians, but not many Americans. William Powers is an exception."

— *Charlotte Observer*

"A searing memoir... recalls the literary travelogues of writers such as Mark Salzman and Bruce Chatwin."

— Jeffrey Pepper Rodgers,
contributor to NPR's *All Things Considered*

"*Blue Clay People* is written in a clear style, with a narrative structure that keeps the reader's attention." — *San Francisco Chronicle*

Praise for *Whispering in the Giant's Ear* by William Powers

"As an aid worker living in Bolivia, Powers did not just witness the change; he was immersed in the action, forced to juggle the country's internal conflict with his environmental organization's mission of saving the rain forest.... What results is a deeply personal and informative chronicle of Powers' ambitions, the Indians' ambitions and perhaps most importantly in a country as physically diverse and dramatic as Bolivia, nature's ambitions." — *Publishers Weekly*

"A rip-roaring chronicle of the struggles and compromises, doubts and determination needed to implement the Kyoto accords — an international agreement setting targets for industrialized countries to cut their greenhouse-gas emissions — in Bolivia." — *Newsweek*

TWELVE
— BY —
TWELVE

ALSO BY THE AUTHOR

Blue Clay People: Seasons on Africa's Fragile Edge

*Whispering in the Giant's Ear: A Frontline Chronicle
from Bolivia's War on Globalization*

TWELVE
— BY —
TWELVE

A ONE-ROOM CABIN OFF THE GRID & BEYOND THE AMERICAN DREAM

WILLIAM POWERS

New World Library
Novato, California

New World Library
14 Pamaron Way
Novato, California 94949

Text design by Tona Pearce Myers
Illustrations by Hannah Morris, Morridesign.com

Excerpt on page 213 from "After Making Love We Hear Footsteps" from *Mortal Acts, Mortal Words* by Galway Kinnell, copyright © 1980 by Galway Kinnell. Reprinted by permission of Houghton Mifflin Harcourt Publishing Company.

Excerpt on page 214 from "Prayer" from *The Past* by Galway Kinnell, copyright © 1985 by Galway Kinnell. Reprinted by permission of Houghton Mifflin Harcourt Publishing Company.

Excerpt on page 239 from *The Quotidian Mysteries* by Kathleen Norris, copyright © 1998 by Kathleen Norris. Reprinted by permission of Paulist Press, Inc.

Library of Congress Cataloging-in-Publication Data
Powers, William, date.
 Twelve by twelve : a one-room cabin off the grid and beyond the American dream / William Powers.
     p.   cm.
Includes bibliographical references and index.
ISBN 978-1-57731-897-2 (pbk. : alk. paper)
 1. Sustainable living—United States. 2. Alternative lifestyles—United States. 3. Self-reliant living. 4. Green movement—United States. 5. Environmentalism—United States. 6. Conservation of natural resources—United States. 7. Powers, William, 1971– I. Title.
GF78.P68 2010
333.72—dc22   2010003839

ISBN 978-1-57731-897-2
Printed in Canada on 100% postconsumer-waste recycled paper

g New World Library is a proud member of the Green Press Initiative.

10 9 8 7 6 5 4 3 2 1

You need not leave your room. Remain sitting at your table and listen.
You need not even listen, simply wait. You need not even wait, just learn
to become quiet and still, and solitary. The world will freely offer itself to
you unmasked. It has no choice; it will roll in ecstasy at your feet.

— Franz Kafka

There is another world, but it is in this one.

— Paul Éluard

CONTENTS

PART II: TWELVE

PREFACE

AT THE BEGINNING OF 2007, I returned to America after a decade of aid and conservation work in Africa and Latin America. It was a rough homecoming. More than simple culture shock, I felt increasingly disillusioned. Though many of my projects abroad were successful, reducing poverty and protecting local rainforests, a destructive global system hammered at the broader picture. For example, Nobel laureate scientists have predicted that global warming could cause half of the planet's plant and animal species to become extinct in just a few decades. My creed — *We can learn to live in harmony with each other and nature* — was stressed to the breaking point.

I landed in New York City and began asking myself a daunting question: How could humanity transition to gentler, more responsible ways of living by replacing attachment to things with deeper relationships to people, nature, and self?

Fortunately, I stumbled upon someone with some clues: Dr. Jackie Benton. The first time I met this slight, sixty-year-old physician, she was stroking a honeybee's wings in front of her twelve-foot by twelve-foot, off-the-grid home on No Name Creek in North Carolina.

She struck me as someone who had achieved self-mastery in these confusing times, but discovering how she'd done this would prove to be a riddle intricately connected to the house itself.

At once poet and scientist, Jackie slowly revealed to me a philosophy that is neither purely secular nor purely spiritual. People call her a "wisdomkeeper," a Native American term for women elders who ignite deeper questions in us. Wisdomkeepers differ from what you might call Wise Ones. Wise Ones lay it all out for us — here's your life's blueprint. Wisdomkeepers dig to the Latin root of the word *education*, "drawing forth" what's already inside of us, and embody the curious original meaning of the word *revelation* (*re-velar*): "to veil again."

Over the course of eighteen months, I exchanged letters with Jackie and visited her community several times. But most significantly — and, frankly, it still feels astonishing to me — I came to live, alone, for forty days, in her tiny house in the spring of 2007. This book tells the story of what happened there. I didn't plan to live 12 x 12, and I certainly didn't plan to write about it. But as I told friends about Jackie and her biofuel-brewing, organic-farming neighbors, about the striking setting of the No Name Creek wildlands, and about the profound changes the experience wrung out of me, they overwhelmingly encouraged me to share the tale. So here it is, presented as a loose chronology of my time in the 12 x 12 — framed in two parts, twelve chapters each — along with twelve of Jackie's Socratic thoughts, placed periodically and marked with the symbol 🗐. However, 12 x 12 solitude also helped me synthesize wisdom from indigenous people I met during a decade abroad; I've included some of their stories as well, so the book ranges far beyond the house's dimensions.

Jackie did ask one thing of me: that I change her name. Her path, she explained, is increasingly private. She is glad this story is being told — so long as it doesn't draw more people to the 12 x 12. Out of respect for her wishes, I've disguised her name and certain identifying details, such as the names of surrounding towns and neighbors.

Finally, I've included a brief appendix to suggest further reading and action, and I have an expanded and regularly updated version at www.williampowersbooks.com.

By sharing this journey in a very intimate fashion, I hope to help release fresh questions and insights about where we are, where we are going, and ultimately, how we might uncover hope for personal and global healing.

PART I

TWELVE

1. THE SHAPE OF THE WORLD

"I KNOW A DOCTOR who makes eleven thousand dollars a year," my mother said.

I looked up, suddenly curious. "She's an acquaintance of mine," my mother continued, passing me a basket of bread across the dinner table. "Lives an hour from here in a twelve-foot by twelve-foot house with no electricity."

I noticed my father's empty seat next to her and felt my chest tighten. He was still in the hospital. We still weren't sure if they'd been able to remove the entire tumor from his colon. I'd come down to North Carolina from New York City, where I'd recently settled after several years in Bolivia, so that I could be with him as he recovered.

My mother went on: "She's a tax resister. As a senior physician she could make three hundred thousand dollars, but she only accepts eleven so as to avoid war taxes. Did you know that fifty cents out of every dollar goes to the Pentagon?"

"Hold on. So this doctor —"

"Jackie Benton."

"— Doctor Jackie Benton, she lives in a *twelve by twelve* house? That's physically impossible. That bookcase is twelve by twelve."

"She doesn't have any running water, either. She harvests the rainwater from her roof. Haven't you heard of her? She's a bit of a local celeb."

I stopped eating and looked out the window. The rust-colored sky above my parents' condo hovered exquisitely between orange and red. I could hear the hum of the refrigerator, the rush of cars going by. That distinctive sky momentarily brought me back to Lake Titicaca in Bolivia, beneath a similar red-orange glow, and the echo of a question a shaman had asked me: *What's the shape of the world?*

Something moved inside me. I looked over at my mom and asked, "Do you have any way of contacting Dr. Benton?"

"I have her mobile number," my mom said. "She keeps it off but does check messages every now and then. People are always trying to reach her. And that's made her even more reclusive."

JACKIE DIDN'T CALL BACK. As the days turned into a week, I left several unreturned messages on her voice mail. Meanwhile, when I wasn't visiting my father in the hospital, I asked others in town about this mysterious doctor. She provoked a range of opinions and was called everything from "commie" to "saint." As I eventually learned, Jackie had been a communist in the early 1970s; once, while counter-protesting at a KKK rally in Greensboro, five of her communist friends were shot to death by Klansmen. The police knew who did it, but the good-ol'-boy perpetrators were never prosecuted.

Jackie went on to marry one of her leftist friends, had two daughters, and settled into a life of doctoring; she mostly worked in the state system, attending to African Americans and undocumented Latin Americans in rural clinics. As a mother, she taught her kids symbolic tax resistance as they grew up — like not paying the telephone tax and taking $10.40 off her 1040 form each year, with a note to the IRS saying it was to protest defense spending — while leaving her more radical activism behind. She divorced but remained close friends with her ex-husband. When her daughters went away to college, she continued to work full-time but lowered her income to eleven thousand dollars to avoid paying any taxes at all.

Even those who were offended by her admitted she was a child of the South, sprung from local soil, and most people spoke of her with respect, whether deep or grudging. After all, she'd given up all that money, dedicated her life to serving the poor with her doctoring, and survived on the radical edge of how simply one can live in America. She'd also developed a unique blend of science and spirituality, creating a kind of third way that appealed to secular and religious perspectives alike. "Jackie's a wisdomkeeper," one of her friends told me. When I asked what that was, she said, "Wisdomkeepers are an old tradition, goes back to the Native Americans. They're elder women who inspire us to dig more deeply into life."

If Jackie had any wisdom, she was guarding it. You couldn't exactly look her up on Google Maps. Her dirt road didn't show up on any map. More than that, she wasn't living 12 x 12 just as an expression of simplicity. She chose those tiny dimensions, as she chose her tiny salary, for pragmatic reasons: in North Carolina, any structure that's twelve feet by twelve feet or less does not count as a house. It's considered to be a tool shed or gardening shack — if it's even considered. If you live 12 x 12, you don't pay property tax and don't receive electric lines, sewage, or roads from the state. So I was leaving voice mail messages for someone who, from a certain official point of view, was invisible.

During that time, a family friend in Chapel Hill invited me to run in a local 5K race. He said, "Come on, it'll get you out of the hospital and give you a break from calling... What's her name?"

"Jackie."

"Right. Plus you'll love the place where they're holding the race."

As we drove in his SUV through Chapel Hill and onto the highway, he enthusiastically described the hills, forest, and lake of the race site, but I was baffled when we arrived at an industrial park. Sure, it was green. But the hills were landfills covered with sod, the lake artificial, the woods a monoculture. The place was spawned by AutoCAD, not Mother Nature. Like a bad toupee, it looked all the worse for trying to be something it wasn't.

I ran amid two hundred others past the high-tech military suppliers, between the human-made forests and lakes, and I realized it wasn't just the aesthetics of the place that bothered me, but what it symbolized: the Flat World.

New York Times columnist Thomas Friedman presents the phenomenon in a positive light in his best-selling book *The World Is Flat*. Technologies like the internet, he observes, are breaking down hierarchies. Thanks to bandwidth, companies can easily outsource certain jobs to India, China, and elsewhere; hence, people now compete on equal footing, according to talent, on a globalized economic playing field. World capitalism, guided by government incentives, will save us from environmental collapse, Friedman further argues, by inventing clean technologies to allow for the increased global consumption.

It's not an argument to be taken lightly. Though world inequality is unfortunately on the rise, the "flat" system has led to quick economic growth in certain countries like India and China. In our ever more interconnected world, environmental and human rights horrors can be more efficiently exposed. In theory, a world that's flat gives us previously unimaginable intellectual and economic freedoms, so why was I feeling the Flat World blues?

Friedman didn't invent a flat world, but rather his metaphor articulates a truth about the way we have come to imagine the twenty-first century. The metaphor carries a host of negative connotations: The world has hit a flat note. Industrial agriculture creates a flat taste, and multinational corporations flatten our uniqueness into *Homo economicus* serving a OneWorld™ Uniplanet. A once-natural atmosphere has been flattened by global warming: every square foot of it now contains 390 ppm of carbon dioxide, though up until two hundred years ago the atmosphere contained 275 ppm (and 350 ppm is considered the safe upper threshold for our planet). Rainforests are flattened to make cattle pastures; a living ocean is depleted and flattened by overfishing; vibrant cultures are steamrolled to the edge of extinction. Have the well-rounded objectives of America's Founding Fathers — life, liberty, and the pursuit of happiness — been flattened to a single organizing principle: the unification of greed?

When the 5K race was over, I left the awards ceremony and looked into the lifeless water of the lake beside Dow Chemical. Since returning to the United States, I felt something wasn't right with me. I'd been a squid out of ink, the joy squeezed right out of me. I closed my eyes and traveled back to Bolivia, to the banks of Lake Titicaca and the particular moment I'd remembered while sitting with my mother.

It happened just three months back. Two friends, she American and he British, were getting married. They'd lived in Bolivia for years, working with the country's indigenous people, and an Aymara shaman was going to marry them. Before the ceremony began, I stood with the shaman as we admired the most extraordinary sky, a rusty orange-and-red blend, and the famous Andean lake, which was the size of a small sea, its unseen far shores in Peru. We stood at thirteen thousand feet, and the light cast a gossamer shimmer over three distant islands. Above them, the jagged Andes.

The shaman looked out over the landscape and asked me, "What's the shape of the world?"

Farther up the lake, I saw the bride and groom mingling with other Bolivian and American friends, all dressed in their finest. About half the Americans lived and worked in Bolivia; the other half were just there for the week. Honamti, the shaman, was dressed in an olive jacket and jeans and looked nearly iconic, his long hair tied back in a ponytail, an ambiguous expression in his dark eyes.

"The world?" I finally said. "It's round."

"How is it round?" Honamti asked.

I showed him, putting my two pointer fingers together in front of me and drawing a downward circle.

"That's how most people imagine it," he said. "But we Aymaras disagree."

He was silent for a long moment. Alpacas and sheep grazed in the distance, shepherded together by an Aymara woman in a colorful, layer-cake skirt. A pejerey leapt from and plunged back into Lake Titicaca, sending out rippling circles. "We say that the earth is round, but in a different way," Honamti finally said, and he traced an upward circle, the opposite of how I'd drawn it, beginning at his belly and finishing at his heart. He traced the shape slowly. Amazed, I watched it spring to life in the landscape. His upward stroke began with the lake, curved up the sides of the Andes, and finished gloriously with the dome of the sky.

"And it's also round like this." This time he traced a circle that began at his heart and went outward toward the lake, finishing two feet in front of his body. And the earth took that shape, as the lakeshore curled into the base of the distant mountains and then into the sky's horizon, a perfect outward circle.

"And it's also round like this." Keeping his hands two feet in front of him, he traced a slow circle back into himself. The circle finished at some hidden place inside, the outward world circling into our inner world.

Somebody called over to Honamti; the ceremony was to begin. But before the Aymara man turned to go, I asked him, "Which of the three is it? What's the shape of the world?"

He answered by repeating: "What's the shape of the world?"

I opened my eyes: the lifeless Dow Chemical lake before me, Honamti's question/answer echoing in my head. Did the world have to be flat? Was it too late to imagine other shapes?

"YOU'RE A MAN WITHOUT A COUNTRY," my father said, looking up at me from his sickbed.

I looked out the hospital window: three smokestacks blew gray smoke into a gray sky. The backs of adjacent six- or seven-story gray-brick buildings. Beside me, the muted beeping of an IV drip; the smell of fast food and Ben Gay. Fluorescent lights and the television's flicker illuminated my father's slightly ashen face.

Suddenly, and despite the dreary surroundings, I felt a rush of love for him. He'd given me gifts of stability, diligence, and an appreciation for the power of ideas. He was telling me, his thirty-six-year-old son, that I was a man without a country not in criticism but out of love. He was right: acute culture shock had pushed me into a kind of exile.

I touched him on the shoulder, pushed the hair back off his forehead, remembering something from my childhood. One year, during the Fourth of July barbecue, he taught me how to grill London broil. On that humid day the forested spaces around our Long Island home were alive with box turtles. This was before urban sprawl defined the island, before our magical woods were cleared for McMansions. My sister and I found a turtle and brought it home and set it loose. *Billy*, my dad called over to me, *I want to show you something*. As I watched his hairy forearm expertly flip the meat, I loved him. The sound of fireworks in the distance; a red, white, and blue flag up on its pole, where my father raised it every public holiday. I felt organically connected to my home, my family, and our prosperous society; to the yard, the turtle-filled woods, the smell of meat grilling.

The sound of sizzling meat drew me out of my reverie, back to the hospital room: a Wendy's ad on TV, reminding me of the hospital's preferred food option. My father dozed off to the sizzle of burgers and a corporate jingle, and I walked through the labyrinth building, past hundreds of patients, to the source of many of their health problems and heart disease: greasy hamburgers. UNC Medical Center had outsourced meal service to Wendy's.

I brought a tray of burger and fries to a table by the window. Outside was a parking garage, its asphalt stacked five stories high, packed with vehicles — the source of many of earth's health problems. I checked my voice mail; still no response from Jackie. I considered calling her again but decided against it — I'd already left three messages. Beyond the parking lot, a monoculture of pines and the highway to the mall. I tried to *feel* something for the landscape, but it lacked shape.

Worse, doubt gnawed at me that the past decade of my professional life had been for naught. I'd labored incredibly hard as a humanitarian aid and conservation worker in places like Liberia, Sierra Leone, and Bolivia. Part of my job was to help people living on the borders of the rainforest improve their lives economically while defending their forest. I've got a toolkit: ecotourism, sustainable timber, nontimber forest products, shade-grown organic coffee, political organizing and advocacy. In the end, the logic goes, if the rainforest pays, it stays. If these folks earn their living from it, they'll protect it from the multinationals coming to cut it down, whether for mahogany, for soy and sugar plantations, or for iron, gold, and diamond mines.

I have helped create rainforest-protecting municipal reserves, indigenous areas, and community forests that have successfully resisted logging, mining, and industrial farming. But these efforts have been trounced by the global trend. Have I been merely rearranging the deck chairs on the *Titanic*? From 1998 to 2008 the world's rainforests have disappeared at a rate of an acre every two minutes, approximately 1 percent a year. At this rate, in forty years we will have destroyed the last of them.

When I fly over the rainforest into these places, I feel the irony. Planes spew dangerous global warming gasses into the stratosphere that hasten the desertification that fuels rainforest decline. I don't want to get on the plane, and yet, I have to get on the plane.

I get on the plane. Below, there's West Africa's Upper Guinea Rainforest. There's the Bolivian and Brazilian Amazon, Central Africa's Congo River Basin Rainforest, Central America's Monte Verde cloud forest, and the final remnants of India's forests collapsing under the weight of a billion people.

Still, it's marvelous that we have some rainforest left. Sometimes, especially in the so-called megadiverse nations like Peru, Bolivia, and Indonesia, the strange green animal below stretches 360 degrees as far as I can see, bulging slightly in the middle distance, then softening out to the thin line of the horizon. That olive and lime green pelt sometimes looks so exquisite that I ache to reach down from the air and stroke it. It's like the back of an enormous animal we thought extinct but that still lives, reclining below in soft curvature.

But when this animal's side comes into view, I see the burns in its fur — ten-acre clear-cuts fed by logging roads like snaking arteries thick with virus. Sometimes fresh fires still burn, but I can't hear the monkeys' screams of terror under the plane's engine. When the fires are gone, there's a pure black deadness to the skin — and it's time to land amid the charcoal, the stumps. A million species flee or die; only one species moves in.

"ON THE HILLSIDES OLD CROPS DEAD AND FLATTENED ... murder was everywhere upon the land. The world soon to be populated by men who would eat your children in front of your eyes and the cities themselves held by cores of blackened looters who tunneled among the ruins and crawled from the rubble white of tooth and eye carrying charred and anonymous tins of food in nylon nets like shoppers in the commissaries of hell."

Granted, Cormac McCarthy's *The Road* was probably the worst possible thing to read during my reentry to America. But there I was anyway, a few days later, reading the novel in my parents' condo parking lot. I recalled that McCarthy suggested his Pulitzer Prize–winning novel is not about some distant future dystopia; it's really about the present time.

Boy, did I need some comfort food. In the supermarket across the road, I walked down an endless ice cream aisle and finally found it: Ben and Jerry's, something I never see in Africa or Latin America, and a real treat. But something was different. On the back of the pint of Phish Food was one word: Unilever. The Vermont duo had sold their erstwhile eco-company to the world's biggest food conglomerate, responsible for denuding the Brazilian rainforest and poisoning field laborers with chemicals.

I put the pint back. As I walked through that windowless, sterile mega-market, with piped-in music, the exit seemed to recede into the distance. I finally reached the door, only to escape into the sprawling parking lot. I didn't belong here — not in fast-food hospitals or condos; not in industrial-park 5K runs or malls. The wisdom I thought I'd gained over the past decade couldn't make sense of the dark direction the world seemed to be taking and of my own complicity in it. Perhaps the shaman was wrong. The world had lost its shape, and I was losing mine.

I felt a vibration in my pocket. My phone. "Hello," I said.

A silence on the other end. Not a long silence, but one full and round with expectation. Finally: "Hi, this is Jackie."

2. | THE LEAST THING PRECISELY

JACKIE SQUATTED BEHIND TWO HEIRLOOM TEA BUSHES, covered with golden honeybees. They explored her skin, her hair, the folds of her white cotton pants and blouse. I could see her stroking the wings of one of them. She was so absorbed in it that she didn't even hear me pull up.

The drive out to her permaculture farm was a collision of the Old and New South. The Research Triangle — which includes the cities of Chapel Hill, Raleigh, and Durham — and its McMansions, pharmaceutical plants, and research universities, like Duke and the University of North Carolina, disappeared as I crossed into Adams County, where Jackie lived. The wide highway narrowed to a single lane with occasional potholes, and the rolling green landscape evoked the Civil War setting of Charles Frazier's *Cold Mountain*. Plantation houses collapsed into themselves, and the old tobacco fields around them lay fallow. Jackie had moved into one of these abandoned, to-be-defined spaces.

She was partly obscured by the tea bushes. At a distance, all I could see was part of her face and a ponytail of salt-and-pepper hair.

I got out of the car and, still unnoticed, walked in her direction. Though it was early April, barely past the last frost, under Jackie's hand two hundred varieties of plants sprang from the ground in manic glory. Later, I'd learn their names by heart: Jack grape and Juneberries; hearty kiwi and Egyptian walking onions. Lettuce sprang up in a neat rectangular bed, and the winter wheat rose skyward. All of Jackie's flora was in motion under a slight breeze, smeared together as if in an impressionist painting, with the muted purples, oranges, and reds against a background of green and brown.

This area was a clear-cut when she moved in, Jackie had told me over the phone. Over the four years of living here, she'd been helping nature heal. Now you could barely make out the gleam of No Name Creek through the thickening vegetation. But I could hear it. It gurgled and bubbled through her two acres. There were some whippoorwills calling out, but otherwise I was drawn by the sound of the creek. It seemed to whisper secrets.

I was so absorbed by the setting, I didn't hear Jackie approach, but suddenly there she was, standing not six feet from me, regarding me with a kind of Mona Lisa half smile. She didn't say anything for a long moment; neither did I. She wore a lined navy blue windbreaker, too big for her, and white cotton drawstring pants. I knew she'd just turned sixty, but she gave the impression of fifty. Health and agility sprang from her whole body and shot from her blue eyes. She wasn't bold or assertive, far from it. She looked at me almost timidly, her eyes downcast.

I noticed several bees still clinging to her jacket, one in her hair, and another on her wrist. As we shook hands, the bee on her wrist made the short jump to my forearm. I stared at it without moving. With a little pull on my hand, Jackie led me over to some rainwater pooled by the tea bushes. We crouched there, and the bee flew off my arm and landed beside the pool. Above us sat a bee box. Jackie told me her Italian bees produced forty pounds of honey a year, enough to give to friends. "Listen to how quiet the bees are," she said. "In a month they'll be swarming, and it'll sound like a freight train." We stayed crouched there for a while, the air around us fragrant with raw honey. A slight buzz mingled with the murmur of the creek. We were surrounded by Juneberries, figs, hazelnuts, and sourwood. The bee that had been on my forearm was now sipping from the pool. Jackie reached down and stroked its wings as it drank. "Sometimes I wake up in the morning out here in the silence, and I get tears of joy."

During the next hour, she led me through her permaculture farm. She pointedly described permaculture as "the things your grandparents knew and your parents forgot," adding that the word is a conjunction of both *permanent agriculture* and *permanent culture*. She said permaculture can be defined as a holistic approach to sustainable landscape, agricultural, and home design. Our conversation consisted of my gawking in amazement and she gently, intelligently explaining the science and poetry of it all. She'd laid out the land in zones.

Zone 2 lay just beyond the fence and, along with her bees, held the crops that were inherently deer and rabbit proof and did not need to be enclosed in fencing: a profusion of native and wild elderberries and blackberries; several pawpaws, the largest edible fruit native to America, which is as plump as a mango; five Southern heirloom apple trees ("Four from Lee Calhoun," Jackie told me, "the dean of Southern heirloom apple lore."); three pecan trees from the yard in Alabama where she grew up; and two medlars, which produce apple-like fruits. "I got them because I was so enchanted by the shape of the plants," Jackie said. "They were cultivated in medieval walled gardens, and eaten at feasts in those days. I use them today for medlar jam." Zone 3 was her forest, which she used for collecting wood, edible mushrooms, and edible plants like pokeweed, and for bathing and meditating by the creek. I asked her about Zone 1, and she said we'd get to it later.

As she told me about the teas she grew, about her homemade jams and boysenberry wines, about the shiitakes she'd planted on a pile of logs, about the rainwater she harvested, I thought of something from Nietzsche: "How little suffices for happiness! . . . the least thing precisely, the gentlest thing, the lightest thing, a lizard's rustling, a breath, a wisk, an eye glance — the least thing makes up the best happiness." All of these tiny things — a bee, a creek, a tea bush — were causing me to loosen up, relax, and feel joy rush through me, the asphalt inside me beginning to crack.

Finally we made it into the core of her farm, Zone 1, stepping inside a green plastic deer fence. A membrane more than a frame, it unobtrusively circled a half acre or so of her two acres and harbored dozens of gardens full of vegetables, herbs, and flowers. There was Brugmansia, or angel trumpet, and Virginia bluebells, native persimmon for wine and preserves, cornelian cherry, mint everywhere, spicebush (for the spicebush swallowtail butterfly), and Dutchman's pipevine (for the pipevine butterfly). But at the center of Zone 1 something stopped me. Was it a *house?* The edifice was so slight that, viewed from a certain angle, it seemed as if it might simply vanish, like looking down the sharp edge of a razor blade. Wait a minute. Sure, I'd seen the structure several times already during our tour (hadn't I?), but it hadn't really sunk in. It just seemed like a little shed or something in the background. *She actually lives in there*, I thought, suddenly feeling like I'd crossed a line by even coming here. I wondered why she hadn't even mentioned the house yet. Was she embarrassed?

I was now looking at a different person. Where I'd seen this remarkable physician with the world's greenest thumb, I now saw a pauper. Something deeply ingrained in me reacted violently to the situation. *She has nowhere else to go.* She continued to talk about the joys of homesteading, but all I could do was nod, mutely, and steal peeks at the horrifying sight of the 12 x 12.

"Would you like to come in for tea?" she asked.

Part of me did not. But she led me toward that terrible, tiny house. To choose to live in anything that small was insane. As we neared it the place looked far smaller than I'd imagined. I'm six feet tall, so it was exactly twice my height at the base. As we approached the house it seemed to shrink, and I imagined the awkward moment when we would both squeeze in and drink the tea standing up, painfully forcing conversation. Four winters had weathered its brown walls. As we stepped onto a minuscule porch, she asked me if I'd mind taking off my shoes.

Why did something paradoxical in me, at that moment, long for something grand? For something that shouted the glory of human beings rather than being practically erased by the thick woods around it? Freud noted that people subconsciously struggle with two opposite but equal fears: being expelled by nature — cast out of Eden, as it were — and being absorbed by nature. This was the latter fear. By scaling down to only this speck of human space, Jackie had been enveloped by nature. No electrical wires, no plumbing. The bubbling creek now sounded almost ominous. I pulled off my shoes, heard the door creak open. I couldn't see inside, didn't want to. I wanted to be back in the plush interior of the car, jazz on the stereo, cruising on the highway back to Chapel Hill. But there was no turning back. I stooped down and entered the box.

From the inside, instead of feeling cramped, the place felt surprisingly roomy. While Jackie brewed tea on her four-burner gas stove, I leaned back into her great-grandmother's rocking chair and looked around. The space was so filled with the richness of her life that its edges fell away. It seemed to expand. Photos of her two grown daughters, of her ex-husband, even of her infamous Klansman father. Jackie said something that sounded a little shocking to me, but I'd later get where she was coming from: "Like a lot of Southern men of his era," she said, "he was a damned racist but had a heart of gold." Everything seemed forgiven. Excerpts from Buddhist and Taoist texts and snippets of poems and spiritual quotes filled the gaps between the photos of her life, a half dozen of them fastened to the ladder that rose up to a small loft, which contained a single window over her mattress and a set of drawers. Books filled a shelf covering one wall: a library of poetry, philosophy, spirituality, and — Jackie's a scientist, after all — technical books on biology, physics, astronomy, soils, and permaculture. I didn't see any on medicine other than a copy of *Where There Is No Doctor*, a manual I had occasionally used as an aid worker. The house had a faint scent of cedar from what she called her "splurge": one of the walls was finished with pure, beautiful cedar from ground to ceiling.

I now count the next few hours as among the most sublime of my life. Later Jackie would say that during our hours together the conversation would dive deep and surface again and again, that we'd go from smiling over the tea, the setting sun, and silence to talking about philosophy.

All the while the 12 x 12, tiny as it was, expanded outward. Outward to her neighbors. Outward to her gardens. Outward to the forest. She talked about her dream: living not only in harmony with nature ("having the carbon footprint of a Bangladeshi") but among a variety of social classes and races. Her two acres were part of a thirty-acre area. Of the thirty, twenty remained wild — through the intentional plan of an ingenious local eco-developer I'd learn more about later — common space she shared with four neighboring families: a Mexican furniture craftsman, a Honduran fast-food worker, an African American secretary, and the fascinating Thompsons across the road, who had moved to the country from a crack-infested trailer park and now struggled to make it as organic farmers.

She talked about a New American Dream that stretched beyond these ethnically diverse thirty acres. Others in Adams County were resisting the Flat World, trying to imagine and live something different. This was one of the only counties in the United States *adding* small farms each year. Land in Adams was still inexpensive enough for the average person to buy, yet there was a large and growing urban market just up the road in Chapel Hill and Durham that increasingly demanded — and would pay a premium price for — organic and local foods. Nationally, their lives tied into the growing slow food, environmental, and antiwar movements, part of a more durable future.

"You might say it all centers around a question," she said as the sun was going down. "Where do you grab the dragon's tail?"

Two deer bolted through Zone 2, beyond the deer fence. I spotted them through the 12 x 12's cedar-side window, slowly becoming aware of the natural activity around Jackie's home. Meanwhile, she talked about her upcoming trip in the next weeks. She had an eighty-dollar Greyhound ticket out west. With a small group, she'd walk a pilgrimage across the desert to the Nevada Atomic Test Site to hold up a sign saying NOT IN OUR NAME. And then she'd be "Greydogging," as she put it, further west to visit other activist friends. After thirty years of doctoring she'd taken a year's sabbatical and was on a sort of pilgrimage to figure out if she would continue in medicine or strike out on a new path.

It was time for me to go. But I wanted to absorb more. "Where *do* you grab the dragon's tail?" I asked, feeling the Bolivian rainforest burning, the climate dangerously warming.

She looked at me and said: "I think you should grab it where the suffering grabs you the most."

As I drove away, the sun was setting. I only made it fifty yards before slamming on the brakes. I looked over my shoulder. Most Americans seem to have a recessive melodrama gene, and I guess I'm among them; I couldn't resist the urge to look back. Through a cloud of dust the 12 x 12 appeared hazy. Jackie's brook, swaying winter wheat, "the least thing precisely, the gentlest thing, the lightest thing." I'm not sure how long I stared back at the tiny house, the seed that becomes a redwood, the atom that turns into a bomb.

I TOLD MY SISTER OVER THE PHONE about my 12 x 12 visit, and she said: "Where do you put that?"

At first I put it in one of those categories we all have: that time when that amazing thing happened. A one-off wonder. Something pure and illuminating that becomes a kind of touchstone. Frankly, I had no idea where to put it. I only knew that I felt a stirring at the 12 x 12, partly because of the way Jackie looked at me. She didn't see a baffled global nomad; she gazed through that and saw what I might become.

In any case, I reluctantly put the 12 x 12 away and prepared to head back to New York. My dad was recovering, walking around, even planning to start jogging again. So my sonly duties were done. That's when the letter arrived.

I found it at midnight — I wasn't sleeping so well at the time — partly hidden in the pile of mail by my parents' phone, addressed to me. I took a sip of red wine and breathed in deeply. The letter was weighty, like a fat college acceptance letter. I opened it.

A slip of paper fell out; on it was a poem by Mary Oliver called "Mindfulness." The poem ran down the page like a long, neat ribbon, each line containing just a few words. As I read it I felt the expansiveness I often feel when reading Mary Oliver's poetry. She talked about her teachers: the world's "untrimmable light" and prayers "made out of grass." But one particular phrase really made me pause. Oliver said her life's purpose, essentially, is to become fully absorbed "inside this soft world."

My heart now beating a little faster, I pulled the meatier pages out of the envelope, several loose-leaf pages of handwriting folded to fit into the small envelope. I unfolded them. "The sky is exquisite now. What a real joy to have you visit." Jackie went on to lay out several pages of facts, calling it "info I forgot to pass on," mostly the names of others in Adams County living in a way that challenged corporate economic globalization — organic farmers, permaculturalists, peak oil radicals, beekeepers, an "intentional community" called Blue Heron Farm, the Silk Hope Catholic Worker, a couple of families trying variations on her 12 x 12 experiment.

From this info she forgot to pass on the fuzzy edges of a story emerged. On one level it sounded like what Che Guevara used to call *gusanos* (worms) that slowly, bite by bite, cause the whole apple to collapse from within. It was the story of two competing visions of how to reshape the Old South and, indeed, the globalizing world. But deeper than that was something more. An extraordinary physician, activist, farmer, mother, wisdomkeeper, and visionary, taking the time that night to notice the beauty of the sky and to handwrite me a long letter in cursive, by candlelight.

As if guided by instinct I flipped over the Oliver poem. In cursive, across the back lengthwise, Jackie had drawn from the exact phrase that had practically jumped out of the poem at me, a phrase that hinted about the shape of the world. She'd written: "A soft world?"

My heart beat increasingly faster as I noticed the letter had a postscript: "P.S. And I really forgot the most obvious: I'll be away till summer, out West. You are absolutely welcome to come and stay in the 12 x 12 for a day or a week or a month or more, and any in and out combination. Just show up — I'll let the neighbors know."

I put down the letter and knew I had to go. I had to face this challenge to find a way out of my despair; to learn to think, feel, and live in another way. The 12 x 12 seemed full of clues toward living lightly, artfully in the twenty-first century. If beauty, as Ezra Pound said, loves the forgotten spaces, maybe so too does wisdom. New York would have to wait. Unexpectedly, I was bound for No Name Creek.

3. | THAWING

IT WAS DARK WHEN I DROVE UP to Jackie's place. Toting a back-pack, I groped my way along paths through a pitch black Zone 2 and into Zone 1, finally making it to the unlocked 12 x 12. I fumbled around for a light switch; naturally there was none. I managed to find matches and light candles. After exploring Jackie's bookshelves and the tiny loft that held her — now my — single mattress, I wrapped up in a couple of blankets and sat in her great-grandmother's goosehead chair for one hour, then two. I listened to the slight mur-mur of the creek, not completely sure of what else to do. As the quiet and darkness pressed in, so too did a mix of joy and trepidation.

Jackie told me how astonished she sometimes was to wake up in a Garden of Eden. I felt no such thing my first mornings there. I rose at dawn, climbed out of the loft, and made a strong cup of tea. Co-cooned in a handmade quilt in the rocking chair, I stared out into the cold gray light: the steam from my tea fogging my glasses and the windows; No Name Creek hardly stirring beneath a partial sheet of ice; the new moon cold and hidden beyond the horizon someplace; the stark 12 x 12 slab of frigid concrete pretending to be a floor.

Without Jackie there, the place seemed completely different. Instead of her contagious enthusiasm and intelligence, there was only me. Me and a bunch of plants, barely breathing. A late frost hit on my third night, causing hundreds of farmers throughout the county to lose their strawberries and tomatoes, but the diversity and native-plant focus of Jackie's farm hedged against the suddenly frozen soil. Some of her plants froze to a crisp and died, but most of them held on.

Whereas I'd seen only the flourishing-of-it-all in the light of Jackie's charisma, I soon realized that, aside from the garden beds in Zone 1, the earth around me was mostly slumbering. Stick season, they call it, with the skeletons of birch and oak and the sticky buds of leaves to come. Stalks of winter wheat, hoary vines on the trellises, and last year's asparagus. And silence.

I walked down to the creek, listened to it murmur, stuck a finger in. Frigid. I yanked my frozen finger out. Beyond the creek, a rolling terrain with more late-winter woods, pasture, and a higher forest beyond the pasture, all of the landscape edged with a crisp gray sky. I stopped for a moment to pick an empty cocoon from a branch, noticing a crack where the butterfly had emerged and flown out into life. As the lifeless shell crunched between my cold fingers, turning to a dry, useless powder, I wondered what in the world I was doing here. Should I have come at all?

I could be helping Liberian refugees, I thought, *saving rainforests in Bolivia, or distributing malaria-preventing bednets*. The things I was trained to do. Or if I was to be in America, I should be making myself useful, working twelve-hour days at the UN pressing for better refugee policies or sending out scathing op-eds and speaking at conferences. But this, pardon me, *dead* place just made me feel the deadness of the society around me even more. That dead pond in the industrial park; the techno-hospital's fast food. Trapped in a looping mind, I reasoned that coming to the 12 x 12 had been a mistake.

At night I'd sometimes light a little bonfire outside and listen to the hiss and sizzle, look into the orange coals, and stare at the stars, as cold up there as I was down below. The fire would die out, and I'd climb the 12 x 12's ladder to Jackie's loft and try to get cozy in her bed. I'd have no dreams at all. It was as if the nonlife, the frigidity of the place, was mirrored in my dreams. In that tiny house, snuggled in a vast forest, secluded in its upper loft, my spirit felt as fallow as the scene around me.

A warm pile of eggs is what would begin to thaw me out. My eleven-year-old neighbor, Kyle Thompson, beckoned to me one morning as I walked up Jackie's dirt road toward Old Highway 117 South. He asked me if I was living at Jackie's, and I nodded. Without further introductions, he took my sleeve and led me over to the important business at hand: a disheveled woodpile, where a Muscovy duck squatted over her nest. With a stick, Kyle prodded the duck gently to reveal a large pile of eggs beneath her in a bed of hay and feathers. "We're going to have fourteen ducklings," he said, a little proudly.

I looked at Kyle. His thick, dun-brown hair flopped above a pair of blue eyes. He had a couple of freckles under each eye and a slight tilt to his head. Though I later found out he wanted to be an engineer, and I had already discovered his love of animal husbandry, his facial expression suggested how I pictured the young James Joyce in *Portrait of an Artist as a Young Man*. I looked back down at the eggs. Kyle spoke excitedly about the ducklings to come, but I was doubtful. Amid the frost-covered wood and gray background, they looked like cold marble, fossilized dinosaur eggs, things not destined to bring forth life.

Kyle was practically the only person I saw during those frigid first days at the 12 x 12. The colorful cast of neighbors Jackie had described — Mexican furniture makers, permaculture pioneers, and even Kyle's parents, the Thompsons — all seemed to be in hibernation. Even Kyle I didn't see much; sometimes I'd spot him a football field's length away, across the field and pond, looking expectantly into his woodpile, talking to the mother duck, trying to persuade life to happen. I was otherwise alone. I felt bare to the point of barren, just another skeleton, like the plants or the dark new moon.

What was I to do? "Not do, *be*," Jackie had told me. In her invitation note, she mentioned that she was not asking me to house-sit or farm-sit. Her guidance was clear: I was simply to sit. It would become apparent that, for all the variety and fruitfulness of her gardens, they were mostly on autopilot. She planted and arranged in ways that minimized weeds by not having rows, and she used plants that needed little water. Permaculture, to Jackie, was to be a blessing, not a burden. Her motto for her gardens was the same as the motto of her house: Think small. No, not labor in her fields but rather labor with her fields — and also observe the fields. I realized how fortunate I was to be able to take this leisure time; I'd been frugal during years of work abroad and had savings. So now, like much of nature, so still, just sitting, the minerals, the trees, the water in the pond, I too began to feel my anxious mind slow down as the days passed and I tuned into nature, slipping into what the Chinese call *wu wei*, an alert inactivity. This is not considered sloth but a kind of "waiting" in the esoteric sense of the word: present, attentive, as when Jesus said to "be like a servant who does not know at what hour the master will return." An outward nondoing; an inner readiness.

The world was numb; I was numb. But numb isn't dead. Kyle called me over to the woodpile, pointing out the very first hairline crack in one of the fourteen duck eggs. I finally felt that something might actually happen. That if I waited patiently enough, the world might reveal itself to me.

ALL THE SURPRISES AT JACKIE'S helped to gradually thaw me out. Perhaps there's a "cure" in the practice of curiosity. With no electricity, piped water, or any of the conveniences we are so accustomed to, I was forced to see everything anew. The first puzzle: How in the world was I to bathe?

Jackie didn't leave an instruction manual, an "Idiot's Guide" to living in a 12 x 12. There was no shower, of course, and the creek was still too darn cold. But so was the rainwater Jackie harvested from the two gutters running off the 12 x 12's roof. I took one bucket shower, cursing as I cupped freezing rainwater over my head, before I discovered a five-gallon rubber diaphragm on her back porch labeled "Sun Shower." The directions were on the side of it, and I followed them, filling up the rubber bag and letting the morning sun heat it. Midday or evening, I strung it up in a tree beside the 12 x 12 and felt the positively *hot* water stream over my body, which became a sensuous daily pleasure. I appreciated every bit of that hot water, and it was all the lovelier knowing that its energy came directly from that day's sun, producing no dangerous greenhouse gasses. And the runoff watered the gardens; nothing wasted down a drain.

I began to appreciate water. It felt so immediate. Instead of being invisibly piped into my home from some deep aquifer or distant reservoir, it fell from the sky into the pair of fifty-five-gallon tanks beside the house. When I arrived they were full; when I left, ditto. All of my dishwashing, laundry (I followed Jackie's lead and used only biodegradable soaps), bathing, and cooking water simply came out of the sky, passed through my hands, and then went directly back into the earth to water the food I ate.

Less appealing was the dilemma of the toilet. Instead of a flush toilet, I discovered that Jackie used a five-gallon composting toilet under the porch out back. It featured a regular toilet seat, but there was no chemical-filled cesspool belowground — just a standard white bucket. Throw some fresh-smelling cedar chips in after every use, and there was absolutely no foul odor. The conundrum occurred when the bucket started to fill. And fill. How to dispose of it?

I fingered along the spines of Jackie's scientific books, until I came to one with a rather nonthreatening title: *The Humanure Handbook*. For twenty-first-century homesteaders like Jackie, it's the bible of composting toilets. So many designs! True to her simplicity, Jackie'd chosen the simplest model, the concealed five-gallon bucket, the contents of which, *The Humanure Handbook* informed me, I was to simply compost. Yes, in fourteen weeks human feces are soil just like any other soil and can be ploughed back into your garden. So I carried the bucket over to the compost pile, intending to follow the *Handbook* and dump it right over my eggshells and carrot peels. But at the last minute I couldn't go through with it. The science notwithstanding, I felt queasy over the aesthetics; I grabbed a shovel and buried the contents deep in the woods.

Adjusting to life without electricity was relatively painless. I've worked in subsistence economies around the world and have gone for short stints without electricity. The only oddity was that I was in the heart of the world's richest nation — but living a subsistence life. No humming refrigerator, no ringing phones (I decided to go cell phone free in the 12 x 12), and none of the ubiquitous "standby" lights on appliances — those false promises of life inside the machines. Instead: the whippoorwill's nocturnal call, branches scraping quiet rhythms in the breeze, and groggy No Name Creek. Looking east from the 12 x 12 toward the creek into the ink black night, without the slightest glimmer of industrial society, I thought, *Could I really be inside the borders of a high-tech superpower?* To the west, I could barely make out the Thompsons' porch light, and José's and Graciela's lights cast a glow on the trees above their homes.

Fire replaced electric light. Sparks from outdoor fires would briefly escape gravity and reflect off the creek, before disappearing into the massive dark sky and the flaming white points of the stars above. Most luxurious of all, each night was blessed with the glow of candles. On the eleventh night, I noted in my journal, I lit the candles without even thinking about it. I simply came in after a hike, struck a match, lit them, and began cooking, candle lighting having become as automatic as switch flipping. The house glowed from the inside like a jack-o'-lantern. Sometimes I'd step outside and look in through the windows, a dozen or so candles inside, as cheery as a birthday cake — the 12 x 12 point lit with primordial fire amid dark woods — and I'd feel this smile spreading across not just my face but my spirit as well, lifting me with a feeling of emotional weight-lessness.

"THEY'RE ALMOST HERE," Kyle practically whispered with excitement early one morning. I jogged behind him up to the woodpile. All of the eggs were laced with cracks. Little beak tips had begun to poke through.

"Where's the mom?" I asked.

"She's over there eating with the others. But she left this to warm the eggs." He stroked the blue feathers, interlaced with straw, that partly covered the eggs.

As we walked together down to No Name Creek, Kyle talked of Boy Scouts and of the coyotes that threatened their ducks. When the weather got better, Kyle wondered, could he and I bike together to the post office? Sure. We skimmed rocks along the creek; they'd sometimes slide along the final traces of ice on top before plopping to the bottom. I wondered about his parents and my other neighbors; I was eager to meet them. We were silent for a while. The water gently complained, muttering over stones, as if annoyed at having been woken up too early. In the distance, a truck hurried down Old Highway 117 South and then was silent. We heard the flap of a hawk's wings, and then it swooped down over the creek, splashing for a fish, coming up empty.

Kyle talked about predators and prey. He speculated as to when the duck eggs would hatch. *Don't do, be.* I sat there, completely content, listening. Instead of listening with one ear, as I sometimes do when faced with life's deadlines, with multitasking, I used both ears. Real listening is prayer, I would find, as the weeks passed at the 12 x 12. Perhaps the mistake we make in attempting to pray is that we do all the talking. Slowing down, I would find it so much easier, more pleasurable, to be with children as I let them, and myself, simply be.

I spent a lot of time walking, aimlessly, hours at a time. Sometimes an entire day would pass out there in the woods, along Highway 117. One day I followed No Name Creek down to where it met the old railroad tracks and then walked along them. It was a numb day. I wasn't thinking or feeling much. I didn't feel overwhelmed by the great silence or the solitude, nor did it feel particularly peaceful. The earth was cold and hard beside the tracks; the trees rose by the thousands in bare brown attention. Shoe sole on railroad tie, the silver rails a mute metallic shine. I saw a path into the woods and spontaneously took it.

The path was wide at first but soon narrowed to the width of my body, before abruptly ending. But I kept going, bushwhacking into the brush. A stack of clouds moved across the sky like an iceberg, gradually covering the sun. The air had no scent at all; I just felt the cold in my nostrils, saw my breath as I struggled through a briar patch, scraped my sleeve on a cluster of thorns, passed through a narrow clearing before plunging into a deeper, darker part of the forest. I finally stopped, out of breath. I looked back and saw no sign of the trail. I was utterly alone.

In the midst of this silence, four words gathered in my mind. A little phrase from Rumi that Jackie had handwritten onto a white card and left out — for me? — on top of other cards on a little stand in the 12 x 12. It read: TRADE KNOWLEDGE FOR BEWILDERMENT.

I walked on, and the forest opened into a meadow. A fleck of purple caught my eye — the season's first wildflower. I touched the dew in its four petals, hints of yellow in its translucent pistils. I lay down next to it and turned my head to the side. Around it were a thousand of the same species, the dead husks of last year's flourishing.

Pent-up emotion rose from somewhere inside, searching for the fire exits. Death was all around me in those thousand brown husks, the skeletons of trees, the washed-out sky. It was different from the death of hospital fast food, industrial parks, and the felling of rain-forests. Those aren't really death but resignation: giving up on our-selves, our world. The death around me in the woods held desire for life in every detail.

The next day, the duck eggs hatched. It was the first warm day; spring nudged into the landscape, and the sticky oak buds opened slightly, a thousand winks of green. Fourteen fuzzy, noisy ducklings squeaked for food in the woodpile nest. "They're fully feathered," Kyle boasted. I noticed their diverse colorings, the scoop of their wet, quacking bills. And my neighbors, until this moment merely rumors, came out of their houses to see what the commotion was all about.

TRADE KNOWLEDGE FOR BEWILDERMENT*

---

* In the 12 x 12, Jackie keeps a stack of cards with handwritten sayings or questions, like this one. She puts a new one out in view on a little stand each day. I followed her rather Socratic practice, even adding some of my own to her pile. Doing this deepened daily life because, at several points of the day, I would notice the card and be brought into mindfulness. In the spirit of this practice, I include twelve of them at different points in the story.

4. CHICKEN

*It is not too soon to provide by every possible means that
as few as possible shall be without a little portion of land.
The small landholders are the most precious part of a state.*

— Thomas Jefferson to James Madison, October 28, 1785

MIKE THOMPSON — KYLE'S DAD — walked toward me down the
gentle hill from his house, a bucket of feed swinging in each hand. He
was a portrait in reds: rosy cheeks, a tomato red shirt (in black block
letters: SUPPORT ORGANIC FARMERS), and a pirate's red goatee, hanging a full six inches off his chin, hiding his Adam's apple. I could see
a reflection of Kyle in him: a tilt of the head, a similarity in the easy
offering of his smile. On other days, I'd notice a blend of introspec-
tion and unease on Mike's face. He'd be putting up a hog pen or
feeding the chickens, and he'd have another look, as if doubtful his
organic dreams would actually flourish. But on this day he had a glow
around him as if he'd found his place on the earth. In a huge splash
of dry grains, he dumped out both pails of feed, emitting a little
whoop as he did.

Winged creatures rushed at Mike and me, aiming for the seed
piled at our feet. The farm around us was a chaotic swirl of birds.
Along with turkeys and several species of ducks, from Muscovy to
Pekin, were several breeds of chickens — chaldrons and chanticleers,
redcaps and rose combs. Local North Carolina finches, cardinals,

n array of sparrows mixed in with the others. The end result was a *Beyond Thunderdome* version of an aviary. And it descended upon us.

On the periphery of this pleasant madness, there were the hogs (just two when I first moved in), goats, dogs, and cats. And kids. Two of Kyle's younger brothers, Greg and Brett, tore out of the house like caged wildcats suddenly let loose. They dashed toward Mike and me, right through a swarm of fowl that were flying off the pond toward us and honking like mad over the expectation of food. The two giggling youngsters grabbed my hands to break their stride. More fowl accumulated around my feet, hundreds of them from elsewhere in the farm. Then came the boys' brother, Zach, skidding into the fray on his BMX bike. Their guardian goat, a long-horned Billy who protected the chickens from foxes, leapt atop the roof of a small chicken house, posing proudly in regal profile. A fresh wave of ducks and geese, sensing the food, alit from the pond, soared in, and crash-landed in the grain.

Out of this chaos, I felt a tug on my sleeve and looked down to see Kyle. "I found a chicken for you," he said.

For a moment I didn't know what he was talking about. But then I recalled a conversation we'd had while I bought eggs from him the previous day, about getting some poultry as well. "Yes, the chicken meat. Do you have some ready?"

"No, but I have a chicken," he said, pointing into the swirl of chickens and ducks around us. "There it is. That's yours: that white broiler."

I saw it, but only for a second. A nice five-pound chicken, strutting around in the free air, not squeezed into a chicken factory pen. It soon vanished in a swarm of color as other birds swooped in. "How much is it?" I asked, and immediately regretted the question. What did it matter? There was no doubt I would buy that chicken, and many more chickens from this family, even if it were twice the price of a factory-farmed chicken. I looked around at all this genetic diversity, this happy dance of people and animals, and suddenly wanted to buy all of their chickens. I wanted to support this.

Their endeavor was a tenuous one. The Thompsons, as was immediately apparent from the disorganization of their operation, didn't know a whole lot about farming. They'd bought a bunch of animals and let them loose. Mike and Michele Thompson, now in their early thirties, started having kids in their teens, raising them in an urban trailer park in North Carolina's Research Triangle area, and going on welfare. It was only when the drugs and knives, so common in the trailer park, directly threatened their kids that they decided to sink all of their money into a mortgage for this remote piece of land, put a simple prefab house on it, and improvise an organic farm. But the tough life Kyle had lived up until then was reflected in his eyes; he had that too-mature-for-his-age look even as we playfully skipped stones along No Name Creek.

However, as I discovered from our early conversations, Mike and Michele weren't just fleeing a dangerous urban life; they felt animated by a kind of Jeffersonian dream of becoming independent freeholders. They both wore big smiles and talked energetically about their farm and children. They wanted to live by sweat and gusto. They chose the organic model partly out of idealism, but also because this premium niche market was the only route open to small farmers, since big companies like Gold Kist can crank out conventional factory-farmed chickens much cheaper.

Kyle took me over to their front porch and opened a shoe box with holes poked in the top. A single duckling. I asked him where the other thirteen were. "Coyote raid," he said. "They got all but one."

I looked down at the single duckling, a little horrified, picturing the coyote downing them one by one, like popcorn. "I'm so sorry," I said.

"It's fine," Kyle said. "There's two more batches on the way." He pointed to two other mother ducks, sitting on their freshly laid eggs — reminding me of *Leela*, the divine play of the Hindus, where the forms on earth spontaneously replicate themselves by the hundreds, the thousands. Down by the pond, Mike was dumping another two buckets of feed randomly, two of his kids leaping in it, another twirling an inchworm on its silk in each hand, a hundred birds fluttering for what they could grab. Everyone and everything seemed to be laughing and dancing. In the competition with factory farms, and considering the way mainstream America is organized, could this pay the bills? Michele did some tax preparation part-time — she was trained in basic accounting — but the family was up to its neck in debt. For them, the farm simply had to work.

I GRADUALLY BEGAN TO NOTICE a mysterious smell. I hardly noticed it at first because I was so enraptured by Jackie's budding gardens, the 12 x 12's solitude, the rush of No Name Creek, which had changed from an end-of-winter sluggishness to a cheerier spring flow, flush with rainwater. But after a while the smell was impossible to ignore. It was noticeable only under certain wind conditions and at particular places on my long walks into the surrounding countryside, where it would creep into my nostrils and send a wave of discomfort through me. It was the stench not of death, but rather of the absence of both life and death. The unpleasantness of an overflowing ashtray.

The smell — which I wouldn't identify until later — was usually covered over by brighter ones. The fecund scent of thawing earth, the fresh scent of my skin after a rainwater solar shower, budding wildflowers. Jackie's storied fields came into fuller life. Storied, because her dozens of beds contained seeds, roots, and bulbs given to her by friends and family — tulips from one of her daughters, Honduran herbs from Graciela's *finca* south of the border — and as they bloomed, fruited, and flowered each year, so would their presence in Jackie's heart. She'd left out a colorful, unfolded map in the 12 x 12 that showed the names of her plants as well as stories about the giver of the seed.

There was Aunt Daisy's scuppernong, a variety of muscadine grape with sweet yellowish fruit from the aunt of one of Jackie's best friends. "Aunt Daisy died a few months from her hundredth year," Jackie noted on her map, "an African American elder and wise woman." Another "well-adapted bunch purple grape" — the Jack grape — came from Tom Franz, who found it three decades ago on his nearby farm; journals indicate it may have been established a century ago.

I followed the treasure map to ginger lilies from Jackie's sister and onward to spider lilies from the old homeplace of "Daddy's people," her mother's yard, and "the gardens of the home place of my great-great-grandmother." She noted: "Spider lilies are all over my childhood lawn. We always took them to the teachers when school started." I discovered columbine and green-and-gold, beautiful native wildflowers that Jackie got from her adoptive godmother, who was a legendary activist and, she noted, "my beloved mentor and friend. I have many plants in my gardens from her, and it is as if I walk with her in the mornings." These were next to her dear elder cousin's mums, "splendid in the fall" and her "John Jamison apple tree from my dear friend John, who was proud to have been named outstanding Black farmer in the county one year. Wonderful hours in his kitchen listening to his stories."

There was beautyberry, which grows along roadsides all over the South, but "this one is from the Murdock home place in Ronark, Alabama. The house my great-grandfather built for my great-grandmother when they married." A fig tree from an activist friend in Chapel Hill. Fragrant flowers near the 12 x 12 door: Osmanthus, aka fragrant tea olive, "sweet scent of my childhood. It perfumes the

air on summer nights, as do four o'clocks from my sister's garden,
nicotiana (flowering tobacco from Analisa), datura, or devil's trumpet, so fragrant at night." Plus American hazelnuts and rugosa
rose (for rose hips) and native wildflowers from other relatives —
Solomon's seal and Solomon's plume; dogtooth violet, skullcap, and
amsonia — making the whole swirl of life around the 12 x 12 a glorious blueprint of nature, love, and memory.

Her map brought to mind Thoreau's observation that it's
perfectly fine to build castles in the sky — just be sure you put foundations under them. Jackie's air castle — a sensual, productive relationship with a few acres; being mindful and fully present; living on
a low-carbon diet — bloomed in full color before my eyes. Her castle took transpiring, photosynthesizing form on the earth's surface.
She put foundations under her dreams: some seeds, some science,
some art. Each day I'd walk out at sunrise into a gently transformed
world. New shapes, smells, and shades of color, the hang of a tiny
fruit, the wrinkle of a leaf, the ambitious shoot of a straight stalk.
Glory be.

Along with the mysterious smell, another wafted over to the
12 x 12: the smell of a working farm. One day Kyle saw me from
across the pond and ran over to remind me about the dangling issue
of the white broiler. He pointed it out again, in the swarm of fowl,
and I told him I'd take that one plus another.

"Okay," Kyle said. "Would you like to take them with you?"

"Like this?" I said, a frown growing on my face. "But they're
alive."

He looked up at me through blue eyes, a little puzzled. I tried to
clarify: "They need to be slaughtered."

"Yes," Kyle said, innocently. "You're going to slaughter them."

I shifted my weight from one foot to the other. A moving wall
of chickens, turkeys, and ducks was all around us. Kyle was now
joined by two of his brothers; the three blond boys stared at me with

an earnest, expectant intensity. I was fully acquainted with the relevant theory: if you eat it, you should be able to kill it. Someone else shouldn't do your dirty work. And if I couldn't kill a chicken, perhaps the only honest response was to become a vegetarian.

Kyle filled the silence: "My dad can show you. It takes one hour."

"How about we talk about it later?"

"I'll ask my dad. He shoots them in the head."

"Sorry?"

"Yes, that's how he slaughters 'em."

"Sometimes," six-year-old Greg jumped in, "the head gets shot off the body, and one time it was hanging by just a little skin." The three brothers giggled, and the four-year-old launched into another head-shooting anecdote, the bloodiest so far. More hysterical laughing.

Kyle then assumed an authoritative pose again, shushing his brothers and pronouncing: "There's two ways to kill a chicken."

"I thought you cut its throat," I said.

"That's the other way. But it's harder. I recommend blowing its brains out."

Feeling a bit stunned by this turn of events, I told the boys I needed to think about it. As I hustled back to the 12 x 12, I bumped into my furniture-maker neighbor, the forty-something José, from Mexico. He handed me a plastic bag of feathery seeds, explaining it was an herb for Mexican cooking that he'd brought from Michoacán for Jackie to plant. Enthusiastically, José invited me to his sanctuary, his woodworking studio. When Habitat for Humanity helped him construct this house — the ribbon was cut only a year before — this studio wasn't part of it. He built it himself. He opened the lock on the front door and smiled as he led me inside. José's shop was filled with the smell of fresh wood. Colorful paint was splashed on the walls like a Jackson Pollock painting. He proudly showed me his tools, the latest band saws and dowel inserters, and some of his furniture.

It was beautiful work. Fine tables and cabinets, mixing his native Mexican folk art with contemporary style. He worked into the night crafting this furniture and sold it door-to-door in Siler City. When I asked him why he put in such long hours, he said, "It keeps me out of the chicken factories." Hundreds of his fellow Latin Americans manned the blades, conveyor belts, and trucks of the Gold Kist factories not twenty minutes away. "I don't like that much blood," José added.

But José had a problem. People in North Carolina were not used to buying handmade Mexican furniture from door-to-door artisans, so business was difficult. He'd been able to scrape a living together selling to other Mexicans, but now, with Wal-Mart in Siler City offering cheap Chinese-made furniture, selling his furniture was even harder. Scrambling, José found a job as a handyman for a Pittsboro-based company that produced piping for various manufacturing processes. Still, José's dream was to make beautiful furniture full-time.

He invited me into his home, Habitat for Humanity's standard two-bedroom. José disappeared into the kitchen to fix something for us while I sat on his sofa watching his thirteen-year-old son, Hector, kill chickens with a shotgun and pitchfork. The computer game was called RuneScape.

"I kill these chickens for their bones," he said. "I need more bones." He pronounced the word *bones* with a strangely elongated *o*.

"You see," he said, showing me the screen, "I've already got 3,200 bones."

"3,201," I said with a gulp, watching him pitchfork another one.

My eyes drifted to the open window, as the setting sun painted the sky orange and crimson over No Name Creek. The colorful rays illuminated the silk of several spider webs attaching the window to surrounding bushes, and as I watched the different-sized spiders labor — each in its own way — it occurred to me that my neighbors were trying to become the equivalent of free-range chickens: free-range people. They were extracting themselves from the most poisonous parts of globalization and were in the midst of an exciting, if quixotic, experiment to create a fruitful life on the margins.

How difficult it is, and how elusive, I thought. A plump, half-dollar-sized spider grasped a cherry red flying ant in its pincers. In the neighboring web, not one but rather a hundred spiders the size of poppy seeds had spun an intricate, three-dimensional web. Two spiders, two strategies; nature splintering itself off, playing the odds. Both of the strategies worked. I looked over at José, who was running his hand gently along a gorgeous antique-accented dresser he'd made in his shop, and felt a tinge of pity: he could hardly sell such beautiful wares. Though he had escaped the industrial chicken factories, and the Thompsons had escaped a monoculture of doublewides, both families were still surrounded by a pervasive blight. "Look!" Hector cried out, showing me the screen of his video game. "I pitchforked five more chickens." Out the window, the plump spider downed his cherry red ant while the pinhead spiders entombed gnats in silk.

WHILE I WAS WALKING IN THE WOODS ONE DAY, a loud *crack* startled me as a branch snapped above my head. I cried out and covered my head; above, an enormous hawk took awkward flight. Branch and leaves fell to my feet, followed by something slower, fluttering down. I plucked it out of the air: a long white feather.

I brought the feather to my nose. It had a gamey scent that triggered something primitive in a remote, rarely used part of my brain. The tip of the feather was still sweaty, as if dipped in invisible ink. I pantomimed writing cursive in the air, strange symbols in an unknown language, and then slipped the foot-long feather into my pocket.

I felt tingly, sweaty from exercise. I hadn't seen a person all day, lost somewhere in the deep forests around Jackie's. Wildness. Feeling the feather, I smiled inwardly at the surprise of scaring a hawk from its sleepy perch. I took the feather out and again traced strange characters in the air, this time more slowly. I put it back into my pocket, walked a few more steps, stopped. What the heck had I been writing? And, beyond my feather-traced haikus, what a beautiful lexicon, all of this: feathers dropping from the sky into my hand; the first wildflower of the season; my neighbors' wild mass of fowl; the great silence of the 12 x 12. I walked on.

I crossed out of the woods again and onto a winding country road. Whistling, twirling my feather, feeling buoyant, except . . . there was that mysterious smell again, growing stronger, a smothered scent. I sniffed the feather in my hand; no, not that. The feather smelled like a night in the forest, a naturally pungent smell. This other, very different odor increased with every step until it was a full-throttle stench. The first vehicles I'd seen that day roared past. I'd arrived at a perfect railroad crossing gate with its red lights, complex hinges, and long straight wood. And then, to my left, I saw, like a nightmarish mirage, the source of the stench: a monstrous chicken factory.

KEEP OUT. BIO-SEALED, read one sign in flaming red. Another sign: GOLD KIST POULTRY CENTER. Behind the signs was an absurdly manicured lawn, like an estate photo from *Town & Country*, and a dozen or more "houses" — long, rectangular warehouses for the poultry.

By now the smell was almost unbearable. On the warehouses, circular fans blew out feathers and the stench of chicken waste. These chicken houses were identical to the others I'd seen on the drive to Jackie's. They each "did" tens of thousands of birds a day, feeding the Gold Kist empire. (Gold Kist was the country's third-largest chicken processor until it was purchased in 2007 by the even larger Pilgrim's Pride. Gold Kist kept its name; the combined company is the world's biggest of its kind, surpassing Tyson.) Mike Thompson told me that, in addition to mutilating their chickens through beak searing, tail docking, and ear cutting, Gold Kist was experimenting with featherless chickens to eliminate inefficient plucking, along with beakless chickens that couldn't peck at each other, something they tend to do as they go nuts over being confined to a tiny dark space their whole lives. When chickens peck at each other, they spoil what they are to us: meat.

Later, out of curiosity, I would visit an industrial chicken factory, one of a hundred throughout that part of North Carolina, nearly all of them producing poultry for giant companies like Gold Kist. The first thing I noticed was how dark they are. Factory farming began in the 1920s soon after the discovery of vitamins A and D; when these vitamins are added to feed, animals no longer require exercise and sunlight for growth. This allowed large numbers of animals to be raised indoors year-round. The main problem that occurred with this kind of intensive confinement was disease, but in the 1940s the development of certain antibiotics took care of that. Unfortunately, factory farming causes suffering and pain for animals and is a scourge to the environment. I couldn't believe the suffocating ammonia smell inside. Around me, thousands of birds were caged so tightly that they weren't able to move; movement would make them more muscular and less tender to chew. And it was oddly quiet, as if these genetically manipulated creatures had been bred to hush up. Their silence was probably a side effect of all the hormones, antibiotics, and other chemicals pumped in so that they could be, mercifully, slaughtered as 3.5 pounds of product in seven weeks.

What chance did Mike and Michele Thompson — and their six kids — have against this? In front of the bio-sealed Gold Kist factory, I looked down at the feather in my hand, the wild quill that had fluttered out of the sky. The contrast between the freedom of that hawk, flushed out of an evergreen into the morning sky, and the industrial birds numbed by chemicals, deprived of sunlight and freedom, suggested a frightening metaphor for the way we humans have come to live in a flattening world.

IT SMELLED LIKE CHICKEN at Bobby Lu's Diner in Siler City, ten miles up the road from Jackie's. As I walked through the restaurant to an open booth, I noticed that nearly all of the fifty or so customers were eating chicken. Broiled, fried, cordon bleu; fat chicken legs and breasts, chemically pumped-up Gold Kist pickings.

Having seen, and smelled, the bio-sealed Gold Kist factory, I felt nauseous and skimmed the menu for something that wasn't chicken. I ordered a cheese sandwich with taters and salad. The customers, nearly all of them white, seemed to have a nearly identical glow, or lack thereof, a kind of sheen. I wondered what the effect of eating chemically enhanced food over decades has on our bodies. Do we become like factory chickens when we avoid exercise, work and live most of our lives indoors, and eat chemically altered food?

Also, is there an unconscious effect of being so close to the source of so much pain? Maybe I was imagining things, but I could almost feel the Gold Kist factory's dread in the air, an invisible violence like radio transmissions.

I had spent much of the past decade in places where humans still live in relative harmony with nature and one another, in the Global South where the land hasn't yet been domesticated, nor culture industrialized. Sociologists point out that American kids today can identify a thousand corporate logos but less than ten native plants and animals that live around their homes. Are we, like Gold Kist chickens, evolving in artificially manufactured, rather than natural, ways?

THAT NIGHT, UNDER THE STARS, I made myself a second meal: over an open fire beside the 12 x 12, I grilled my five-pound broiler.

In the end, I had decided that it wasn't in me to kill a chicken myself, and Mike did it for me. Perhaps in the future I'd see it differently and be able to participate in that natural process: steward an animal's healthy growth; take its life, with reverence; and ingest its energy into my own. I wasn't there yet. However, it certainly was in me to support the Thompsons' free-range agriculture. I sat down to eat, alone, with care.

In each bite, all that flavor connected with the Thompsons. After seeing the Gold Kist plant and its chicken in Bobby Lu's, I appreciated the Thompsons' efforts even more. They were taking a stand and attempting, on their quirky little farm, to heal a ruptured relationship with the earth's natural rhythms. In the fire and moonlight, I looked at each bite before I ate it, smelled it, felt the flesh on my tongue, exploring the texture and the taste.

Mindful eating restored some of my balance, but not all. I was too aware of how complexly interwoven our society's problems are. Each time I biked up the highway, I'd feel the asphalt harden inside. At the Quick-N-Easy convenience store, four miles from the 12 x 12, I sometimes encountered fights, nagging, and even viciousness between people, as if our factory-farmed Flat World causes us to go a bit nuts and peck each other. Once when I was shopping there, a man yelled at his wife in the parking lot: "Maybe if you didn't pick on her she wouldn't cry all the time!"

"Well, I didn't know she was in a picky mood," his wife answered. Doors slammed.

Another time in the parking lot, I watched a banged-up TransAm pull up beside my bike. A man, around thirty — with a Confederate-flag bandanna on his head, tattoos, and a torn, sleeveless shirt — flung his door open, slammed it, and yanked open the back door. He pulled out a small boy, who looked to be around six, and pulled down his pants. "Ouch," the boy protested.

"Just stand here and piss because you won't fucking wait!" his dad said, and then: "Hurry up!" But now the boy couldn't go. His dad shook his hips, and the boy's urine finally flowed and pooled around the back tire of my bike.

"Damn it, you don't even say thank you," the man said as he pushed his son, whose pants were still half down, back into the car. They hadn't seen me.

As I biked away from the Quick-N-Easy, my tire left a short trail of urine. I had a 12 x 12 permaculture retreat, but where did this family go? Tires squealed and the family's car raced past me, the wife smoking a cigarette. Her son bawled, her husband fumed, and she cast a vacant stare out the window, all of us breathing the odor growing around us on a dull wind: the stench of chicken factories.

5. | WARRIOR PRESENCE

WHAT IN THE WORLD DO YOU DO?

This is the question I started asking myself at the 12 x 12. In Jackie's permaculture paradise I felt increasingly energized by pulsing growth, humble simplicity, and the gentle sound of No Name Creek. But bike a mile up the road in any direction and it was Cormac McCarthy's road. This dichotomy begged the question: How could I maintain Jackie's level of positive energy under any circumstance?

I wanted to talk with Jackie about it, but she was Grey-dogging west, without a cell phone. So I emailed her, and a few days later she replied with the phone number of a friend's where she was staying, and I immediately biked to a pay phone and called her.

It all gushed out. I told her not only about the chicken factories and the conflicts at the Quick-N-Easy, but about an inner dilemma: As an aid worker, I am confronted by global inequality all the time. Just as the Flat World chicken factories and industrial parks suck the presence out of me, so too does the pillage of the Global South's forests, mines, and oceans in order to fuel our Northern economies.

And many of the countries in the Global South try to replicate this awful example.

At first, Jackie didn't say anything. I could tell she was listening deeply. I continued, suggesting that perhaps I needed to *do more*, more to help those in need. This has been my typical response: join the battle; ship metric tons of food to internally displaced people; combine community ecotourism with political advocacy; research and expose corporate greed.

Finally, I was all talked out. Still, Jackie didn't say anything. In the silence I remembered what she'd told me when we'd first met, and repeated it aloud now: "Don't do, be."

Jackie let out a little laugh. "Well . . . yes . . ." she said.

I frowned and said, "But isn't that what you told me?"

Jackie began to speak. She spoke for a long while, and what emerged was a unique approach to living in today's world, a blend of spiritual passion and secular practicality. I later came to synthesize her approach in very simple terms: see, be, do.

First, she explained, see the problem. It could be anything: resentment toward a family member; a homeless woman by the curb; a government plan to fund a bigger nuclear bomb instead of better schools. Often we look away from problems — we're busy earning a living, going to the ball game, or being depressed. This, Jackie told me, is a core error. Every one of these so-called problems is there to teach us. Either we face it, and grow toward that higher level of consciousness, or it comes back again and again, in one form or another.

Once we've garnered the courage to see the problem, it's not yet time to act. Jackie suggests that first we *be*. This is the hardest part: going to that solitary place that I'd begun to discover in the deepest part of the woods beyond the 12 x 12. Some people call this place God, but others call it intuition, or the "still small voice," or grace, or simply presence. The name doesn't matter. It is merely a signpost for an experience we either understand directly or barely at all. For example, imagine you'd never tasted honey. I could describe "honey" for days and you still would have no real comprehension of it, but one taste would bring instant understanding. When we find a way — be it through meditation, music, prayer, your child's eyes, a shooting star, anything — to become present, we can look at problems fearlessly and with clarity.

Jackie's final step — do — is then as natural as drawing breath. You hand the homeless woman a sandwich; forgive no matter how you've been injured; join a peace study group to confront the nuclear issue with others in your community. Or take one of a thousand other actions.

As fascinating as all of this was, I resisted Jackie's message. "But you're a *doer*," I said. "While doctoring for thirty years, you've also regularly completed the Selma-Montgomery march, done the School of Americas protest in Georgia, and so much more. And soon you'll be marching across Nevada in a protest against nuclear weapons. You're not about sitting around contemplating."

After a slight pause Jackie said, "Both Einstein and Jung said the same thing in different ways: the world's problems can't be solved at the same level of consciousness at which they were created." She added that do-gooding, however outwardly noble, tends to bring the do-gooder into the blight: the same level of consciousness that creates problems like the global ecological crisis. Hence, the archetypes of the burnt-out aid or social worker, the jaded inner-city teacher, and the compromised activist. "There is someplace absolutely essential *beneath* the doing," she said, "and it's the most important part."

"How do I find that place?" I asked.

She replied: "Have you asked the creek?"

THE WOODS ARCHED above No Name Creek, their color wrung out, browns against a pale sky. I sat, listening to the creek gurgle and murmur on its stones. An hour passed, then two. Three. The sun had peaked and dipped westward when I began to put something together. In twenty years of meditation and spiritual search I've noticed that the people who really "get it" in the sense of beautifully blending inner peace with loving action have something in common. It doesn't seem to matter whether they are Buddhist, Hindu, Jewish, Catholic, or born-again pagan. They have what might be called "warrior presence." In other words, they face larger problems just as they face their personal problems — as Einstein and Jung suggest we do — on a *different* level of consciousness than the one at which the problems were created. Instead of allowing the negative forces of a flattening world to flatten *them*, those with warrior presence maintain beauty and control in their interior space, through being fully present in the moment.

Was this what Jackie was suggesting? I'd been by the creek for four hours now, maybe five, and I felt more alone than ever. But, remarkably, I did not feel lonely. Whereas loneliness is clingy and needy, solitude — I increasingly sensed — is expansive and luminous. You can feel lonely in a 5K race with hundreds of others or even at your own surprise birthday party. This is because inside each of us is a place of absolutely no connection to others. That place is like a bottomless open well. We try to shine floodlights into the well, fill it with toxic rubbish, or board it over with activity and routine. But if we don't befriend the well — if we're not strong in solitude — then on one level our relationships can be tinged with insecurity.

It occurred to me, beside No Name Creek, that by living 12 x 12 Jackie has been cultivating an interest in the well; leaning over, peering in. She has the genuine confidence and lightness of spirit of those who have taken the interior journey. She whispers into solitude's well without fear of the voice that might come back. Ducklings, like the ones the Thompsons raised, develop alone in their shells and — though they rub feathers with others during their brief lives — they essentially live alone and die alone. We are like those ducklings. If we lose ourselves in material things, anxiety, work, and personal dramas of various sorts — and thereby miss our beautiful interiority — then perhaps we miss ourselves.

A doctor friend in New York City once told me that when she looks through an ordinary ophthalmoscope, she can see through the retinal wall clear to the edge of the brain. It's that close. And the brain, seen like that through the eye, looks like what it is: a gray glob. When we look out at the world through our eyes, who or what is doing the looking? Am "I" that gray glob? It's so mysterious. I stood there in the forest, feeling my heartbeat, aware of the creaking in the trees above, shivering slightly, beginning to sense that we humans are nature become conscious of itself.

See, be, do. Yes, I thought, being was indeed the most difficult part in an era where clutter — in both stuff and activity — eclipses the sweetness of solitude, the aliveness of the present moment.

I got up and walked away from the creek, the sun now hanging low to the west. I looked at the 12 x 12, a muted orange light reflecting off its windows. It's one thing to ponder warrior presence in the peace of the woods. But I knew it would be difficult to live it. At some point, my 12 x 12 retreat would end, and I wondered if I'd be as strong as Jackie when the inevitable challenges came. Would I be capable of drawing from deep wells of optimism, compassion, and pragmatic action, regardless of the shape of the external world?

6. | LIVING WELL

THOREAU WRITES IN *WALDEN* that he had more visitors during those two years in the woods than at any other period of his life. Just as my curiosity led me to visit Jackie in the woods, so too did my curious family and friends begin visiting me.

I'd chosen not to bring a mobile phone to the 12 x 12, and so I was anxious the night my friends Dan and Gwen, cell talkers both, were coming to dinner. I cringed at the thought of metallic ring tones and jargon-laden work talk echoing through the 12 x 12, an annoying reminder of the technological bulldozer currently flattening the world.

They arrived abuzz with energy in a station wagon (its sole bumper sticker: "I'd rather be smashing imperialism") with their two-year-old son, Pete. Longtime urbanites, the late thirty-something couple had moved to Chapel Hill six months earlier because of a job offer. Dan disappeared with little Pete as I cooked pesto pasta on the propane-powered, four-burner stovetop while chatting with Gwen.

When dinner was ready, we called for Dan and Pete. No response, so we wandered along the dirt road and finally found them over at the Thompsons' farm. Dan was pulling his giggling two-year-old son out of the deep mud — and thereby getting covered in mud himself.

Noticing Dan's woeful expression over the mess, Michele Thompson tried to comfort him, saying, "Oh, my kids do that all the time." But the urban Dan and Gwen became increasingly anxious over their single child. I wondered how it was that Michele, with six kids, always managed to maintain a state of apparent harmony.

Dan passed the muddy Pete to Gwen, trying — failing — to brush the mud off his white shirt. Meanwhile, Mike Thompson heaped feed among the goats, chickens, and ducks, driving them into a Pavlovian frenzy. Kyle came running down in his Boy Scout uniform and threw additional cups of feed into the animal swarm. Along with Pete, three of the Thompson kids formed a chorus line and danced for the animals. Michele momentarily disappeared into the house, then came waltzing back down with her infant, one of the cutest little Buddhas I've seen. I took her in my arms, and she smiled up at me with her big eyes, fat lips, and tiny teeth, squirming in all her uncoordinated perfection. Gwen peppered Michele with questions about bantams and Muscovys, while kids ran around with handfuls of eggs, baby chicks, and feed. A swirl of fowl, mammals, and humans in a buzzing state of joyful chaos.

As we walked back around the pond toward Jackie's, the amazed Gwen said, "It's like Bolivia."

"Like Africa," said Dan.

"It even smells like Bolivia — or Africa — chicken shit, and the stale water in those rusty wheelbarrows." They had had little idea that this sort of life was being lived less than twenty miles from their own house.

They'd brought the most exquisite chocolate truffles, which looked vaguely aristocratic and especially lovely displayed in the 12 x 12. The truffles proved scrumptious, as did the pesto pasta, salad fresh from Jackie's garden, and caper bread with local cheeses. As we munched away on the porch, Gwen said, "It tastes so much better outside, like when you're camping."

"We are camping," Dan said.

We drank ginger tea and savored Equal Exchange dark chocolate and some of the truffles. "The rest better go into the refrigerator," Gwen said.

"What's a refrigerator?" I replied.

"Yeah," Gwen said, laughing, "what the hell is a refrigerator?"

The whole evening buzzed and popped with a sort of relaxed electricity, partly because of the absence of electricity. I found that to be the same with all 12 x 12 visitors — a kind of wonder and good feeling animated their visits. Riddles and puzzles abounded in a tiny house secretly hiding in the middle of an empire. Instead of acting out the expected roles of thirty-somethings at a polite dinner party, we turned into little kids exploring each object, each being, each moment.

Dan loved the bees and the asparagus ("so that's how it grows"), and Pete discovered Jackie's metal lizard sculptures hiding behind the shiitakes. As we picked tea leaves, I explained that they were heirloom teas that Jackie was bringing back to life, Southern substitutes used during the Northern trade blockade during the Civil War. Gwen picked mint, collecting it in a small bundle using a blade of a grass to tie it together. Dan yanked up green onions for their own kitchen. While I was chopping the tomatoes, I asked them to go outside and cut some lettuce; they did and washed it in cool rainwater, which they hand-pumped into the kitchen sink from the plastic tank outside. It gushed onto the greens and splashed onto Gwen's shirt.

They asked me how I was doing. I told them I was surprised how normal it felt. My bathroom showers were easily replaced by outdoor solar showers; I'd automatically fill the five-gallon diaphragm with water at night, and it would warm up in the sun all day.

Instead of a flush toilet, a composting toilet. Instead of a refrigerator for veggies, Jackie's garden. Most luxurious of all, each night was blessed not only with moon and starlight but with the warm, inspiring glow of candles. The stars and candlelight gave the place a meditative feel that evening. Pete fell asleep in a bundle on the floor. Dan explored Jackie's aphorisms, taped above the table and on the ladder, and read aloud: "The difference between actually very serious and actually very funny is actually very thin."

He laughed and his eyes jumped to a group photo. "Which one is Jackie?" he asked. Gwen and Dan both stared for a long time at her, that aquiline nose, those blue eyes, and the long, pepper gray hair. They continually asked questions about Jackie, her background, the Thompsons, and Adams County's other quirky characters. They weren't going to give up their electricity, piped water, and plumbing, but they left still asking questions, and they drove home questioning. Gwen told me later they still sometimes puzzle over the riddle of Jackie's 12 x 12.

As they were leaving I felt happy, centered, and energized. Yes, their cell phones had gone off during the evening, but it hadn't bothered me. It was simply part of who they were. Then, under the stars, my mind wandered to my past ten years of work in the Global South, and I felt a pang of guilt over what I'd often been doing: punishing people for living sustainably, for living like this. Sure, at times I'd been shipping food and medicines to people on the edge of starvation — in postwar countries like Sierra Leone and Liberia. But in other projects my own ethnocentricity over what it means to "live better" allowed me to drive a fancy white jeep into subsistence communities — ones that already had *enough* — and preach the gospel of Ever More. Subtle, to be sure. I wasn't preaching shopping malls and superhighways, but rather better clinics and schools, more efficient agriculture, the standard aid fare, the rhetoric of conventional Western wisdom. But isn't the end result of all that to turn "them" into "us"?

A shooting star blazed across the sky, its ember trail leaving an afterglow. Looking up into the heavens, I considered a fundamental question: Is the modern project, the flattening world, ultimately leading us to greater happiness, health, and environmental sustainability? There's so much we can learn from the cultures of the Global South. I thought of Honamti, on the bank of Lake Titicaca in Bolivia, his world circling in three ways. That day he also told me about the Aymara idea of "living well." He said the Aymara do not seek to improve their lot in a material sense. The idea is not to live better, but to *live well*: friends, family, healthy body, fresh air and water, enough food, and peace. Jackie joked once that she was "downwardly mobile." A lot of people would call her poor. But perhaps she had consciously scaled back from the paradigm of living better — with its high levels of environmental destruction, collective anxiety, and personal depression — to living well, something more akin to Aristotle's golden mean, the lovely midpoint, where many in the world still live, and live quite well.

FOR JACKIE, SIMPLICITY ISN'T A PURITANICAL ASCETICISM. It's not about denial; rather, it's a creative process. Jackie isn't trying to inspire people to live 12 x 12. She told me once that those are the correct dimensions of *her* life, as a single person with grown children. Those who live with families, with kids and relatives, the majority of people, obviously require larger dimensions. So, where is the point of enough for each of us?

For me at the 12 x 12, "enough" definitely included a car. Absolutely. No doubt about it. Isolated deep in the country without electricity, water, phone, or an internet connection (though I did bring a laptop for writing), I needed a car for pragmatic reasons as well as to provide a kind of emotional escape valve from so much nature. Still, I found myself inclined to bike everywhere. I'd brought along a twenty-six-dollar used three-speed I'd picked up in a thrift shop in Chapel Hill. Most days I'd bike up and down Jackie's lane with Kyle Thompson; I also began using it to go to the post office in Pine Bridge, and the shop in Smithsville, four miles up the road, or ten miles into Siler City. The bike became a way to exercise my body and to lift my spirits. Instead of being cocooned in plastic and metal, insulated from the world, I was flying free, fully exposed to the sun and wind and the grit of life. Instead of the angry groan and poisoned cough of a combustion engine, I had silence and the constant respiration and heartbeat of a living world.

The car belonged to my parents — they had two and were happy to let me use one during my time in the 12 x 12. For the first few days I was glad to have it, using it to get around the rural area. Then, without even realizing it, I stopped driving.

The car sat idle for a full week, then another. With my bike I moved more slowly, and the world grew larger and more interesting. I biked country roads through the rolling farms and woods, and the landscape revealed itself to me in depth and nuance. But there was one problem. I was the only one biking out there in the middle of rural North Carolina, so I was an oddity. There are more vehicles in the United States than people. Not having a car is generally viewed as one step away from living out of a shopping cart. The stares I'd get as I biked down Old Highway 117 South ranged from blank to scowling. That's when Mike Thompson taught me the North Carolina wave.

"It's like this," he said. He pretended to be holding handlebars and flipped two fingers and a thumb off the grip for a long second. And put them back.

"That's it?" I said. "Nobody's going to see that."

Mike laughed. "Just try it."

On my next bike trip to check email in the Smithsville Public Library, I flashed an NC wave to the first pickup that passed. The results were instantaneous: a flash of two fingers and a thumb while the driver gripped the steering wheel. I tried it again. Another NC wave returned. As an experiment I tried a hand-in-the-air, *buongiorno principessa* wave a few times and was met immediately with suspicious frowns. The NC wave was a kind of secret handshake that proclaimed: I'm from here, too.

Buoyed by this new insight, I read my email at the little library, chuckling over a satirical article a friend sent me from *The Onion*:

> CINCINNATI — The blank, oppressive void facing the American consumer populace remains unfilled despite the recent launch of the revolutionary Swiffer dust-elimination system, sources reported Monday. The lightweight, easy-to-use Swiffer is the 275,894,973rd amazing new product to fail to fill the void — a vast, soul-crushing spiritual vacuum Americans of all ages face on a daily basis. . . . Despite high hopes, the Swiffer has failed to imbue a sense of meaning and purpose in the lives of its users.

Biking home, I asked myself: Did that car in front of the 12 x 12 imbue me with a sense of meaning and purpose? Blissfully, I exchanged NC waves with truck drivers and older men on porches. I noticed the sun, the wind, and my heart racing; pulse up (thump, thump, thump), the heart banging on my rib cage like sweaty, joyous palms on a drum, the butterfly spreading and drying its new, wet wings, and I was home quicker than ever. Up Jackie's lane, waving across the pond to Mike in his bright red shirt, and wheeling into Jackie's world. The slight, subtle abode, opening its door, smelling Jackie — her spices, her clothes — now mixed with my smells — my cooking, bread, cheeses, and the sweat on the previous day's shirt.

AFTER A DECADE LIVING IN GLOBAL SOUTH countries that often seemed as spiritually rich as they were materially poor, I couldn't help asking myself about simplicity.

I came across the work of a psychologist at the University of Pennsylvania, Dr. Martin Seligman, who had managed to cut rates of depression in clinical studies. He calls his method "positive psychology."

In contrast with our mainstream therapy culture, which tends to focus on what's wrong, Seligman focuses on what's right — the factors that contribute to our general well-being, a state of inner joy and security. He found that three elements contribute to this: positive emotion, engagement, and a sense of meaning and purpose.

The first factor, positive emotion, is necessary but not sufficient. If it's bought for the price of Prozac or a bottle of wine, it's transient. To last, it must come out of the second two factors.

The second, engagement in the moment, is akin to how you feel listening to an amazing live jazz show or symphony orchestra, a sense of being "lost in the music." This engagement can happen anytime, whether you are painting, gardening, or cooking. When you are in that state, if someone were to suddenly interrupt and ask what you were feeling, the answer would probably be: nothing. Absorbed in the moment, you've transcended the narrow ego and become, in a real sense, one with the task at hand.

The third factor, a sense of meaning and purpose, happens when that activity you're so wrapped up in also contributes to a larger cause. In other words, complete engagement in shopping or NASCAR may give a temporary buzz, but it leaves an existential hangover.

Jackie, I noticed, cultivated the second two factors in her life. She was completely engaged in her permaculture, activism, and doctoring, and all of these contributed to a higher purpose. The first factor — positive emotion — then flowed naturally, as when she told me she wakes up with "tears of joy" in the 12 x 12. As love is seemingly without limits, so too are these more intangible factors. None of the factors of genuine well-being are closely linked to material possessions. All material possessions are subject to habituation, a waning interest with repeated uses. Think of that first bite of ice cream: bliss. The second, also delicious, but perhaps 80 percent of the first. The third, yum-yum; the tenth, ho-hum. So the cliché that "money doesn't buy happiness" is grounded in this phenomenon, habituation.

Jackie was pursuing a kind of positive psychology, not a preachy austerity; still, did her neighbors feel judged by the existence of such simplicity right next door? The Thompsons, after all, had an ordinary-sized house, three bedrooms in all, plus a nice-sized living room, a TV, and all the other electrical appliances.

Even so, looking at things through Long Island suburban eyes one day, I wondered how Mike and Michele plus six kids — eight people — could live comfortably with just three bedrooms. Until one day, while chatting with Michele Thompson on her porch, she said rather curiously: "I don't know why we built such a big house."

I didn't say anything, looking over at a colorful Muscovy taking noisy flight from the pond. I looked at the house again. Too *big*? Quite the contrary, it was a prefab house, not that big at all. "We all sleep together in one room anyway," Michele continued. "So that's two bedrooms too many."

Inadvertently I frowned slightly. It just seemed weird that eight of them would sleep in a single room. Seeing my reaction Michele explained, "We sleep with the baby and littlest one in our king-sized bed, and the others either squeeze into the bed with us, or curl up together in their sleeping bags on the carpet below! Now that Zach's fourteen he sometimes sleeps in one of the other rooms, and Kyle has been known to join him. But there's always at least one of the three bedrooms empty."

What was a little odd, perhaps, from one perspective was perfectly ordinary from another. Most of the world's families sleep together in a single room. From the Gambian *kunda* to Tibetan *mongour*, necessity and tradition has Mama Bear, Papa Bear, and the Baby Bears all together in the same den. In Turkey, a census showed the most common place married couples had sex was the kitchen — one of the few spaces they could sequester away for some privacy. Going back just slightly in human evolutionary time, we find *Homo sapiens* sleeping together in communal tents or caves, not just with eight members of the nuclear family, but in clans of thirty or forty. So the Thompsons, by homesteading, were simplifying their material lives and increasing their sense of warmth and togetherness in a way that is quite natural in 99 percent of human history and even in most of the world today.

DID I REALLY NEED THE CAR? Two weeks had passed without using it, and I began to wonder.

I recalled my years living and traveling in villages and cities throughout Africa, India, and South America, enmeshed in communities of people who lived outside modernity, who walked and biked — and swam — everywhere. In large cities like La Paz, Bolivia, and Freetown, Sierra Leone, less than 2 percent of people own cars, mostly because they can't afford them. When I lived in those places, I watched the locals and tried to emulate them. Squeezing five to a tiny taxi in La Paz you could cross the city for a quarter. Rapport usually developed among fellow passengers in such tight quarters, leading to some fascinating conversations.

In the Bolivian Amazon, the indigenous Chiquitano people have no cars, and barely any roads — the river is their highway. They engage in what I came to call Amazon swimming, where they combine pleasure and function into a seamless activity. Instead of swimming directly up the Amazon tributaries to do the chore at hand — weeding a field, visiting a relative — they backstroke in a lazy, curvy pattern, sometimes chatting with a friend as both swim. They might stop midway to eat wild pineapple springing up on the river bank somewhere. I began to do this in Pine Bridge, taking the circuitous route down dirt roads for diversity or going out of my way to visit new neighbors and friends.

All the while, in front of the 12 x 12, that one-ton monstrosity of metal, plastic, and rubber sat as a nagging reminder of Western excess. I got in it once and turned the key, the motor roaring to life, blue smoke shooting out of the tailpipe. I turned it off and walked down to No Name Creek. Before I even reached the banks I knew what I was going to do. I knew that having that car in that place at that time was too much. I'd crossed the elusive threshold of living well. In this situation, the car didn't add anything. In fact, it rather complicated my life. Each day, one more unnecessary decision: drive or bike? With fewer options, I'd feel and be freer. And, anyway, why did I have to get anywhere faster than two wheels or two feet could take me?

I called my mom and told her. Silence.

Finally, she said, definitively: "You're keeping the car."

I tried to explain, but she told me there was no public transport in the area. I said I could take the bike ten miles to Siler City, lock it up, and get a bus from there, but she insisted.

"You're *keeping* the car," she said, "and that's my final word." I knew it wouldn't be easy to get her to take the car back. I figured the only way to convince her was to bring her out to the 12 x 12 so she could see for herself.

THE STRENUOUS CONTOURS OF ENOUGH

7. ‖ MOM AND LEAH VISIT

I DROVE BACK TO CHAPEL HILL and picked up my mother, and we drove back to Jackie's. Instead of relaxing in the deep countryside, however, she grew increasingly anxious as the quiet isolation swallowed us, and particularly as we turned onto Jackie's dirt road and parked in front of the 12 x 12.

"Now you're *really* keeping the car," she said, a horrified look on her face as she regarded the miniature house on No Name Creek. I remembered my own first reaction: embarrassed for Jackie that she lived in such cramped quarters.

In awkward silence we walked through Zone 1 and entered the house. My mother sank into the old rocking chair and soon remarked at how surprisingly roomy the place felt. We brewed tea from rainwater, picked mushrooms and asparagus for the evening meal, and watched the bees — as Jackie had predicted, they were now "swarming like a freight train" around the hive. After her initial wilderness shock, my mom blended rather easily into 12 x 12 life. Perhaps it was because she had a reference point: she'd served as a Catholic nun for fourteen years. Amid Jackie's material simplicity, my mom talked about entering the convent at age eighteen. She'd wake up joyfully in her cloister at five AM each day to pray in silence. When she left the convent at age thirty-two to marry my father, she had almost no material possessions.

Nor did my father. He'd been a Catholic priest for fifteen years, mostly in the Brooklyn diocese, leading the Spanish Mass for Latino communities. It was the progressive sixties, and disillusioned with the slow pace of Church reform, he left the priesthood to start a family. He met my mom at a Peter, Paul, and Mary concert and lured her out of the convent with love poetry. Then came my sister and me. My parents became college professors, and we moved into a middle-class home on Long Island, where our backyard was a forest of pines and oaks with a maze of contemplative walking paths that dead-ended or looped into themselves. My father baptized my sister and me at home amid their group of intellectual Catholic friends from the university. In our house, there was a sense that every object — from the piano to the Renaissance paintings to our gardens — spoke of that-which-is-more-than-just-human. I think it was this unusually contemplative upbringing that opened me up to the idea of living 12 x 12 and also what led my parents to have an entry point for understanding it.

My mother and I hiked deep into the woods, past abandoned farmhouses, stopping to pick grass and feed it to two horses, one beige and one patterned like a chocolate chip cookie. On the way back, as the sun dipped deeper into the western sky, she told stories about my childhood, ones I'd heard a dozen times. We wondered aloud about the thirty-acre intentional community — Jackie, the Thompsons, José, Graciela — whether that kind of harmony between humans and nature could actually be brought to scale in twenty-first-century America.

We were almost back to No Name Creek when we both saw it at the same time: a big snake, not two feet from us.

We froze. It must have been six feet long and was dark brown, a constrictor by all appearances. Not the least bit worried about the pair of tool-making bipeds standing before it, the snake ribboned its way into a bit of bush and climbed the nearest tree, a twenty-foot oak sapling. My mom and I stood in rather awed silence as it muscled itself straight up the thin trunk. The tree had few branches, so the snake gracefully utilized any available niche to hold its lower body as it arched and wound itself skyward until its pointy head rose above the sapling's tip. Then it turned quickly into a right angle, eyeing a larger pine tree several yards away.

It eased itself up still higher, now seeming to defy gravity. Half its length rose as a straight broomstick above the tree, and it shook the tree back and forth, trying to get within jumping range of the pine, but its efforts were in vain. The pine was simply too far away, and the snake, if it did attempt the leap, would certainly fall to its death onto the rocks below.

"Help it out," my mother urged. I stepped past the bush and pushed the sapling. It swayed under the efforts of the snake, and as it swayed forward I leaned into it. Our joint effort bent the sapling far enough for the snake to finally take courage. It leapt.

Suddenly the snake was suspended in the gap between the trees. In slow motion, this slender cord soared through the air, its body like the bends of a river. It landed, crouched in the pine needles, and then foot-by-foot graced its way up the pine until its head rose above the highest pine branch.

At the end of the day, my mother drove herself home in the car. I waved good-bye as she reversed onto Jackie's lane. The sound of the motor softened, then disappeared. The dust settled on the lane, and a blanket of silence covered Jackie's little homestead. The place where the vehicle had been wasn't empty; spaciousness filled the gap, the elusive contours of enough in the ripening leaves of the forest.

I biked down to the bridge, gazed down at No Name Creek, lost in thought. My mother and I hadn't talked about theories of living better vs. living well or the perils of degrading and erasing subsistence cultures. It was the snake that changed her mind about the car. The silence and strength of it brought her back to those reverent five A.M. moments in the chapel, incense burning, when she was a young nun obedient to a vow of poverty. The snake didn't possess anything in this world, but still it rose to the tallest branch, proclaimed and celebrated its being. Do we really need so much more than that snake? Do we need Hummers and Sony Playstations? China cabinets and electronic sensors in our running shoes?

I TOOK LOTS OF LONG WALKS. Rambles, you might call them, without specific route or time frame. The day after my mother's visit, while rambling, I did an experiment. I tried to see the world around me in "color patches." In a book at Jackie's, I'd been reading about recovering cataract patients at the turn of the nineteenth century, and several used this expression to describe their first experience of vision after being cured. Each place they'd fix their eyes was another glorious set of colors. One patient was exhilarated by the fact that everyone looked different; another asked the doctor about the black stains on paintings. "Those are shadows," the astounded doctor explained. The world looked beautiful to me, seeing it as if through freshly cured eyes, one color patch after another. I looped around from the tracks onto the highway, back to Jackie's. My sense of whimsy sobered as the colors came to represent strewn garbage under my feet. Old 117 South's shoulder was littered with Coca-Cola, Fanta, and Diet Sprite cans; Jack Daniels and beer bottles; paper and Styrofoam cups; Snickers and Three Musketeers wrappers; cigarette packs. New grass sprouted around the colorful debris, tentacles enclosing it bit by bit until it would disappear from sight all summer, reappearing, if faded, in the dying grass of fall. It just seemed wrong. Spotting a plastic bag, I began collecting trash.

The bag filled quickly, and I grabbed another one that had

snagged onto a bush. As I filled the new bag, I tried to connect the faces of the drivers and passengers in the minivans, SUVs, pickups, and sedans passing me with the rainbow of trash I walked through; I could not. All I saw were beautiful faces, and I began to wave. That slight nod, the lift of wrist and flash of those two fingers. Sure enough, the hands came out the windows, not to toss an empty Marlboro packet at my feet, but to snap an NC wave.

They chuckled at this fool. The dark pleasure of schadenfreude. They liked the fool for being carless, worse off than they. They liked him for picking up their trash. I didn't even have to initiate the NC wave. People started waving first, and I felt happy. It didn't matter that Dr. Pepper was dripping down my pant leg and onto my shoe through a hole in one of the bags. I found myself whistling and waving, everyone exchanging the greeting, until one person in one car didn't return my wave. In fact, the car stopped, turned around, and headed back my way, stopping beside me. The door opened — and out stepped Leah.

Lost in my long walk, I'd forgotten about her visit. She looked angelic, her blonde hair, freshly washed, falling over her shoulders. A corded wool sweater. Her blue eyes radiated intelligence along with dismay. She looked at me, horrified, this guy with a three-day stubble and sweat pouring off him.

I stretched out a hand to shake, then realized it was shellacked in Dr. Pepper. We shrugged awkwardly. "I bet you're ready for a nice hot bath," she said, trying to ease the tension. Then she remembered there was no bathtub at the 12 x 12 and backpedaled, "I mean..."

Back at Jackie's, I'd forgotten to put the solar shower bag out to warm that morning, so I scooped cups of cold water over my body behind a bush and lathered up. Meanwhile, Leah wandered through Jackie's gardens, trying to respect my privacy by not glancing my way. She squatted by Jackie's bees and remained there, engrossed, for some time.

Leah and I had met a year ago. I was on a book tour, with readings every evening, media interviews, and daily travel, all the while getting up before sunrise each day to work remotely on my rainforest conservation project back in Bolivia. When Leah first called me, I was in the *Christian Science Monitor* studio in Washington, DC, having just finished an interview about Bolivia's indigenous struggles for the rainforest with Terry Gross for the NPR program *Fresh Air*.

"I'm Leah Jackson," she said, "producer of a radio program based in Chapel Hill." Leah asked me some pre-interview questions, and a week later, she came to a reading of mine in Chapel Hill. Coming up to me afterward, she said she couldn't fit me into her radio show, but she offered to buy me a coffee if she could ask some informal questions about my work. "One of those alumni interviews," she said. We'd both gone to Brown University; she'd graduated eight years after me. We went to Cafe Driade, sipping cappuccinos in a small garden while she grilled me on everything from ways to avert species extinction to structuring op-eds.

At that time, her light blue eyes were almost hyperactive, shifting nervously as she flipped from one topic to the next. Her energy was scattered. She'd had two car accidents in the previous month, and she was restless after three years with the same show; she longed to be a reporter, not a producer, to have more control over her stories. She was also caught in a cycle of breaking up and getting back together with her boyfriend of two years, now a soldier in Iraq.

During the past year we had exchanged the occasional email, and when I came to Chapel Hill to visit my father in the hospital, we had met for dinner at Glass Half Full in the town of Carrboro, Chapel Hill's funky little brother. I almost didn't recognize her. She'd just returned from Senegal and Mali and was tan and more beautiful than I remembered. She talked passionately about the inequality she'd experienced in Africa, and the way Western corporations were raping Africa's natural resources, colonialism under a new name. She came across as self-assured, content with her job and life in Chapel Hill, the very same job she'd hated a year before. She had also permanently ended her relationship with her military boyfriend, started going to therapy with a spiritually inclined psychologist, changed her diet to organics, and begun a rigorous Zen meditation practice. Little in her external life had changed — same job, same little beater of a car, same apartment — but her perspective was completely different.

All wasn't fabulous. The spiritual path brings perils; Leah now felt more sensitive to her own hyper-individualism, as an only child of divorced parents, shuttled throughout her Colorado childhood back and forth between the front range and western slope of the Rockies. "I'm well acquainted with saying good-bye," she said. She also noticed how she tied her self-worth to stuff, living constantly at the edge of her budget, still immersed in the consumer pattern even as she awoke to it.

When I told her about my plan to stay out at the 12 x 12, her eyes lit up. She wondered aloud if she might come out to visit sometime, saying it might help her "sort some things out."

I finished the shower and put on a light green button-down shirt and my faded blue jeans. Then we wandered down to the creek. She hadn't stopped smiling, and as we crossed the creek and headed out into the forest, she said, "This is so brilliant out here. It's perfect."

We bent down in unison to admire a spider web. But nature is a now-you-see-it, now-you-don't kind of thing. The sunlight turned the web into a fragile tangle of shimmering swords. Then clouds passed over, the light dimmed, and the web was broken glass. "Thank you for popping into my life," she said.

She talked about her ex, James. He was a West Point graduate who had been sent off to Iraq. His was primarily a desk job, but still. Their biggest fights had been about the war. He wanted to serve his country; she felt he was being used in service of a lie. She followed him faithfully to rugby matches around the state. He wanted to marry her, said he'd try to get out of the military and into politics, eventually. She couldn't picture a life moving from military base to military base, socializing with other military folks, taking their kids to rugby matches.

"So why did you stay with him that long?"

"After growing up in my family — divorce and a general lack of communication — he and his family showed me what a real family should be, what love is. Love is something that's slathered on.

"In the same way, my job. The reason I've spent four years there really is because it's a caring, supportive *team*. Everyone works together, supports each other. Between that and James's family I've learned that it's possible for me to have that kind of cooperation and love in my life."

We'd come to a sharp bend in No Name Creek. We stopped and lay down on the mossy banks, listening to it gurgle past. She took off her shoes, got up and wandered around, staring at the grass.

I lay back and looked up through the trees, just barely showing their sticky buds, into a blue sky. After a while Leah came over and said, "I have a gift for you."

She led me over to a patch of clovers right at the creek's edge. My eye caught it immediately. Amid the near identical plants, one stood out: a four-leaf clover.

I touched it. "I can't believe you found this," I said. I'd never found one.

"They're everywhere once you have eyes for them."

Later beside No Name Creek, Leah dangled two caterpillars from their silk like tiny puppets over the book she was reading: *My Name Is Chellis and I'm in Recovery from Western Civilization.* In it, psychologist Chellis Glendinning argues that our fast pace, technological and chemical addictions, and lifelong traumas are linked to our dislocation from the natural world. She uses examples from nature-based societies to show how to reconnect to the living world.

As I boiled water in the 12 x 12, I watched Leah by the creek; she seemed lost in thought, staring past the caterpillars into the woods. Her shoes were off, bare toes curling into the mossy bank. I walked down to the creek with two steaming cups of chamomile tea and handed her one. She dropped one of the caterpillars onto a leaf and carefully accepted the cup in her two hands like an offering.

I moved a finger to intercept the silk thread of the remaining caterpillar, and let it dangle before my eyes. We were both quiet for a while, lost in our own thoughts as the creek flowed by. I dipped a toe in. Still cold, but not the freezing water when I arrived in early spring. The day was half gray, with intermittent light streaming through the clouds; the sun mostly hidden. A breeze from the east suddenly brought the smell of the chicken factories, and I felt myself seize up a little, flattening and hardening to my surroundings. I made an effort to come more deeply into mindfulness, feeling the small perfection of the creek's warming waters. A rebellious fragment of light broke through on the edge of a cloud, bejeweling the creek's surface with a hundred diamonds.

Then they were gone, and the surface was gray again. I looked at the inchworm dangling from the silk in my hand and said to Leah, "Think of how nature makes things compared to how we humans make things." We talked about how animals don't just preserve the next generation; they typically preserve the environment for the ten-thousandth generation. While human industrial processes can produce Kevlar, it takes a temperature of thousands of degrees to do it, and the fiber is pulled through sulfuric acid. In contrast, a spider makes its silk — which per gram is several times stronger than steel — at room temperature in water. Humans manufacture ceramics with similarly high temperatures, but the abalone makes its shell in seawater by laying down a small layer of protein and precipitating the calcium out of the seawater around it. The abalone shell is "self-healing" because cracks within it actually strengthen the ends of the cracks so they don't get bigger, unlike, say, an auto windshield. We're just now learning to make dental ceramics this way.

"Imagine we could design our built environment as gently as the caterpillar," I said, noticing how the 12 x 12, from this angle, looked so slight that it faded into the natural background.

Leah touched the silk thread, which the caterpillar makes benignly from the protein fibroin, and placed the dangling black caterpillar back on a leaf. "And think of its metamorphosis," she said, "in its cocoon, a churning of natural juices, enzymes — and out comes a butterfly. Where are the toxics in that?"

We decided to explore Siler City. Because I only had the one bike, we took her car. Along the four-lane highway, we passed Wal-Mart and other box stores, finding Siler City's Main Street abandoned. The box stores had turned the old downtown area into a ghost town: stores boarded up, hardly anyone on the street. The seizing up I'd felt by the creek, that nagging tinge of hopelessness, slid into me again. For a moment, I was certain that the world would slip, inevitably, into a genetically altered, overheated place of lost uniqueness and forgotten joy.

But instead of *being* this negative state, I simply observed it. I was coming to realize that the ideal of warrior presence is not a constant state. Today, I consider it a peak that I scale up, often slipping off, but I can always see it there. Even those rare humans who have lived lives of total love write intimately about their fears. Mother Teresa, for example, revealed in her private diaries an entire lifetime of doubt, a current of negativity that she battled daily. Gandhi, too, wrote of his weaknesses, his feelings of greed. Martin Luther King Jr. said once: "I have so much to do that I shall spend the first three hours in prayer." If these heroes had to struggle daily to overcome the world's negative mental-emotional force field, imagine how much more the rest of us must struggle to maintain warrior presence.

Leah and I wandered on foot into one of the few downtown businesses that wasn't boarded up, a Mexican grocery. We stopped in front of a wall filled with clear plastic bags of herbs, leaves, teas, and spices from Mexico. Leah picked up several, each eliciting a different memory from visits to her mom's home in Mexico. Her mom retired from financial planning at forty-eight and, with her third husband, bought a house with an ocean view. There, she'd been living for the past few years, neither happy nor unhappy. Leah said that her mom described this state as a "permanent vacation," piña coladas accompanying every sunset.

Out on the street we passed a domestic violence counseling center, the signs in English and Spanish. "And there's Triple-A," I said.

"AA, you mean. Alcoholics Anonymous, not the automobile club."

"Of course," I said, squinting to discern an odd sign that read "Holy Congregation of the Bladder" in front of a tiny church that seemed recently opened. "What strange salvation," I said.

"Salvation from what," said Leah. "Urinary tract infections?"

Whatever was not boarded up seemed to be either an odd religious cult or a substance abuse program. We didn't pass more than a handful of people on the street. I thought of my neighbor José, who told me he'd walked backward into America. He'd crossed illegally at night through the Arizona desert and said he'd heard the *federales* counted the number of Mexicans who came in by looking at the footprints in the sand. "I walked in backward," he said, "so they'd think I was going back to Mexico!" Had I, too, walked backward into America? Compared to the slow-living subsistence cultures where I'd spent the past decade, Siler City seemed devoid of life. The town is more than half Latino — most are workers in the dreaded chicken factories — and Mexicans and whites alike drove along the Wal-Mart strip in oversized pickups, loading them with "Made in China" junk.

Is this what America is becoming? Are we as a society accepting a corporate personhood? Just as our personal legal liability has been shifted to the corporation, it seems that we have given ourselves up entirely to this arrangement, as though we are no longer liable for the maintenance of our own souls. Limited-liability living. It's impossible for me to believe that in our deeper, silent selves we really prefer the efficiency of Siler City's box-store strip to the humanity that used to exist downtown. I thought of the colonial plazas throughout Latin America, where people today stroll for hours, greeting strangers under palm trees; Gambia's *kundas*, where extended families share everything; the bustle and color of outdoor markets I've walked through in India.

Of course the Global South is also being colonized by Wal-Mart — now the biggest retailer in China — and its corporate ilk. Nevertheless, substance and traditional cultures exhibit a resiliency that works against the trend, and they tend to be faraway places that are harder for the corporations to reach. We in the West are subject to marketing's relentless bombardment from birth. A South Carolina friend told me about a competition they had in her third-grade classroom: the teacher put them in groups of two, with the task of identifying as many corporate logos as possible. "That first time, we only confused the Black Hawks with Suzuki," she said. "By the end of the year, we could all name hundreds of corporate images. At the time, we thought it was so much fun."

We generally think that colonization is something that happens only in other countries, but aren't we in America also being colonized, constantly and relentlessly? Which is easier for corporate-political power: controlling people a continent away or those right next door? Americans watch an average of four hours of television a day. Our creative action is limited by an accumulation of regulations, taxes, and rules to an extent that eclipses much of our individuality. As Leah and I walked through the dead zone of what used to be Siler City, she talked about how she felt complicit in the way cities like this are changing. "I *am* a consumer," she said. "It's not even software that I can remove. It feels like it's built into my hardware."

Just as we were beginning to feel down, we began to notice a change. As we walked into the very heart of Siler City, like little wild-flowers bursting through cracks in asphalt, stubborn shoots of life emerged between the boarded-up shops and nineteenth-century to-bacco warehouses: a tiny café, a pottery studio, a shop selling paint-ings and sculpture.

This was Bradley's work. In my mind, I put the pieces together. Before she left, Jackie had mentioned Bradley Jamison several times. He taught permaculture at the local community college and was pres-ident of a company he started, Environmental Solutions, through which he bought up large parcels of land, a hundred or two hundred acres at a time, and made them available for eco-communities. The thirty acres that Jackie, the Thompsons, Graciela, and José lived on had been one of Bradley's purchases. His idea: Maintain a beautiful natural landscape by putting only a few houses fairly close together, and leaving the rest as shared natural space for the community — for hiking, fishing, meditation, gathering firewood. Bradley insisted that physically buying up the land was the only way to permanently hold back sprawl. And permaculture was the key to living sustainably on it.

Bradley also had a vision of how twenty-first-century urban spaces should look, and he'd begun dabbling in Siler City, pressing the town to provide tax incentives to attract artists and small busi-nesses. Leah and I wandered through this revitalizing space and talked enthusiastically about it on the drive back to the 12 x 12. She dropped me off there as the sun was setting, saying she had an out-of-town trip planned the next week but hoped to visit again. I told her she was more than welcome.

I BUMPED INTO BRADLEY A COUPLE DAYS LATER, while hiking near the spot where No Name Creek meets Old Highway 117 South.

A pickup pulled over and a bearded man got out and shouted over to me.

A little startled, I began heading back into the woods along the path, and he continued after me. I spun around, calling to him from a distance: "Can I help you with something?"

"I own this land," he said. "Can I help *you* with something?"

"*Bradley?*" I said.

He nodded, approaching me. He was nothing like I pictured. He had a shaved head, smoky beard, and red baseball cap, much too big for his head, that read "Libertarian Party." His body was tight, sinewy.

I explained I was living at Jackie's and he nodded, saying he was busy and only had a moment. He talked about how he allowed eleven-year-olds into his permaculture courses at the community college, saying, "If people want to learn sustainable living, why should the government tell us how old they have to be?" Then he extended his tiny hand, passed me a business card ("Environmental Solutions, Inc., Bradley Jamison, President"), and he was gone.

Bradley was so busy, evidently, because his Siler City idea was evolving into something bigger. Along with encouraging eco-development in rural areas like Jackie's, he wanted to roll into towns. His most ambitious plan was to buy up a massive tract of land abutting Siler City's shell of a downtown. There he would develop an ecological community using permaculture principles — dense concentration of family houses surrounded by a large, thriving green space — but with a difference. Bradley would cluster the human settlements right around Siler City's dying downtown and thereby revitalize its businesses through ecologically inclined residents wanting to shop locally.

A related development trend was then going on in North Carolina's Research Triangle: Southern Village outside of Chapel Hill. I'd been there once, before coming to the 12 x 12. It's a massive village

— 550 single-family homes, 375 townhomes and condominiums, and 250 apartments — but none of it seemed like Levittown suburban monotony. The designers had created a beautiful town plaza: an organic co-op grocery, clothing stores, bookstores, and jewelry shops ringed it and seemed to thrive. Though it has the positive effect of allowing folks to feel more community and walk and bike everywhere, there are big drawbacks. Southern Village has no expansive green spaces to speak of, just the thousand dwellings. It also duplicates Chapel Hill's downtown, thereby actually putting a bit of a strain on its economy by creating two competing centers. And it's very expensive. Very little affordable housing was included in the design, so Southern Village is populated with mostly white and Asian professionals, employees of the hospital and university. A little too lovely, too planned, Southern Village lacks the authenticity, charm, history, and spontaneity of an old tobacco town like Siler City.

Bradley's dream wasn't to create a Southern Village from scratch, but rather to adapt and reshape what already existed, so that people could feel the nurturing cycle of personal authenticity, robust community, and connection with nature. Residents of Bradley's eco–Siler City, once it was completed, could grow their own food organically, exchange it in farmers markets, create and sell art in the new galleries as part of the growing tourism economy, and perform any number of services virtually over the Web, while still living in and maintaining a wild, beautiful place.

There was just one problem. The town council and other powerful people in the community had launched a legal effort to stop Bradley from doing this. To them, his vision sounded like an effort that would hold back development. These were people who could no longer hear the earth beneath the asphalt. People, I had to admit, not unlike me.

8. STAN CRAWFORD'S GARLIC FARM

I'VE BURNED INCREDIBLE AMOUNTS of fossil fuels trying to save the planet from environmental destruction. I have globe-trotted incessantly: Asia, Africa, South America, Europe. It's the irony of my profession: corporations are destroying the environment globally, so we have to save it globally. That's the battleground. You might say a bit of jet fuel has even slipped into my bloodstream. The very bread I eat, the clothes I wear right now, are powered by humanitarian jet-setting: To earn my keep, I think locally and act globally.

I get to airports early. Then there's nothing to do at all, and the waiting becomes a kind of freedom. If I can find an empty gate, I sometimes do yoga. Catch up on some reading. Listen to beautiful music. Breathe. Then board the plane. Blocking out the other passengers' stress, the announcements about oxygen masks, and the pilot's ritualistic announcements of feet-above-earth, I do a twenty-minute silent meditation, relaxing my entire body. Then more sublime literature, music, maybe some unobtrusive yoga postures in an empty space near the kitchen. Before I know it, I'm there.

Not long ago, I had a layover in Denver's über-modern new

airport, which lies twenty miles outside the city on the high plateau where the Midwest meets the Rocky Mountains. The architects brilliantly pointed one of the airport's wings due west, and the west-facing wall is constructed almost entirely of glass. The effect: beautiful sunsets over the Rockies. During my layover I happened to catch one. My gate was near this wall of glass, and the sunset that afternoon washed the entire west wing in Technicolor orange, red, and clamshell pink. Outside, snowcapped peaks shone brightly through the color spectrum.

When I snapped out of my trance, I noticed something almost equally remarkable. No one else was watching the sunset. Hundreds, if not thousands, of people were gathered at nearby gates, lost in their rituals: reading the *Denver Post*, watching the CNN broadcast, buying fast food for their kids. A few had their eyes closed, perhaps napping or engaged in soothing rituals like mine.

We took off into darkness, and I somehow forgot all of my little rituals. I was in shock. The cabin seemed to press against me. I looked down into the darkness, a million electric lights below, and knew that — in more ways than one — I'd left the planet.

I WAS BORN INTO THE BURGEONING ENVIRONMENTAL ERA, shortly after the first Earth Day. One of my earliest memories is from July 4, 1976. I was five years old. My parents took my sister and me from our Long Island home into Manhattan to see the fireworks extravaganza for the American bicentennial. I can still see the color and feel the firepower that rose from those dozens of barges in the Hudson and East rivers, our collective national pride blooming so colorfully in the sky. As a kid, the Fourth of July always contained a hopeful feeling. It tasted like the promise of something, though I had no idea of what.

Eating hot dogs in fluffy white buns, drinking Coke, and watching fireworks, I knew my country was great. I'd help my dad hang the stars and stripes in front of our colonial home, then watch him get the grill going. The stickiness of summer settled on our skin. The feel of salt on me from a day at our Long Island Sound beach, the taste of mustard — all of it felt to me like freedom. I'd watch my dad expertly flip burgers and roll the hot dogs on the grill, and I would picture my grandfather before him laboring for thirty years in the Hudson & Manhattan Railroad, a subway connecting Manhattan with New Jersey; for forty years before that, my great-grandfather worked in a potato field in Ireland.

The mythology of my childhood: America got us out of serfdom, delivered a richness unimaginable to our ancestors back in the Old Country. Summer drives across the country, a large suburban house, my parents' tenured professorships: all of this confirmed the myth. We epitomized the American Dream. And like most myths, it is partly true. I owe much of my intellectual and personal freedom to America's political and economic system, and I am incredibly grateful for that. But over the years, it became apparent that the dream could end. Or that the dream was less attainable for some than others. What seemed to be unlimited economic growth took on darker shades.

As I grew up, Long Island was being paved over, the small farms and the remnants of wild forests near my house disappearing forever to become ten million uninspired cul-de-sacs. The Native Americans who used to live in those forests were long gone by then. I got to know them obliquely through the names of my town (Setauket), my nursery and elementary schools (Cayuga and Nassakeag), and the nearby river (Nissequogue); no one I asked knew what these words meant anymore. My friends' parents worked for Grumman, a military contractor helping to produce nuclear weapons. Beyond the safety and prosperity of my upper-middle-class life was something I didn't have a word for yet: ecocide, or the destruction of our planet by our current economic model. Until then, it had invisibly fueled our lifestyle, but the effects were now surfacing.

V. S. Naipaul, accepting the Nobel Prize in Literature, said that all of his books were about his "areas of darkness." Naipaul did not write about what he knew. He wrote about what he did not know, what was darkest in him, because it fascinated him so much more. He grew up behind walls in the Caribbean, in a comfortable middle-class Indian merchant family on Trinidad. Beyond the walls were colonialism, corruption, exile: his themes. In Naipaul's masterpiece, *A Bend in the River*, Salim cannot find home. An Indian abroad, like Naipaul, he's no longer at home on the African coast with his illiterate merchant parents, nor in India, nor in an immigrant area of London. He eventually comes back to Africa, not to the coast, but to the lonely interior, to a no-name town at a bend in the river. He finally finds home: nowhere.

On the surface, I come from somewhere: suburban Long Island, where I was born and lived until I went to college at eighteen. But is it possible to be *rooted* in a *suburb*, or is this oxymoronic? I've often reflected that those monotonous spaces clash with the notion of being somewhere specific. Suburbs are entangled in twenty-first-century globalism, in a single Flat World culture that has become a ubiquitous nowhere. My Long Island rootlessness flowed naturally into a kind of jet-fueled global nomadic life, in which I lost an essential part of adulthood: finding one's proper place.

Naipaul's area of darkness is a colonial system that degrades the human spirit. My area of darkness is the price of my privilege, an ecocide that degrades and poisons the human being while it destroys our very host, Mother Earth. The global economy gobbles up authentic places and vomits up McWorld, increasingly turning our collective proper place, this planet, into a dystopia. I'm a child of ecocide, caught in a catch-22. How can I get on that plane — yet how can I not get on that plane — knowing that an estimated half of all species today could become extinct due to the effects of climate change? This is my area of darkness: a living earth, no longer underfoot.

WHILE HOEING THE GARDEN at Jackie's, taking five-gallon solar showers, harvesting my own teas, throwing cedar chips into the composting toilet, I tentatively rekindled a relationship with the earth. Blowing out the last candle at night, awakening with the sun in the 12 x 12 loft, I remembered that electricity doesn't come from a socket; tomatoes don't come from a supermarket; water doesn't come from a pipe. Everything comes from the earth. It's fine to grasp this intellectually, but to once again touch, breathe, and eat this reality feels like reconciliation with a loved one after a long feud.

Through her 12 x 12 and afterward, Jackie became an earth mentor for me. Humans are nature become conscious, but civilization forgets this natural connection. Earth mentors not only maintain this consciousness but can spark it in others. At the eleventh hour of the environmental crisis, we probably need earth mentors to connect us to our host planet much more than we need gurus and tele-reverends to connect us to the cosmos beyond. Connect to the earth, to yourself, and you've connected with everything; try to connect to everything by other means and fail.

My time in the 12 x 12 was like an internship with Thoreau. It was as if I was with him on Walden Pond, feeling my thoughts thinking through his, my spade cutting earth next to his, our four ears, together, listening to jackdaws and jays. I felt the presence of Aldo Leopold, John Muir, John James Audubon, Loren Eiseley, and Ed Abbey, all earth mentors. Imagining these mentors by our side improves the quality of our connection with nature.

I've been blessed by having not just one earth mentor but two. When I was a younger man, organic garlic farmer and writer Stan Crawford of Dixon, New Mexico, took my hand and led me joyfully out of civilization. If the flattening world of corporate-led global-ization sometimes sounds like really bad Musak turned up high, Stan-ley Crawford sounds like John Coltrane playing to a room full of friends.

I was twenty-four when I first met Stan, and when I looked up into his clear eyes I could practically hear "A Love Supreme" play-ing in the background — bouncing off the mesas behind his adobe house, out of his El Bosque Small Farm garlic fields, and off the tip of the phallic rock pillar beside them that he jokingly called Camel Cock (a wordplay on the camel-shaped Camel Rock up the road toward Santa Fe). There he was, gray-bearded and six foot three, esteemed author of *Mayordomo*, *Petroleum Man*, and the best-selling *A Garlic Testament*, good friend of literati like Barbara Kingsolver, John Nichols, and Bill McKibben. There he was in a pair of dirty overalls with a hoe in his hands. I followed him out into a field, to weed some rows, in silence, the cool winds coming off the Sangre de Cristos, the gurgle of the river running in front of the field.

Stan paid me six dollars an hour to work with him, two days a week. He first taught me the word *permaculture* and its basic tech-niques, and I applied those techniques the other five days on my own back-forty, a sprawling piece of land on the Rio Grande with a small vineyard, just a twenty-minute bike ride from Stan's. I'd worked out a kind of sharecropper's arrangement with the vineyard's absentee owner. I had his singlewide trailer and an acre on which to farm my own blue corn and squash; he got a third of my crop plus two days of my time tending his vineyard.

I'd arranged both the vineyard-sitting and garlic mentorship through the Northern New Mexico Organic Farmers Association. I was ecstatic. Never before had I cozied up this close to the earth. After the suburban Long Island childhood and college in a big East Coast city, I'd come to Santa Fe to teach seventh-grade gifted and talented students at a Native American boarding school. But I was again in a city. Now I was bathing in the Rio Grande each morning before planting blue corn, tomatoes, quinoa, amaranth, and nearly two dozen other native and exotic food crops under a full moon, just as my Native American, Hispanic, and Anglo farmer-neighbors did to ensure a strong harvest in fall.

After my day spent planting, night fell. My hands were calloused from the shovel and hoe, my muscles sore and spent. The full moon illuminated the empty spaces that would become my blue corn, intercropped with beans (they pole on the corn) and squash (ground cover that suppresses weeds), and my contoured vegetable and herb beds. Permaculture, as I was learning from Stan, likes natural curves instead of straight lines, intensive planting, and mixing crops intelligently, such as fruit, nut, and hardwood trees. I'd put the theory into the ground, and now, under the moonlight, I saw just a blank page, an expanse of moist earth.

Stan inspired me. He'd found a playful balance in life between laboring in the open air for seven months and writing in his adobe studio for the other five. He and his Australian wife, Rose Mary (their two children were already through college), had purchased their acres in the late sixties, built their beautiful house brick by adobe brick by themselves, and lived, without bosses or time clocks, in creative freedom, largely outside the system.

People in the area labored with the earth and then played. Saturday nights, everyone gathered at the Foxtrot Tavern for an exchange of organic pest control tips and off-color jokes and for dancing to bluegrass and indie rock. Rural northern New Mexico couldn't be farther from the tenured world of my parents, from the East Coast establishment. Dancing manically around me were farmers, winery owners, artists, writers, silver and turquoise jewelers, small-town teachers, and yoga instructors. "What do you do?" I asked one guy. His reply: "Water in summer, snow in winter," referring to kayak and ski instructing. I'd just read Jack Kerouac's *On the Road* and felt some of that bohemian, spontaneous energy explode as the nights stretched on at the Foxtrot. More than dropout beatniks, Dixon's folks were cooperating with nature rather than opposing it, sculpting, growing food and wine, painting, teaching, and making a living, if barely.

Stan writes in *A Garlic Testament* about "the pound weight of the real," the actual wrinkled dollars that are exchanged over a box of organic garlic at a farmers market. I'd weigh a pound, hand that weight to a customer, and accept the greenbacks that would pay my wage and Stan and Rose Mary's farm expenses. They were constantly "snatching from the cash flow," as Stan put it, living without savings right on the edge of subsistence like most of humanity. Yet that's exactly what bound them with others. A kind of barter system existed in the area — I shear your sheep, you midwife for me — as well as a traditional communal relationship over irrigation that centered around maintaining tiny dirt canals called *acequias*. This wasn't just pragmatism; I sensed a real passion and spirit that comes from subsistence. I saw it again all over the Global South, where living along the contours of enough, without much surplus, keeps you on your entrepreneurial toes and linked to others through reciprocity.

Sometimes other laborers joined us. On spring solstice day, twenty of us gathered at Stan's to harvest garlic. (Garlic is planted in fall and harvested in spring.) It was one of those Ansel Adams days in New Mexico, with the lines of the mesas carving a sharp edge into the sky. Stan himself stooped a little, squinting out into all that beauty with an artist's eye, a gently discerning gaze. Then he shrugged and bent down to pull the first garlic bulb out of the ground. We followed his lead. Pollen floated in the chilly air as we pulled up garlic all morning. At one point I threw a bunch of garlic a little roughly into the crate, and Stan said, "Careful with my babies." We stopped at ten; Rose Mary and their daughter Katya brought a pot of miso soup into the fields, and we drank it out of cups. The picking conversation was often revolutionary. During a discussion about a proposed hazardous waste dump in the area: "Gandhi didn't just talk about nonviolence in an evil system," a salt-and-pepper grandma farmer said while pulling up garlic beside me. "He was all about *noncooperation*."

Another friend of Stan's, an artist from Santa Fe, talked about cultivating a posture of "maladjustment with Empire" in yourself.

"But everything is tainted," someone else said, wiping dirt and sweat from her brow. "We're feeding nuclear Los Alamos."

"Right," the artist said, "but you stay maladjusted to the general evil. That's true noncooperation: not letting Empire inside you."

Stan hardly participated in such discussions. He hovered a little over every situation, Miles Davis's "So What" coming off the mesas; a softer, clearer place. But he wasn't aloof; after all, he was touching the earth right there beside us. I reached down and touched it, too. When pulling lettuce from my own acres beside the vineyard, I reached down through the lettuce leaves, the lower part of the plant smooth like a lover's inner thigh. Sliding my fingers deeper, to where the lettuce met the moist earth, I sank them a bit into those depths and then coaxed the whole plant loose. Made a salad out of it; took it inside. "Don't let the Empire inside you. Stay maladjusted to civilization," someone would say, and Stan nodded, or didn't, pulling up another top-setting garlic plant, placing it into a pile, the pound weight of the real. I think Stan took pleasure growing dissent in his fields, along with garlic, chilies, and statis flowers. His life was so obviously maladjusted to Empire — why talk about it? His very presence, such a wise, well-known intellectual and novelist, hoeing a row right beside you, elevated everything in our midst.

The summer was coming to an end, and a new semester awaited me back at Santa Fe Indian School. I harvested the first of my squash, zucchinis, and blue corn and packed my little Nissan hatchback with them, driving it into the school parking lot and giving produce to the other teachers. They *oohed* and *aahed*, joking that they knew what

I'd done with my summer. Teaching during the week, I continued to work at Stan's on the weekends. I found that the experience with Stan and the anticivilization Dixon crew blended easily into my teaching. I was no longer the Ivy League expert here to impart knowledge; I was student to these young Native Americans. One day they told me their story of Jesus: Jesus, they told me, continues to fight an ongoing battle with Murosuyo, a Native American god. They duke it out in the sky and on the ground. The stakes are the fate of the earth. Just as Jesus seems to deliver the final death blow, Murosuyo tackles him in the heavens, and they fall together through the clouds and into a lake, and so it continues. I found it fascinating that their culture and environment are still hanging on today through Murosuyo's efforts. My teaching became an exchange of ideas.

I played Super Bowl commercials in the classroom, and together my Native American students and I "deconstructed" them. This was, in part, an idea encouraged by the state of New Mexico. The Green Party, powered by thousands of off-the-gridders like those I'd befriended in Dixon — who lived in pockets throughout the state — had increased their power in the state legislature and had worked with citizens' groups to pass mandatory "media literacy" for all New Mexico schools. I went through the in-service training and then explored, with my twelve-year-olds from the Navajo, Hopi, and Pueblo reservations, the ways marketers manipulate us by linking their brands to emotions like love, belonging, freedom, sexuality, and fear.

I showed a commercial with an SUV conquering a mountain, and an Apache student, Monique, correctly labeled the lie: "Freedom!" she cried out.

"Love and belonging," another student suggested, noting that the male driver was accompanied by a beautiful woman and rosy-cheeked children.

A Hopi student raised his hand. Frowning, he grew angrier as he spoke. His point, eloquently delivered, was that "crossing our sacred grounds with that noisy thing" did not mean love or belonging. He said that, to be more truthful, the gas-guzzler should be driving past the retreating glacier that its greenhouse gasses were melting.

I found these media literacy sessions as deliciously subversive as the chatter in Stan's fields. Thanks to citizen pressure, the very nation that produced more global warming gasses than any other was arming a million New Mexico students with the intellectual tools to *reject* consumerism.

AUTUMN ARRIVED. On one of my last days at Stan's (before the tractor was oiled and tools stored for the winter), a half dozen of us harvested a fall crop of squash and basil for the farmers market. Stan and Rose Mary cut basil on either side of me. I could hear the brook whenever the gentle wind stalled; the sky was a powder-puff blue, the mesas a ridiculous paste of orange, and I felt whole and alive, cutting wrinkly basil leaves, placing them in my wooden crate, the lively smell.

Stan seemed elsewhere, "Kind of Blue" on the breeze, perhaps already in his next novel. *Clip-clip* went his shears. How many basil sprigs had he chopped in his thirty years of farming? *Clip.* The breeze picked up and I couldn't hear the brook, just the swaying trees above, and the smell of chemise and sage mixed with the basil. Stan stood up to his full, lanky height and ran earth-covered long fingers through his beard, looking out into the direction of the wind as if for a sign. Then he sighed, almost imperceptibly and went back to clipping.

In Stan's fields an idea germinated in me that would much later coalesce into a kind of general principle: be in Empire, but not of it. As the years went on, even as a Yankee pragmatism kept me cinched to Empire, I'd try to follow this, walking up to the edge of radicalism. I wouldn't jump over, but the heat of the flaming edge, in Dixon, in Chiapas, Mexico, in Bolivia, in Liberia, and especially on the banks of No Name Creek, kept alive the embers of noncooperation, a healthy maladjustment to ecocide.

The long workday ended. Stan went to the till to fish out my wages. Wages that I could certainly use with my low teacher salary and high Santa Fe rent. But wages I couldn't accept for the community of this fall day. "Stan, I won't take your money for this work," I said, in twenty-four-year-old earnestness. "There's nothing I would have rather been doing today."

Stan looked at me from his heights, his blue eyes suddenly animated, and he patted me on the shoulder and invited me to a late lunch of foods from his farm. I'd later realize that this, more than anything else, is what Stanley Crawford cultivated at El Bosque: an awakened, generous human spirit and, therefore, a new earth.

MALADJUSTED TO EMPIRE

9. WILDCRAFTING AND COUNTRY STEAK

AS THE DAYS AT JACKIE'S PASSED, and the cold earth softened, buds and tendrils began finding their shape, and I increasingly thought about heroes. My heroes are mostly people you never hear about. They quietly go about creating a durable vision of what it means to be an American and a global citizen. These are the people whose spirits nourished me as I hoed the rows at Jackie's place, people like Stan Crawford, Bradley, and Jackie herself. As the world flattens, they give hope. They are what I call *wildcrafters*, people shaping their inner and outer worlds to the flow of nature, rather than trying to mold the natural world into a shape that is usable in the industrial world. Wildcrafters leave a small ecological footprint. They don't conform to any outward program, manifesto, or organized group, but conform only to what Gandhi called the "still, small voice" within. I consider much of the dispersed "antiglobalization," pro-sustainability movement to be connected to wildcrafting. Wildcrafters inhabit the rebel territory beyond the Flat.

But one morning at the 12 x 12, as a particularly strong stench of the chicken factory blew in, I asked myself how people like Stan,

Jackie, and Bradley find the inner strength to resist ecocide. As if in
answer to this question, I discovered a copy of Gandhi's autobiography on Jackie's bookshelf and began reading it each night in her
great-grandmother's rocker. I knew Gandhi's famous quote — "Be
the change you want to see in the world" — but the question still remained: *How?* In his autobiography he talked about how he was convinced that absolutely anyone can achieve what he did; he was simply
an average person who decided to transform himself.

This transformation happened gradually when, as a young
lawyer in South Africa, he decided there shouldn't be a gap between
his convictions and his actions. Each time he identified something in
his outer life that contradicted his inner beliefs, he decided to make
a change. For example, believing it wasn't correct to eat meat, he immediately cut meat out of his diet. When he realized that buying
British clothing supported the colonial system that oppressed his people, he began wearing a dhoti, spinning the cloth himself. And so he
continued, one quick relinquishment after the next, until his outward
actions gradually came into harmony with his beliefs. This not only
built his character but inspired the confidence of others, turning him
into the great, humble leader who would free hundreds of millions
from the colonial yoke. In his own words, Gandhi was incredibly
clear: changing yourself is the key; no external achievements, however noble, can replace that.

From the rocking chair, I regarded the 12 x 12's floor, a white
slab of bare cement. So stark. An unadorned slab of rock surrounded
by two full acres of breathing earth. Jackie later told me that she had
mirrored Gandhi's transformation, relinquishing one hypocrisy at a
time, a gradual, deliberate evolution. She didn't want to support war
taxes, so she reduced her salary to eleven thousand dollars. She
wished to have the carbon footprint of a Bangladeshi, so she went
off the grid.

Bradley, using his skills and interests, was doing something similar. He didn't like the suburban sprawl he saw rolling into Adams County, so he began buying up large tracts of land and turning them into environmental eco-housing. Seeing that our educational system was perpetuating ecocide, he established innovative sustainable agriculture programs at the local community college. It was remarkable to feel the ripple effect of the courses he taught there, from horticulture to eco-design, from beekeeping to turning native plants into tinctures, medicines, and foods. Bradley shaped Jackie's skill set, and she in turn inspired Bradley with her ideas. And they are part of a larger constellation of wildcrafters. My direct neighbor, José, made traditional Mexican furniture by hand. The Thompsons had left the city to produce organic chicken and pork. Lisa, up the road, was a social worker who'd bought ten acres and was slowly transforming herself into a small farmer. And a fascinating father-son team, Paul Sr. and Jr. — whom I was eager to meet — had purchased thirty acres outside a nearby town and had followed Jackie's lead and built several 12 x 12s.

Like Gandhi, these wildcrafters made one small change after another in their lives and watched their inner and outer lives slide into harmony. They were beginning to inhabit a place I'd later come to see as the creative edge.

This idea first came to me in the 12 x 12, but only after leaving Jackie's did I fully grasp the extent to which these folks are shaping their inner lives first, then moving on to shape their outer environment through living beyond paradigms — including paradigms of environmentalism. Wildcrafters, those who work with nature's flow rather than against it, do this in a place that is, in the end, simultaneously internal and external: the creative edge, a dynamic geography.

Wildcrafters on the creative edge have social and political impacts beyond their numbers. For example, the several hundred wildcrafters in Stan Crawford's Dixon were only a few of the tens of thousands in New Mexico creating healthy, near-carbon-neutral communities. They voted on and passed innovative policies like the mandatory "media literacy" courses in schools, and they have grown the state's Green Party into a force in state politics. Nationally, the Green Party has around two hundred elected officials, including members of city councils in Boston, Cleveland, Minneapolis, Madison, and New Haven, and numerous mayorships. In Europe, Green Party inroads are stronger still; in Germany, the world's third-largest economy, the Greens have controlled the powerful foreign minister position and other cabinet posts.

This growing political and economic resistance, sadly, comes not from our elected and corporate leaders, but rather from *gusanos* (worms) that gradually eat away at the apple from within; when it collapses, it decomposes and becomes soil so something new can grow. I have several friends, for instance, who are *gusanos* within the California system, working on the creative edge of health care, education, business, and conservation, laboring to turn their state into something approximating their vision of America, in the hope that it will inspire the rest of the country as a model.

What is particularly fascinating about the *gusanos* in North Carolina, my 12 x 12 neighbors, is that they did not choose to wildcraft in progressive Europe or in funky California, Vermont, or New Mexico. They're in the conservative rural South. The late Jesse Helms used to have a lock on this area of North Carolina. The Thompsons, when they escaped to experiment on their new ten acres, were in a sense in rehab. The trailer park, the weapons and crack, neighbors in prison, the constant drone of commercial TV — all of this gone, cold turkey. They now opened their front door to a profusion of birds, a pond, a dark stretch of forest — to No Name Creek.

While musing over all of this, one morning I noticed a cocoon attached to the deer fence. Was it from last year, or from a caterpillar that had already gorged itself on spring leaves and gone into an early cocoon? Around the 12 x 12, dozens of different-sized, -shaped, and -colored caterpillars and inchworms dangled from silk strings and attached to budding leaves. I came to marvel over the miracle of that cocoon and the transformation of one organism into a completely different one.

Really, we've got the story wrong. We imagine that the caterpillar, knowing that it is time, goes to sleep in its womblike cocoon and wakes up a smiley, happy butterfly. That's not what happens. As biologist Elisabet Sahtouris explains, the caterpillar devotes its life to hyper-consumption, greedily eating up nature's bounty. Then it attaches itself to a twig, like the one on the deer fence, and encases itself in chrysalis. Once inside, crisis strikes: its body partially liquefies into broth.

Yet, perhaps guided by an inner wisdom, what Sahtouris calls "organizer cells" go around rounding up their fellow cells to form "imaginal buds." These multicellular buds begin to bloom into an entirely new organism but not without resistance. The caterpillar's immune system still functions and thinks that the imaginal buds are a virus and attacks them.

But the imaginal buds resist — and ultimately prevail — because they link together, cooperatively, to become a beautiful butterfly, which lives lightly, regenerates life through pollinating flowers, and migrates over vast distances, exploring life in ways that would have been incomprehensible to the caterpillar.

Jackie, Bradley, the Thompsons, and the other people I was meeting were undergoing this transformation, not alone but in a network of hundreds of thousands of other "imaginal buds" throughout Pine Bridge, the United States, and the world. By allowing themselves the space to change, instead of clinging out of fear to what they knew, they were embarking on this transformative journey.

BUOYED BY THIS EVOLVING REALIZATION of wildcrafting, the creative edge, and the possibility of transforming from caterpillars into butterflies, I found my spirit lighter than ever at the 12 x 12. One day I biked to Smithsville, rolling along South Main Street (the town was so small that there was no North Main Street), whistling and exchanging NC waves with the good folks in passing cars, until I arrived at Rufus' Restaurant. My stomach growling, I decided to go in for lunch.

The place was a quarter full, and I peered under the empty tables looking for an outlet to plug in my laptop. As I stooped, a waitress came over and cleared her throat: " 'Scuse me," she said. "But may I *help* you with something?"

"I'm going to eat here," I assured her.

"Under one of the tables?"

Chuckling from the other waitresses. Some of the conversations stopped. I reached up to pat down my hair, cowlicked as it was from my bike helmet; I probably looked crazy.

"I'd like a table where I can plug in my laptop."

A completely blank stare.

"My notebook computer. It hardly uses any electricity."

"See that clock?" she said.

I looked across the room at an electric, unplugged DRINK PEPSI COLA ICE COLD clock stuck at 2:04 and 13 seconds. I sat down under it and plugged my laptop into the empty socket. One of the waitresses had been trying to hold in a big old laugh; when our eyes met, our mutual smile was the pinprick that caused her to burst. She was still chuckling and shaking her head when she came up to me and asked in a friendly Southern twang, "What can I get ya?"

"What d'ya got?"

"Well, we've got country steak. It's not on the menu, and it comes with slaw, pintos, taters, fries, creamed potato, any two."

"What is country steak?"

"Cubed steak."

"What's that? Hamburger steak?"

"Oh no, it's meat that's been cubed."

"So, cubes of meat. In sauce?"

"Gravy, yes. But it's been cubed and put back together. How do I explain this? Mary!"

Mary groaned, as if to say, "How many *times* have I explained this?" I glanced around the restaurant interior; the decorations had been hanging on the walls for decades, mostly soda pop posters with long-dead ad campaigns like "Drink Dr. Pepper. Good for Life" and "Mountain Dew, it'll tickle yore innards." Another slogan, the text inside a three-foot-wide bottle cap on the wall, read obscurely, "Thirsty? Just whistle." *Whistle for what?* I thought, the brand it was meant to elicit unknown to me.

"It's fried" came an impatient Southern twang from the other room.

"Fried," repeated my waitress.

"Fried," I said.

"And it's good!"

"Okay, I'll take your word for it."

"With what?"

"Creamed potatoes. And slaw."

"Yeah, I think it's cubed cow, because I've seen it in the cow section at the grocery store."

"Hold on," I said, "so we're not completely sure what animal we're talking about?"

She sighed and said, "I know it ain't chicken."

There was good humor in our banter, but only later would I realize the ironies and complexities. For instance, I unconsciously judged Rufus' for "backwardness" for not understanding the twenty-first-century lexicon 101: the laptop plug-in. Yet wasn't my very presence there a Flat World advertisement, sidling up and whipping out my portable computer? That community still had what Bradley was trying to foster up the road in Siler City: life centered around people, not machines.

Then there was a more insidious undercurrent: racism. During three visits to Rufus' I never saw an African American person. By virtue of my white skin, I was basically a member of the club, hence the easy repartee with the white staff. Similarly, at Bobby Lu's Diner in Siler City, I didn't see any Latinos — despite the fact that Siler City is half Latino. Other restaurants in Siler City were purely Latino.

There's a grocery outpost a few blocks from Rufus'. Once, when the restaurant was closed, I went in and asked the clerk, a hirsute, heavily tattooed man in his forties, if they served food. He sighed and said, "Nope." Behind his head hung chewing tobacco packets, raw sausage links, and packets of beef jerky. The remainder of the store was filled with possibly the world's widest selection of 40-ounce beers and malt liquors.

The only plausible lunch food was a Hot Pocket. I held it up, frozen stiff in its colorful little package, and asked if I could microwave it. "Sure," he said. He was a man of few words, but not the guy who burst in next. This man's voice boomed through the outpost for the next several minutes, as my Pocket got hot. He was already in midsentence as the front door flung open, a heavyset African American man with long braids tied into a ponytail, trailed by his wife. "... Oh do I see it. I see it! No, not the milk." — his wife was pulling a gallon out of the refrigerator — "It's this!" He hoisted a cold Colt 45 over his head like an Oscar.

"I've been dreaming about it all day, since I woke up at five A.M. This is it, this baby ..."

Even as the man paraded up and down the aisles with his enormous malt beverage hoisted high, his wife lugging milk, bread, and TV dinners, two others were already lined up to buy 40-ounce bottles, including the quiet guy with a bushy, uneven mustache. He'd already opened his Colt 45. He took a long swig and then stared at the black man with intense, squinted eyes.

The overweight black man had by now twisted open his

40-ounce and proceeded to kiss the label, work his tongue up the neck and into the opening. His wife, burdened with groceries, said, "Save some of that action for me." Without the slightest hint of a smile, the clerk accepted food stamps for the groceries and cash for the beer. Before following his wife out, the man stopped tonguing the bottle long enough to say to the deadpan clerk, "Thank you, boss, for saving my life." He then took a giant swig and disappeared on tiptoes after a perfectly executed curtsy.

I felt ambivalent about this little drama on South Main Street. The two whites, the mustached man and the clerk, eyed the black man with obvious contempt. Was it purely about race or also about social class? Can you truly unbundle the two when racism is so deeply imbedded? The black man, though humorous on the surface, was also tragic: grossly overweight, on food stamps, already dreaming of his first 40-ounce during five A.M. insomnia. Was he resisting and transforming the racism around him or conceding defeat?

"THE AMERICANS, THEY DON'T LIKE US," my Honduran neighbor, Graciela, said to me in Spanish. "*Sabes que son los* 'red-necks,' *verdad?*" — "You know what rednecks are, right?"

She was hosing down her lawn very unevenly, soaking one spot to flooding and then breezing over the patch beside it. Her husband was late again. For both Graciela and her husband, this was a second marriage; they each had teenage children from previous marriages. He worked three jobs; two involved landscaping on the side, with his main job "processing" thousands of chickens an hour in the Gold Kist factory. That morning, I saw him tear down our gravel road in his black mini-pickup, late for work. The first time I went over to introduce myself to them, he was guarded, evidently wondering why I spoke Spanish, why I'd chosen to stay in a shack with no electricity — sizing me up to see if I posed a threat. Like the vast majority of Siler City–area Latinos, he was illegal.

"We're like slaves," Graciela said, staring at the water gushing out of her hose. "We work all the time, and it's never enough to pay the bills." Though she was only forty-three, the lines etched in her face made her look a decade older. She had a barrel-shaped midsection, large chest, and solid arms from her day job housecleaning and evening work at McDonald's.

As we spoke, a wave of empathy washed over me. Hearing the Spanish, I felt as if I was back in Latin America, where I'd lived for five years, and where, on so many occasions, I had seen giant multinational companies underpaying people in sweatshops, on industrial soy plantations, and in fast-food restaurants. Was this any different? She was barely earning enough to get by. Yet Graciela was one of the lucky ones. Of Siler City's thousands of Latinos, she was one of the few who owned a house, thanks to the nonprofit group Habitat for Humanity. She praised Habitat on several occasions, saying that her mortgage was only four hundred dollars a month, including taxes, which was considerably less than she had been paying for rent. My mother, while visiting me at Jackie's, remarked: "You can tell Graciela's family loves their house." There was the tidy lawn, newly planted flowers — even a little doghouse with a lightbulb that glowed at night.

One day, arriving home in her greasy McDonald's uniform, Graciela said to me: "Life seems good here if you're American. But only if you're American."

José, in his identical Habitat home across from Graciela, was less open. Though he was incredibly friendly, and he would invite me over to dinner and into his woodshop to see a newly crafted piece of furniture, he always seemed guarded. When we'd talk about certain topics, he'd clamp down or change the subject. I wondered if he was undocumented, even though he'd been in the United States for two decades.

At one point I said to José, "I never see your son playing with the

Thompson kids." It seemed odd, since Mike's eldest son, Zach, was the same age as Hector.

"Oh, he doesn't like to play so much," José said.

"He likes to be alone?"

"No, he plays with Graciela's kids all the time, just not with the Americans."

It always threw me off a bit when my Latino neighbors referred to "the Americans" as if they were a separate ethnic group, and perhaps one not to be melted into. I noticed a struggle in José's face, as if figuring out just how to say something. Always diplomatic, he never wanted to stir anything up. "My son says that — what's his name, Mike?"

"Yes, Mike Thompson," I said, surprised that after a year living here he wasn't sure of his white neighbor's name.

José continued: "He says Mike looks at him in a certain way. Maybe . . ." — he hesitated, then shrugged — "maybe a racist kind of way."

10. | WHITE

THERE'S A POWERFUL DOCUMENTARY called *Dare Not Walk Alone* about St. Augustine, Florida, a city that Martin Luther King Jr. targeted in the 1960s as a place to challenge racist segregation laws. Weekly protests and vigils were held, but violence eventually erupted, including a white hotel owner pouring acid on black children who had jumped into his pool. Images of that incident and others shot around the world, and these events contributed to the passing of the 1964 Civil Rights Act. Afterward, the white elites of the town retaliated against blacks by cutting them off economically and wiping out evidence of the civil rights struggle. Even the old slave market had no sign of ever having been a slave market — not one historical plaque existed in the town. The film ends with two black sisters visiting the church where they were once brutally cast out for being of the wrong race. Members of the white congregation receive the sisters in a powerful act of reconciliation, hugging and weeping, letting decades of pent-up shame spill over. The white congregation needed forgiveness more than the sisters — who had gone on with their lives — needed to forgive.

We need more of such healing. There's a parallel between how we deal with race and how we deal with ecocide. In both cases, we look away. This denial weighs heavily on our individual and collective consciousness. Just being aware reduces the burden. Jackie helped me face my own unconscious racism when she said to me, during one of my visits, "I admire you for throwing it all away."

I shifted from one foot to the other. We were standing in Zone 2 of her farm, beside the beehive. I asked her what she meant.

"Since you're white, and a man, you have everything open to you: power, privilege. And yet you're working in places like Liberia and interested in a 12 x 12. You've sacrificed your birthright."

Jackie helped me see that part of understanding racism is understanding white privilege. Challenging this requires a deep personal commitment to constantly reflect on and root out the ways we've been conditioned by false constructs of race. I find that listening allows me to overcome some of my subconscious assumptions. During my stay in the 12 x 12, I listened to Spike Lee's explanation of how racism works in the film industry; listened to José and Graciela talk about how they experience racism in twenty-first-century America. The more I listened, the more complex it all seemed. Jackie's comment about my "birthright" includes nationality and gender along with race. As I was seeing firsthand in the relationships between my neighbors and in town, racism is often a complex stew of status, income level, culture, and history. While there has been progress — most notably the election of the first African American president — structural racism remains deeply embedded in our society. Just consider the fact that there are nearly as many black people under some form of correctional supervision (in jail or prison, on probation, or on parole) today as there were slaves during the peak of slavery in 1860.

During one of my walks, along Pine Bridge Church Road, I came to an overlook. Below, a lone farmhouse sat in a freshly tractored field. The wide, two-story house had collapsed into itself, sad in its little nook between two hills, as desolate as a scene from Faulkner's *The Unvanquished*. As I looked at that house, a relic from plantation times, I thought of the slaves who once toiled there, and the reality of slavery suddenly became physically real. Black people had been treated like property on this very soil, in that old house. I wondered: Has our society ever come to terms with the extent to which our wealth was built on the backs of people who were considered less than human?

"MY FRIEND JULIANA LIVES IN THE CHICKEN COOP," José said.

I was about to bite into a taco over at José's, when I froze and frowned. Leah was at the 12 x 12 for her second visit, and José had invited us over to his place for a meal. I looked at Leah, dumbfounded. I finally said to José, "*Una persona quien vive en un* 'chicken coop'?"

Yes, he said. He then talked about how lucky he was to have his Habitat for Humanity home, since he also didn't have to live in the "chicken coop."

"José," I said, "what do you mean?"

The "chicken coop," we discovered, was a housing project of doublewides just outside Siler City where the Mexicans and Central Americans who worked the Gold Kist factories resided. Leah, her journalist radar homing in on a story, wanted to visit immediately. She spent the night at the 12 x 12 — I gave her the loft and created a bed for myself below out of a sleeping bag atop two blankets — and we drove into Siler City early the next morning, passed the town's bustling box stores and boarded-up downtown, and crossed the train tracks. Before us appeared a sprawling trailer park, *cien porciento Latino*: the infamous "chicken coop." Rows of white single- and doublewides, each one equipped with hula hoop–sized satellite TV dishes. Hundreds of them.

"It's a kind of US Soweto," I said. "A township." We turned the bend to see hundreds more on the opposite side of the road, and beyond, the forest had been felled for more to come. "So this is where we put the cheap labor."

"The Gold Kist chicken factory workers," said Leah, "plus the seasonal farmhands, the gardeners, the maids, and Wal-Mart stackers . . ." Leah's voice drifted off as we pulled in and drove among the hundreds of identical trailers. Leah's forehead wrinkled. "This is how our *Gastarbeiter* get screwed," she said, using the German word for "guest worker." "Greedy landlords build places like this and then gouge these folks with outrageous rent. They're undocumented, so they can't protest."

I'd seen this all over the world; the global capitalist system zeros in on the cheapest labor. On a work trip to Delhi, India, I witnessed thousands of identical shanties just up the road from a sweatshop where thousands of people produced clothing for wealthy European designers for pennies an hour. In Bolivia's El Alto slums, jewelry and clothing companies have set up similar factory production rows, thousands of Aymara and Quechua people — globalization's refugees. Though the situation is of course complicated, one result is a deluge of inexpensive, industrial-chemical potatoes and corn that has eroded the sustainable rural livelihoods of Bolivia's indigenous majority. It angered me to see people I knew, who had been growing crops in harmony with Pachamama for millennia, now with few options except to sew for terrible wages. In North Carolina, not ten miles from the 12 x 12, the same dynamic was only barely hidden beyond the train tracks.

But as we drove through that Saturday afternoon, Leah and I began to notice something unexpected. This wasn't Eminem's *8-Mile* trailer park, with pistols and ridin' dirty. We noticed *alegria* and community, as people gathered around barbecue grills or on porches; we saw laughter and large gatherings. We passed a birthday party with a child, maybe five or six, swinging wildly at — and missing — a dragon piñata. Leah slowed down further. *Wham!* The boy hit the soft spot under the dragon's neck and dozens of kids broke into a joint scream as they stooped for treats.

And these folks had water, electricity, telephones, roads, and a solid shelter. "It might not be so terrible here," I said.

Leah agreed. "Definitely not. A lot of the Latinos I've met in America, they have a kind of lightness, because they are here for one basic reason: money. And they have this don't-care kind of attitude because they know if all else fails — deportation, it just doesn't work out — they can go back to Mexico. Back *home*. They have a country, a home. I couldn't spin this as a story on 'Apartheid in Siler City.' "

As we crossed the tracks again out of the "chicken coop," we saw the white folks' stately colonials with their dormer windows, gabled roofs, wraparound porches, and sculpted gardens — but not a soul around. No more Latino *alegria*. Who was better off? There were two races, two classes. But there were also folks like José and Graciela, who owned their own houses. And the Latinos here have an emotional and cultural escape route — homelands in Mexico, Guatemala, and Honduras, places with more limited financial opportunities, but homelands nevertheless. We'd found in Siler City something of Soweto, but along with it something else, more puzzling.

FOR TWO STRAIGHT DAYS, THE RAINS FELL. The two fifty-five-gallon rainwater tanks beside the 12 x 12 overflowed; No Name Creek swelled in her banks. The world was liquid. Plants sweated, Jackie's bees beaded up with water, their hind legs thick with honey. Sometimes the sky would momentarily clear, and I'd head out along the tracks or the creek for a walk, but on one of those occasions the skies suddenly turned from gray-blue to charcoal and began dumping rain. I ducked into an abandoned house, under the one part of it that still had a rusty tin roof, and crouched there for an hour, just watching the rain, listening to it, feeling it bead on my skin. I looked up; I wasn't alone. A hawk was in there, too, seeking shelter on a rafter above, the same enormous one that had dropped a feather out of the sky into my hand. Our eyes met, and we both froze. After a while, though, we forgot about each other. I listened to the rain — on tin, on leaves, muffled by the wet earth. When the rain slackened and I continued along No Name Creek, the hawk remained behind.

During those walks the landscape held something back. I'd break away from the creek's banks at random places, heading off through farmers' fields and tracts of wood, along old dirt roads, wherever my instincts took me, sometimes coming to a high point where a hilly panorama would stretch out around me. Everything looked stalky, reedy, as if wanting to burst into a full Southern spring but not being able to. The landscape was thick with history, with inertia, sluggish and melancholy, as if it just couldn't motivate to once again change seasons.

Leah and I began spending weekends together as we developed what the Irish call *anam cara*, or a soul friendship. Without doubt, a romantic attraction was growing between us, but though it was unspoken, we both hesitated to act on that attraction and become lovers. It seemed we were exploring so many feelings and issues that went beyond "us."

We'd usually stay in the 12 x 12, but we once went to her place in Durham. The first time I climbed the outside stairs to her apartment — actually the converted attic of a hundred-year-old home — I was struck most forcefully by the white glare of the entire place. A clamshell-white kitchen, a white sitting-room nook, and a large white bedroom with twin sloping ceilings. She'd taken down the photo of her ex-boyfriend, and many of her old paintings; she had created a fresh blank canvas on which to repaint her life.

The three colorful photos she had up only accented the white further, like parrots flying across a sky of billowing clouds. Indeed, in her apartment I felt a bit as if I was floating in a cloud, buoyed by scents of jasmine soap, incense, spices, and the fresh fruit gathered in a wooden bowl in the kitchen.

We set up a little room for me in her reading nook. Later, we lay side by side atop a comforter on her bed, staring up at the ceiling. The whole place, though by no means ostentatious, felt luxurious compared to the 12 x 12. We talked for an hour, enjoying what novelist Anne Lamott calls "prone yoga," where you get horizontal and let thoughts flow from mind to mouth. We talked about "decolonizing ourselves," how to rewrite our scripts, throwing out the ones that posit consumption as end and not means, that consider the natural environment as a bunch of stuff put there for us to use; the scripts that oppress races, classes, and nature felt hardwired into us. After a while we shifted gears and talked about where our own lives were headed. Leah said into the pure white ceiling: "I'm confused."

"If you're not confused, you're fused."

She got up and pulled me from the bed, saying, "I want to show you something." We went for a walk in Durham. The city has a gritty, hardscrabble feel to it. It's three-quarters African American, one-quarter white. We walked past scores of old tobacco warehouses, many of them being renovated as restaurant and gallery space — the slaves that worked in them and their history covered over with hardly a trace. We walked past the YMCA where Leah worked out, past her office, and into an old neighborhood, circa 1940s, where she was thinking of buying a house.

I looked into her blue eyes, and then down the street. She said, "I'm twenty-eight, and I want a home."

"Will buying a house give you that?"

She looked down the street. "You'd go crazy in a place like this, wouldn't you?" she said.

I followed her eyes down the street, the chestnut trees, old middle-class homes, and shrugged. Much was changing in me, and in that moment, I didn't know.

BACK AT THE 12 X 12 THE NEXT DAY, I spotted the two-year-old blonde head of Allison Thompson bobbing along the dirt road toward José's and Graciela's houses. I'd been watching the movement of a light breeze, which passed like a wave through the trees on the Thompson farm, crossed No Name Creek, and washed through the deeper woods beyond. Seeing Allison reminded me that I had a gift for her.

Actually, it was from Leah, a doll she'd given me to pass along; Leah said Allison reminded her of herself as a little girl. Picturing the smile on her face, I retrieved the doll from inside and strode toward the rabbit fence. I was about to undo the twist tie when I hesitated. Beyond the cute little Allison — who had now been joined by her four-year-old brother, the mohawked Brett — I noticed other people with darker hair and skin, who for a second felt vaguely threatening. Mexican and Honduran teenagers: Hector — José's son — and two of Graciela's kids, ranging between twelve and sixteen. I wanted to give Allison the doll, but another thought crossed my mind: Did I really want to interact with the teenagers? Have them know I'm home? What if the two older ones were into gang stuff? Later on, I'd look back at this reaction as my own internalized racism — I viewed them not as unique people in that moment but through a kind of racial profile. My fingers hesitated on the twist tie, and then I heard Mike's voice booming from down the road: "Allison! *Allison!*"

In a flash Mike reached the 12 x 12's gate, three of his boys in tow. Even quicker, little Allison and Brett, hearing their father's angry voice, took a shortcut between two Habitat houses and headed by a back route toward their own home.

"Have you seen my daughter?" Mike blurted out to me, his face practically cherry red. I told him she'd hung a left back toward his house. He didn't respond; instead he charged in the direction of the teens, his boys picking up steam behind him. I thought of Mike's gun. I'd heard it go off during target practice the day before. Meanwhile, the Latino teens seemed oblivious to Mike charging toward them. They fake-pushed each other, fooling around. When Mike was fifty yards away, the tallest boy looked up and stopped midsentence; the others stopped as well, regarding the angry father and his three blond boys. Everybody froze.

The silent standoff stretched out for a long moment, an incredible tension filling the space between Mike and his boys and the Latino teens. Suddenly I felt myself completely outside of the situation, as if I were a ghost in a movie revisiting his life. I experienced a kind of inner paralysis, knowing only one thing for sure: I didn't want anyone to get hurt. Mike moved toward the teens, his sons right behind him. They narrowed the gap to thirty yards, then twenty yards; the teens didn't move. Then all of sudden Michele's voice rang through the trees: "I got her!"

Mike stopped abruptly, one of his boys banging up against him. "You got her?" he called out.

"Affirmative!" Michele hollered from about a quarter mile away.

Mike hesitated for a few seconds, which stretched out to ten. He seemed at a loss as to how to act. Nobody moved or spoke. His boys looked up to him, waiting for his cue. Without a word, Mike did a 180-degree about-face and marched toward his house, his boys following him, a rapid retreat.

11. FORGIVENESS

"I WALKED BACKWARD INTO AMERICA," José said. "I never finished that story. Of how I came to your country."

José had invited Leah and me to his cherished woodworking studio. He gave Leah the same impassioned tour he'd given me, showing her the beautiful dressers, tables, and chairs that he struggled to sell door-to-door. He told her that Habitat for Humanity made it all possible, as he touched his sliding table saw with reverence. Leah couldn't hide her fascination with the man. He invited us in for tacos.

They were delicious. We happily munched away, *La Fea Más Bella* on the TV in the background. Hector got up early to go play RuneScape on the computer, and eventually Leah followed him in there, sitting next to him. "I'm killing chickens for their bones," I overheard him saying to her.

The touch of mistrust I'd felt from José until that point — the way he'd tiptoe around his past or local racial politics — seemed to fall away as we got to know each other. Leah wandered back in and sat down next to me on the couch. José cleared his throat and said, in Spanish, "I lived in a village in Guerrero, Mexico, until I was one, but our family had constant gunfights with the neighboring family. A historical feud. So my grandmother decided one day that we should leave. We found another place, closer to the city, in the hillside slums, and I lived there until I was fifteen. It was a shack with old mattresses for walls and cardboard siding, with a tin roof and a single window.

"What did I do? I went to elementary school for a few years and then dropped out at age eight to shine shoes in town for twenty pesos a day. Later I sold ice cream on foot. When I was fifteen, my cousin said, 'Nothing is ever going to change here.' Then he mentioned 'America,' but I didn't know what that was."

Leah didn't catch all of this, so José stopped while I translated. She asked José in broken Spanish if he had never even heard of America at that point in his life.

José said, "I had no idea what America was. Sure, I'd heard the word *America*, but it meant nothing to me. Absolutely nothing, like . . . like *a grunt*."

He muted the TV and continued, "In the end, my cousin convinced me that we could make money in America. So we got a train — but went the wrong way and ended up in Guatemala. Guatemala! A week later we were back in Guerrero, ashamed. But soon we did travel north. We crossed the border at night, through the mountains, the desert. We spent three days in the desert.

"At one point Immigration had raked the desert sands to a smooth surface. Perfectly flat and smooth. Why? They did this so they could count the wetbacks who came in during the night. That's why I walked backward into America, to make it look like I was returning to Mexico.

"I saw a dead man, hanging by his neck from a rope in the desert. I finally arrived at a train track. My cousin kept walking, but I risked hopping on a freight car to Los Angeles. That's where I stayed for some years before moving here to North Carolina five years ago."

After a silence, Leah asked him, "America was nothing but 'a grunt' to you as a teenager. What is it now?"

José stretched out his arms to take in the house, the woodworking studio. "All of this," he said. "And freedom. Opportunity. I love this country."

His response began as spontaneous and genuine, but by the time he got to "I love this country," I sensed he was mouthing what you were supposed to say to Americans.

On TV, the soap opera was over and the local news came on. Easter was on the way, and with it rumors of right-wing groups who were planning to once again impede Siler City Latinos from carrying statues of Christ and the Virgin Mary through town. Since 2000, Siler City had been a crossroads of US immigration issues, ever since David Duke, former grand wizard of the Knights of the Ku Klux Klan, had given a speech there in front of four hundred people denouncing illegal immigrants. Some supporters waved American flags; others, Confederate flags. Most Latinos stayed in their homes that day, afraid to come out to counterprotest. Duke was assisted by the National Alliance, a neo-Nazi group, and most of the supporters were from out of town. Racial tensions in Siler City were high because thousands of Latinos had been moving there and taking jobs in the poultry industry, and the city government had written the federal government for help in removing undocumented workers. Days after Duke's speech, the local Latino Catholic church was vandalized.

Since then, a group of white and black parents and the school board have tried to transfer undocumented Mexican students out of local public schools, and Duke has held several more rallies. Siler City has become even more racially divided. In 2006, protestors stormed the door of the town hall to ask for stricter immigration laws, some shouting, "I pay my taxes!"

José looked out the window toward the Thompson farm, toward

Siler City beyond, a huge frown etched deeply into his forehead. I asked him what was wrong.

"I'm fine," he said. "*A veces con un poco de miedo, no más.*" — "Just a little afraid sometimes."   .

IN GREENSBORO, NORTH CAROLINA, in November 1979, the state's Ku Klux Klan and the American Nazi Party killed five of Jackie's young friends in cold blood while they were protesting racism. Luckily, Jackie herself arrived late to the protest. To date, none of the killers have been prosecuted for what occurred in the Greensboro massacre. The Greensboro police were sympathetic to the KKK and weren't about to turn in their buddies.

As Jackie told me when we first met, her father was a Klansman, and he used to rally like the rest in a pointy white hood. Nevertheless, Jackie keeps several framed photographs of him in the 12 x 12. While sitting in Jackie's great-grandmother's rocking chair, I once examined an incredibly tender photo of her parents. Jackie's mother sits in the same rocking chair, looking melancholic, while her father, dressed in a pair of jeans and flannel shirt, stands beside her, hand on her shoulder, looking directly into the camera. The look in his eyes is childlike. On the other side of the 12 x 12 is another photo of her dad. Another is up in the loft, framed by her bed. She loves him.

During my time in the 12 x 12, I kept wondering: How could this be? Jackie's dad went against every principle she lives for. In the days after my lunch with José, as Siler City prepared to deal with more anti-Latino riots, after witnessing Mike Thompson and his sons descend in anger on those Mexican and Guatemalan teenagers, after visiting Siler City's chicken coop and stumbling across the relics of slavery in the surrounding countryside, I felt myself become first annoyed, then angry toward Jackie. How could she turn the other cheek to all this?

These people — the ones who killed her friends in Greensboro,

KKK members like her dad — they had to be brought to justice, didn't they? A mix of fear, resentment, and bitterness grew in me, and there was nothing in the 12 x 12 solitude to distract me from it. So I did what I often did at Jackie's: I walked.

Almost immediately, I realized where part of my feelings came from. I've been physically attacked three times in my life, in Providence, Boston, and Amsterdam. All three times by gangs of young men. In Providence, the attack on me was one of twenty-seven by African American gang members, who were targeting white and Asian college students as part of their initiation. In Boston and Amsterdam, I might easily have been killed or crippled had it not been for luck: the police happened to be passing by. In both these cases, the perpetrators were arrested and prosecuted for violent assault, but eventually they got off without jail time.

Violent attack is barbarian and inexcusable, and I understood what José must have felt, what North Carolina Latinos and blacks, then and now, must feel: extremely vulnerable and outnumbered by a violent group. I vividly recalled my assailants' furious faces, their shouting, grabbing me, punching me to the ground, and kicking my skull and rib cage. They deserved punishment! Forgiveness seemed little more than another word for weakness.

These thoughts pounding in my head, I suddenly stopped walking. There before me, a box turtle was stranded between the rails. His head came in and out of his wrinkly neck. I loved box turtles as a child on Long Island, discovering them hidden amid the fallen oak leaves in the forest patches near my house. I lifted him up and placed him in the woods. His feet found grass, and he bolted forward. So did I. Onward. Something raw rose up in me, a desire for revenge against the people who had attacked me, who continue to attack others. I walked more briskly, then jogged, then ran hard. Nature absorbed some of my pain. A teal blue sky wisped with clouds to the south, a washed-out indigo blue to the north, and a million points of light green, buds and tiny leaves, bursting forth everywhere. I walked into it, walked for five or six miles, and kept walking.

I wasn't going anywhere in particular; I just let my legs lead me. Slowly, my jaw, held tight, began to slacken. I tried to focus on the present moment. I realized I was hardly aware of my surroundings because I was so wrapped up in my inner angst. Off the tracks and into the woods. I felt tingly, sweaty, breathing hard, at first from exercise, but then from a beautiful growing realization: I don't have to be controlled by lower-order feelings like anger and resentment, even when they burn right through me. Cradle the feeling, release it, and come back to the moment. I repeated a mantra from Thich Nhat Hahn that I'd found the previous day in the 12 x 12: *Breathing in I calm my body / Breathing out I smile / Dwelling in the present moment / I know it is a wonderful moment.*

The mantra brought me back. For a moment only; then bitterness returned. *Ah*, I said, a sudden realization. *So this is bitterness!* I walked with it, cradled it like a baby in my arms, and then breathed with it, calming my body and mind, releasing it, releasing bitterness and coming back to the present moment.

Wonderful moment. I came upon several hundred black tadpoles on the verge of death. Their mini-sea of rainwater had evaporated so much that it was now just a shallow puddle. From a distance the tadpoles looked like a swarm of insects on the water, as the top of their heads and their tails protruded. Only as I got closer did I realize they were tadpoles — and that they didn't know anything was amiss. They swam lazily, eating from the pool bottom and siphoning off what landed on top, oblivious to the fact that their pool was drying up.

There were no replenishing rain clouds in sight. I did a quick tour of the surrounding area and found no other water where I could translocate the poor guys. They were doomed, but I reminded myself: frogs themselves are not doomed. Likewise, 99 percent of the little stunted firs, pines, and dogwoods, the tiny saplings shaded from the sun under the tree canopy, were doomed. But trees aren't doomed. Nature played the odds, spreading out a thousand seeds of amphibians, of trees, so that a few might survive.

I sat by the puddle and looked at the black-and-gray creatures, glossy as the sad sinking surface. They nibbled at the wet clay bottom, swerved and sliced one past the next, and some of the large, grayer ones — another tadpole species — rimmed the water's surface with parted lips, sucking off what they could and leaving a thin wake. I fished a tadpole out, put it back, watched it swim away. Dipped a hand into the clay bottom, squeezed silky mud through my hand, and then sank in the other hand. I enjoyed the cool mud, the feeling of the water.

James Holman, a blind nineteenth-century British writer and traveler, said his blindness seldom caused him to miss anything. When they became aware of his condition, people always invited him to "squeeze things" as a way of perceiving them. Perhaps this is what we in a flattening twenty-first-century world must do: *squeeze* things, places, feelings, and ideas until they yield something. I squeezed the mud again, deeper into the earth now, and pulled out my hands, shellacked in deep brown, the sun gleaming off the rippling water that slid down my hands onto my forearms. A breeze peeled back my mud-covered arm hairs and smoothed a little wrinkle out of both my eyebrows as I got up. I walked into the forest with gleaming brown hands.

After another mile, the mud now caked on, I found myself once again at No Name Creek. I put my hands in the creek and rinsed the clay off, took another step and then another, and suddenly realized how different I felt.

Rather than being a tense ball of anxiety, I'd now come fully into the present moment. No marooned tadpoles, moored turtles, or hawk feathers falling from the sky announced the change. My heart pumped away as usual, but my mind had stopped. I smiled. I breathed. All the walking had paid a dividend. I looked down into the creek.

My image shimmered. I could see a face, some eyes, the strawberry blond color of my hair, the blue of my jeans, but all of this was like looking into a bubble. Seeing my translucent image in No Name Creek, I realized something important about Jackie. This is what she's done with her life: become transparent. Later, she would confirm this and explain more: when you become so enmeshed in the fullness of nature, of Life, that your ego dissolves, emotions like resentment, anger, and fear have no place to lodge. She says she still feels these emotions, a little, but more like a dull thud against her mind. They fall away.

What would have happened if she and her friends had taken revenge on those KKK folks in Greensboro, maybe with a tit-for-tat killing? This would have only continued the cycle of violence. Instead, in 2005, she and others came up with a novel idea: to replicate post-apartheid South Africa's Truth and Reconciliation Commission. They created a Greensboro Truth and Reconciliation Commission to hear public testimony about the event and to examine the causes and consequences of the massacre. The Greensboro City Council officially opposed the efforts of the commission, but the process forged ahead and became the first of its kind in the United States. What the commission discovered was significant: that Klan members had planned beforehand to provoke violence at the rally, and that the Greensboro Police Department and the FBI knew this ahead of time. The commission also determined that the white supremacists fired on demonstrators without being attacked first. The commission's 2006 final report laid out a blueprint for continued dialogue and peacebuilding, and through this process of open acknowledgment and engagement, instead of more hatred being fueled, an entirely different result is manifesting: hatred is slowly transforming into healing.

That's what happened in South Africa. Never was there a better case for revenge. For decades, the white minority had practiced legalized segregation, keeping the black majority in separate "townships" or shadow towns, marginalized from economic and political power. If you protested against this, as Nelson Mandela did, you could be imprisoned for decades. But after apartheid was dismantled and blacks took power in 1994, Mandela exhibited wise leadership, and the other cheek was turned. Whites were not only allowed to stay in South Africa, but could keep their homes and businesses. As a result, South Africa avoided the kind of massive bloodshed seen in Zimbabwe, and the country and its economy continued to function for everyone.

JACKIE DIDN'T MEET HER FATHER'S HATRED of other races with a dose of her own. Instead, she decided to walk the Selma-Montgomery march every year in her native Alabama. In fact, when I first met her, she'd just returned from the weeklong event. The original Selma-Montgomery march occurred in March 1965, ending weeks of political and social conflict over voting rights in the South during the peak of the civil rights movement. On March 7, some six hundred civil rights activists headed east from Selma en route to Montgomery. They made it six blocks, to the Edmund Pettus Bridge, before state and local officials met them and attacked them with billy clubs and tear gas, driving them back to Selma. Two days later, Martin Luther King Jr. led a "symbolic" march from Selma to the bridge. After that, other civil rights leaders in Alabama traveled to Montgomery to receive protection to carry out a third, full-scale march from Selma. On March 21, 3,200 marchers left Selma on their way to Montgomery. They reached the capital four days later, at that point 25,000 strong. Five months later, President Johnson signed the Voting Rights Act of 1965, which gave blacks the right to vote. To commemorate the 1965 marches, the federal government created the Selma to Montgomery National Historic Trail in 1996, and today, thousands of people follow that route every March to celebrate the acts of heroism that took place and to continue the process of racial healing. The annual march ends with a rally on the Montgomery green, the exact spot where Jackie's Klansman dad used to rally in his hood.

As I thought back on the three gangs that attacked me, I realized that, to an extent, I had turned the other cheek. After I was attacked by the gang in Providence, I wrote an op-ed piece for my college newspaper encouraging Brown students to volunteer as Big Brothers and generally climb down out of the ivory tower and get involved solving the problems that were the root causes of such attacks. After my Boston attack, the prosecutor tried to get me to press charges against the principal assailant, but I wrote a statement forgiving him, brutal as the attack had been. Had I prosecuted, he would have been denied entrance into the navy. In my statement I wrote that his anger would be better channeled into discipline in boot camp than festering and growing in prison.

As I returned to the 12 x 12 after my long walk, however, I realized there was a key difference between myself and Jackie. Whereas she, from all indications, had evolved beyond anger, I still had it lodged firmly inside me — as I had just witnessed. Eventually, the stay at the 12 x 12 would help me let go of it for good. Yet everything on Jackie's four tiny walls, including the photographs of her father, spoke of only one thing: love. I could not see a negative emotion anywhere. When Jesus said to love your enemies, he of course meant: Don't have any enemies. Instead of letting racism and other forms of negativity inside you, transform them through forgiveness.

⌂

DRIVE ALL BLAMES INTO ONE

12. | SACRIFICE AND SEDUCTION

DOWN BY NO NAME CREEK ONE DAY, I read aloud to Leah from Jackie's copy of the *Tao Te Ching*, Lao-tzu's famous book of Chinese wisdom: "Do you think you can improve the world?"

Without hesitating, Leah said: "Yes."

I paused, and then read on: "I don't think it can be done."

In unison we broke into smiles, and I continued: "The world is sacred, it can't be improved."

"Hearing that," Leah said, "I feel a pressure lift."

"It's our training," I replied. "'You can save the world!' It goes on to say, 'The master sees things as they are without trying to control them. She lets them go their own way, and resides at the center of the circle.'"

I turned my head to look at Leah's profile. Neither of us said anything.

Then she slid the book from my hand and continued reading from it: "Know the male, yet keep to the female. Receive the world in your arms. . . . Know the white, yet keep to the black. Be a pattern for the world."

I felt lighter, in a deep well of time, the forest around us growing more roomy. "I like that," I said, "about being a pattern for the world." The opposites were bouncing around in my mind: male-female, white-black.

"'Pattern' is so much better than 'model.'"

"Who said anything about model?"   .

"Exactly. But we always talk about role models. And model citizens. Sounds as plastic as a model airplane, when we're talking about an interwoven whole."

"Are you a pattern for the world?"

Her cheek tilted toward her shoulder and she shrugged. "Your turn," she said, handing me the book.

"He who defines himself can't really know who he is. He who clings to his work creates nothing that will endure."

"Lose your shtick," Leah said. "The more deeply we try to carve an identity, the less we're ourselves."

"We're cheapened. It's like trying to reduce God to one of its metaphors — the religions."

"Heresy!"

"Perhaps, but the finger that points at the moon is not the moon. You know," I continued, "I had an artist friend in New Mexico. She'd paint these beautiful watercolors on homemade paper. Work on them for hours, for an entire day. And then she'd leave the finished paintings by the river bank to blow into the water and disappear downstream."

"And thus they endured," she said.

This is the type of conversation Leah and I had during those spring days. On the surface these philosophical discussions were ironic because we were at the very same time gazing deeply into the dark waters of industrial chicken factories, at an underclass in sprawling trailer parks, and even at the possibility of racial violence among Jackie's direct neighbors. Did we believe "The world is sacred, and can't be improved"? Quite the contrary; it needed infinite improvement.

As we walked along No Name Creek, I considered this contradiction. According to Eastern thought there is no contradiction because of nonduality: everything is exactly as it should be at any given moment. I couldn't quite accept this. It seemed too easy a way out. Did that include the Holocaust? Six million Jews plus four to six million homosexuals, gypsies, Catholics, and communists dead in Nazi Germany — is that exactly the way things should be? Part of a lesson humanity has to learn? It seemed too much of a stretch.

But gazing into No Name Creek, I realized the creek was two things at once: a crazy pattern of noise and texture on top and a quiet stillness below. Some parts of its surface were particularly rough, and some parts of the bottom, like pools near the banks, completely still. So Leah and I, as we became more immersed in Jackie's home and philosophy, began to become more like the creek: rougher on our surfaces and stiller in our depths. We experienced more forcefully the distinction between *maya* (the illusion of sensory perception as reality) and *dharma* (the invisible, spiritual path). In its deepest essence the creek is neither rough surface nor still depths: it's water.

THE FOLLOWING DAY, walking far up along No Name Creek, I came to an abandoned sharecropper's house. I'd seen them before. In fact — for reasons nebulous to me — it was all the fashion in certain Southern lefty circles to translocate, renovate, and inhabit a former slave or sharecropper house. But finding them abandoned in the middle of nowhere was something quite different. I eyeballed the hard-plank structure to be about twice the size of Jackie's: maybe thirty by twenty-four, far smaller than the abandoned farmhouse I'd seen several days before. The roof had long since caved in, but the walls stood firm. I walked inside.

What was it like to be a sharecropper? In 1874, say, with slavery over but life largely the same? You've got freedom but can't exercise it. That freedom must have seemed scary. You've always lived as a slave, as your parents and grandparents did. It's the way things were done. Now, what options do you have? So you remain on the master's plantation, in a house like this one, receive a little salary; in theory you can leave, but for all intents and purposes, life remains what it was, in bondage.

The woods encroached in and around the place. But I could see that it had been fairly recently inhabited, maybe a decade back, judging from the junk around it. It even had an electrical line, now severed, running up to it, probably pirated electricity. I could hear the gurgle of No Name Creek and see patches of blue through the forest canopy overhead. It struck me that maybe most of us inhabit the awful no-man's-land of sharecroppers, suspended between slave and free. Between Gold Kist and free-range; between 100,000 square feet and 144; between Wal-Mart and homemade.

Recognizing the bind we're all in together, I decided while at the 12 x 12 to experiment with practicing nonjudgment of others. One day up the creek, I saw the most beautiful buck leap a farmer's fence into a corral of four horses. Sensing me, the buck returned to his mate and three babies. There, they grazed, the smallest doe rubbing its light brown face against the mother's, a perfect little kiss. Suddenly: *Bam!* A shotgun rang out in the middle distance, and the deer fled into the forest. Not ten minutes later, the owner of the shotgun blast appeared — a camouflaged hunter in a shiny Silverado pickup. As he passed, we nodded to each other, both of us equally trespassing, so no problem there. Then I saw the bulk of a light brown deer in his pickup cab, and I felt judgment rise. He'd come to shatter some skulls. But I thought: Were I him, I'd do exactly the same. Perhaps he has kids at home to help him skin the deer and roast it. Perhaps they use every single part of the animal. I pictured my own dwindling rations (with no car for a supermarket run) and thought of the pleasure of venison roasting over my own fire.

As I tried to practice nonjudgment, things worsened with the Thompsons. Several times Mike referred to his Honduran and Mexican neighbors as "the Habitat Mexicans." Then I was told that the African American woman who lived in the third Habitat for Humanity house hardly ever came, preferring to stay in her Siler City rental, partly because "she was afraid of Mike and his guns."

When I heard these things, anger would creep in. Then I'd think of something Jackie said to me, a little cryptically, that first day in the 12 x 12: "When you see worthiness, praise it. And when you see unworthiness, trace it."

IT WAS NEARLY TWILIGHT the next time I was with Mike, a week after the standoff with the Latino teenagers. He told me a story as the day faded, with his family gathered around. Michele had their baby to her breast, and the other five kids lingered on the porch in front of the pond, Kyle's shoulder pressed up against mine. Only Mike stood, and he told us about the wolves that came to their farm one night. His family knew the story of the wolves — they'd lived it, just a year before. But they listened as intently as I.

"Half-breed wolves," Mike said, the sun's afterglow giving his eyes a sparkle, "took out a thousand dollars in livestock one evening.

"Two of them, male and female, snuck into our farm when we were in town and ravaged the place. We came back to find bodies everywhere — turkeys and ducks strewn there, there, there, all the way up the road!"

I could imagine the carnage. Imagine how he must have felt to see so much of his work devastated by those half-breed wolves.

"They even got three goats and a hog."

There was a silence. "Did they eat any of it?" I finally asked.

"Nothing," Mike said. "Killed for killing's sake. One of the

Habitat Mexicans captured a half-breed, the male. He'd collared it and came to tell me I should shoot it. Out of revenge. I grabbed my gun, loaded it, and raced over with my finger on the trigger."

He paused, the suspense before the blood-soaked ending. *When you see unworthiness, trace it,* I could hear Jackie whisper. Don't judge. Trace anything you don't like in someone else back to their unique history; then trace it back to yourself because anything you dislike in others is somewhere in you. Mike was trying, against the odds, to live as an organic farmer, Gold Kist becoming more poisonously efficient every day. He and his family were fresh out of a drug-riddled trailer park, trying to make a quixotic dream of sustainability come true in an era of the big, the efficient, the flat. He's quick with a weapon and suspicious of other races, but in his situation, would I be any different?

"When I got to José's, I pointed my gun at that half-breed wolf. My hand shaking, I —"

Just as he was about to finish his story, to deal the deathblow, an eagle's shadow passed over his face. We all looked up; the eagle soared right past on a warm current, in a slow arc over No Name Creek, toward the sharecropper house and out of sight. *He said "José,"* I thought to myself, *not "the Habitat Mexican."* It was the first time I'd heard Mike use his neighbor's name. Beside the porch, tiny white moths rose up in lazy flutter, seeds falling from the trees around us, and I could hear insects crackling in the dead leaves below our feet.

"I looked at it through the sight of my gun," Mike continued. "The wolf was all huddled up and whimpering, and I lowered it. I said to myself: 'I can't kill him. He's just doing what he was born to do.' So I put down my gun, called animal control, and they took that half-breed away."

THE TENSIONS LEAH AND I DISCOVERED at the 12 x 12 — the creek's rough water and its stillness, *maya* and *dharma*, that the world is evil and the world is perfect — seemed entwined with another apparent duality: sacrifice and seduction.

To reduce her carbon footprint to the level of the average Bangladeshi's (that is, to one-twentieth of the average American's consumption), Jackie had made some considerable sacrifices. Ciao, airplanes; hello, Grey-dogging. She also said good-bye to electricity, to home heating, and to piped water. I was living these sacrifices on a temporary basis, but could I make these changes permanently? It was more than a bit scary to picture.

Leah and I talked about what would really change in our lives once our time in the 12 x 12 was over. I'd gotten rid of the car and begun to bike and walk everywhere — put on Jackie's garments, as it were, for a retreat — but my international twenty-first-century life, my *flat* life, was still waiting for me. I knew that unless I changed, nothing would change. That's the biggest test, the only test of the worth of an experience — is the change atomic? Does it get down into the very pattern of your psychological, emotional, and habitual DNA?

I didn't know what would happen. Like a caterpillar, I'd gone into a cocoon and felt my inner world shifting, but I had no idea if a butterfly would emerge or a stillborn half-creature. Would I be wise enough to identify the changes I'd need to make to align my life with the health of the planet? Even if I identified the changes, would I be strong enough to follow through on them?

The seduction of the 12 x 12 experience drew Leah and me in: organic food, fresh air and water, feeling God through feeling good. But looming in the background was the unsustainable lifestyles we both normally lived. Sure, I had the financial resources to drive a car, but is it sustainable? What is the larger cost of this mentality to the planet? I tried to be transparent about my own hypocrisy, of navigating the tensions of mindfulness. I began to see things in terms of what you might call false privilege, or any action that can't be enjoyed by everyone on the planet without compromising our ecosystems. Until that is somehow reconciled, clean living is all seduction and little sacrifice.

ON A LONG WALK ONE DAY, Leah and I talked about living honorably in the environmental era, a time when all of our planet's life systems are in decline. Before we realized it we were a couple of miles into the countryside, near a pond freckled with leaves and seeds. We stopped and sat on its banks.

An hour passed in silence. I let my gaze glaze the pond's surface. A flying insect made perfect circles, two feet in circumference, and then began lazily carving figure eights. After a while I was no longer looking at a pond; it had in a sense seeped inside of me and merged with the nearly two-thirds of my body that is water. Closing my eyes I felt its dimpled surface, its cool foreign depths. The figure eights started to tickle. I was smiling when I opened my eyes. The feeling was more than a little weird to the rational mind. What was going on? Something inside me was shifting. I was getting glimpses into the mystical experience — the sense that everything is intricately connected into a grand unity. It's what Thoreau meant when he called fish "animalized water," or what Whitman meant when he called grass "the journeywork of stars." It's Van Gogh's wheat fields and starry skies bleeding into their background; Gauguin painting people in colors as earthy as the world around them.

"I feel different," Leah said, walking back to the 12 x 12. The sun was setting in red and orange pastels. I looked over at her. Her soft blonde hair fell over bare shoulders, just the strap of a black tank top. A bit of perspiration covered her forehead, matting a patch of her hair. She brought up a hand to push it back, and then her hand came down and took hold of mine. We stopped and kissed for a long while. It wasn't our first kiss. Though we'd initially hesitated to become lovers — as if that would somehow obscure the spiritual and societal

questions we were grappling with — we eventually allowed ourselves to express what we were both feeling. We held each other, and
I looked over her shoulder into the thickening green of the oaks and
dogwoods. Spring was now here.

We walked on. Another mile, then two, and I felt something
catch in my chest, beyond the budding romance with Leah. Is there
any limit to what I, what she, what we humans could become? I felt
a sense of awe, as if all of my former boundaries had melted and I was
now a pile of clay ready for molding.

Back at the 12 x 12, we lit the candles and cooked up a stir-fry
with freshly picked shiitake mushrooms, sipped heirloom tea, and
entered into a kind of stillness that I thought was possible only in
solitude. It was cool outside; the full moon lit up some dark gray
clouds passing over. We heard the first spring frogs calling, and some
cicadas, and saw Venus through the window. I was thinking about
Jackie; she'd emailed me from her Nevada desert peace walk and
dropped a hint that a big change was afoot in her life. I wondered
what it was. And then I wasn't thinking about anything at all.

"There's a roominess to the present moment," Leah said. We
lapsed back into silence for the longest time. Actually we had little
conception of time. Sitting there in Jackie's goosehead rocker, hearing the slightest bubbling of the creek, I entered into a kind of trance.

I felt the house and me overlap with a click; we fell into place
together, fitting each other like shoehorn on heel. A similar thing
would happen again several times when I was alone in the 12 x 12 at
night. But on this, the first time, with Leah, I felt a shiver. Most of the
time, of course, I was just in the little house cooking, baking, writing, dressing, sleeping, marveling at the sky through the window.
But then it would happen, suddenly, on the rocker: *I feel the house
living inside me.* Not metaphorically, but actually inside me, doing
house things like warming, illuminating, freezing, getting dirty, getting clean, boiling, baking, inspiring, being still. Grounded, but

stretching a little toward heaven. Breathing through a flung-open window or door, breathing through my mouth. Inside me.

I was somewhere else. Nowhere, with a tiny house in there. Leah had a look on her face at once bewildered and astonished. She whispered, "Did you feel that?"

I did, and I still do. That's the One Life about which words are only signposts. It's the other world inside of this one, the place beyond contradictions. Are we to find the fullness of life in more things, in faster food and bigger shopping malls? Or is it to be found in the still, the small, the radical present?

PART II

TWELVE

13. CREATIVE EDGES

WHAT'S THE SHAPE OF THE WORLD?

Looking at baby lettuce coming up, the smell of fresh, loamy soil saturating my nostrils, and feeling around at the dewy base of the lettuce for weeds to release, I burst out laughing. An all-out guffaw. It's the wrong question. When the Aymara philosopher Honamti told me, by the blue shores of Lake Titicaca, that the earth was round up into the heavens, round out to the horizon, and round into our inner selves, he was actually trying to destroy the idea of roundness. His trinity of circles — up, out, in — is an allegory meant to smash the idea of our earth as any geometrical shape at all. It's not flat, nor is it, in any lived sense, round. So what is it?

Perhaps the world is not shape but rhythm. As my laughter died, I could hear something in the wind in the trees above; the slightly discordant bubble-gurgle of the creek; the peck-peck-peck of a giant woodpecker over the low baseline of buzzing bees in their hives. The search for a meaningful life is the search for the right chord, getting our rhythm in tune with the cosmic jazz improvised all around us. It's not a national anthem, a pop song, or a tired waltz. It's music that dances unpredictably with the silence all around it, that's a little off-key. The Russian philosopher and composer Gurdjieff talks about the Rule of Seven, where all of our lives metaphorically play out along a scale of seven notes, do-re-mi-fa-so-la-ti at first, but with one or two of the notes always changing, throwing the music into a constantly unstable state. This creates the problems of the world, which are then temporarily solved in the next bar of music. We're germinated to a rhythm; our mother's heartbeat is a conga drum beating beneath our racing little dot of a heart as our limbs, face, and fingernails take shape. It's that beat that we lose when we come out of her.

A year after I left the 12 x 12, I returned to No Name Creek, and Jackie and I stood outside one night under the stars. They shimmered in the sky and on the creek. She left me alone for a minute, disappearing into the 12 x 12, and then returned with a pair of everyday binoculars and handed them to me. *What could I possibly see out here on such a dark night?* I thought. Jackie pointed into the sky, toward Orion's knife.

I chuckled at the absurdity. Without a telescope, what could I possibly see? Nevertheless, I humored her, pointing the low-tech binoculars up at Orion's bow. I traced the clear belt of three stars and then saw the weapon at his side, three dimmer stars, his knife. I squinted through the lens; nothing special. It hardly seemed to magnify anything. Looking at Jackie for help, I noticed her smiling. "Focus on the middle star in the knife," she said.

I looked again. Remarkably, the point of that middle star loosened, blurred as if the lens were smeared. Puzzled, I relaxed my gaze and allowed the image to reveal itself. It wasn't a star at all, but a nebula of stars.

"It's the Orion nebula," Jackie said, "an interstellar cloud of hydrogen gas, dust, and plasma." She explained that it's a star-forming region, where materials clump together to form bigger masses that further attract matter and eventually become stars. "The 'leftovers' are believed to form planets," she said. "So it's not a single star, but a million pieces of a future star."

That nebula is a metaphor for Jackie's effect on me. What before looked like one single thing was actually a million. Edges of the ordinary blurred.

There's a rare and puzzling condition called synesthesia where your senses, in effect, cross. Swiss musician Elizabeth Sulston, for example, hears pleasant chords as the taste of sweet cream. Dissonant, grating chords taste bitter. Sulston, according to a study published in *Nature*, is the first known case mixing sound and taste. Much more common is the blurring of sound and sight, where, for example, the sound of a birdcall "looks blue." Scientists believe the condition originates in the limbic system, a primitive region of the brain associated with behavior and emotion. Even more fascinating, studies on infants suggest that we all start out as synesthetes, but soon after birth, neural circuits are pruned and we lose this ability. "It's not a short circuit in the system," neurologist Richard Cytowic is quoted as saying, "but a primitive mechanism that was somehow lost to the rest of us."

When the middle star of Orion's knife fell apart through Jackie's binoculars, I could practically hear the soft rain of a didgeridoo. I'm no synesthete, but coming into nature, into solitude, at the 12 x 12 broke down boundaries for me, including the boundary between the supposedly distinct five senses. They blurred together at times, forging music. Jackie is a scientist, of course, but she approaches nature with a creative eye rather than a dissecting one. Do this, and you enter a convergent world, where things fit together in fresh ways, rather than a divergent one, where an impatient eye dissects reality to intellectual minutia. I was allergic to hard science at school, but while at the 12 x 12 I opened the scientific books on her shelf — geology, hydrology, organic chemistry, astronomy, plant biology — and the landscape around the tiny house deepened exponentially like cells dividing. Underground rivers surged through channels a hundred yards under the 12 x 12; the Jack grapes out the window turned sunlight into energy and exhaled the oxygen I breathed; the compost pile chomped up old straw, tough vegetable stems, and hedge clippings and made soil; the night sky, seen so gloriously with the absence of electricity at her house, became theater. "There's the cup," she told me, "and that star is the constellation's only named star: *Alkes*. And over there" — she pointed to a spot above No Name Creek — "is the bear driver, which Homer mentions in his *Odyssey*."

At Jackie's, the edges of the "hard" sciences blurred together, and this is exactly where permaculture occurs. One of the books I discovered on Jackie's shelf was Bill Mollison's *Permaculture: A Designer's Manual*, which has sold over a hundred thousand copies, suggesting to me how much the phenomenon is spreading. In a chapter called "Edges," Mollison explains that the edges between ecosystems — for instance, between water and land or a hill and flatland — hold more variety than the middle. This is because they're transition zones where unique and diverse life can flourish, such as amphibians that straddle aquatic and terrestrial areas. Home and farm become sculpture you gently shape, consciously cultivating additional edges, and therefore more richness, diversity, and surprise. Jackie, for instance, created a pond among her beds to foster more edges, resulting in frogs, insects, and aquatic plants. Likewise, I remember puzzling, during my first earth mentorship with Stan Crawford in New Mexico, over how to combine hydrology and biology so as to grow crops most effectively in that dry climate. The solution: I planted my blue corn in the furrows and not on the mounds, where they'd capture more of the scarce rainfall. And so on. Permaculture isn't industrial agriculture; it's art and music afield.

FINALLY, I HAD THE OPPORTUNITY to visit the Pauls, a father-son team who'd left a comfortable suburban life near Philadelphia to wildcraft in Adams County. Jackie wrote to me about them: "The Pauls (Sr. and Jr.) are finishing up three 12 x 12s, much more elaborate than mine, but they have more money than I do. They have thirty-two acres about five miles from me. You might visit them. They're just starting."

As I pedaled along the Pauls' half-mile dirt drive, their small pasture and vast woods opened up to me. They were to be the first people to live on this land, at least in modern times. The silence was immense. Out toward the edge were three 12 x 12s, the only structures on this vast property. I had that African safari feeling all of a sudden, of being in the middle of the veldt, as if a large mammal — antelope, zebra, rhino, hippo — could burst forth at any moment.

As I got closer and parked my bike, I took a closer look at the 12 x 12s; their rooftops stood taller than Jackie's, and they had larger front and back porches. In fact, each of the porches had as much square footage as the entire house. I was dying to peek inside, and almost did, when I spotted an older man waddling out of the forest. "I'm Paul," he said, his handshake much more vigorous than I expected. "Paul Sr., that is. Paul Jr. is dealing with a minor disaster." He was sixty-seven, a retired American studies and religion professor from a Pennsylvania college. Paul Sr. reminded me of photos I'd seen of Robert Frost in his later years: waifish, stooped, distinguished.

We toured the 12 x 12s. Instead of Jackie's simple ladder, they contained actual stairways heading up to spacious lofts. Paul Sr. explained that he and his son would each live in one of them "in Benedictine monastic style," and the third would be for guests, friends, and spiritually inclined pilgrims alike. He said that he and his son rose at three A.M. every morning for contemplative prayer. Though I might have expected a scholar and ascetic like Paul Sr. to be aloof, he came across as downright jolly.

Paul Jr. ran up to us, panting and rubbing his shaved head. "It's worse than we thought!" A particularly fierce storm the previous night had uprooted many of their young strawberries, beans, and other crops. Several of their newly planted fruit trees lay on their sides, toppled by the storm.

In concerned tones, they discussed the damage as we walked from the open fields into the forest, toward their stretch of river, but as we got deeper into the woods, we all became so engrossed in the gorgeous canopy overhead, the birdlife, the blooming flora, that their stress faded away. Paul Jr. picked wild pokeweed out of the ground for the evening's salad. It seemed that every newly sprouting leaf hadn't been there when they'd walked through just a week before. Paul Sr. would pop every other leaf into his mouth, his big blue eyes reflecting the taste — bitter, sweet, tart. I asked him if he didn't worry about eating something poisonous. He said, "Bradley taught us that there's only one plant out here that will kill you, wild hemlock, and I know what that looks like." They said they'd taken Bradley's permaculture course at the community college and attended several of his lectures. Bradley's contracting firm was building their 12 x 12s.

"Look!" Paul Jr. exclaimed. A natural bridge had formed when a tree crashed down across their lovely river during last night's storm. He scampered across it and waved at us with both arms from the other side. Then he disappeared into the forest beyond, in search of herbs for dinner. Paul Sr. muttered something about edible mushrooms and walked along the brook's bank in the other direction.

I could hear the sound of a hawk's wings slicing the air above; the river's rush, a buzzing bumblebee, and the rustle of an unseen animal in the middle distance. I walked the path the other way along the river, listening to the music around me, feeling an excitement with the Pauls similar to what I felt the very first time I experienced an earth-centered culture — in another forest, down in Guatemala.

In 1994, I volunteered for a month in a remote Mam Mayan

community. I stepped out of the bus in Cabrican, where I was met by Raul, a Mayan man and local schoolteacher who was to be my host. Through my twenty-two-year-old eyes, the lightly touched landscape seemed alive; it was Gaia, the animate earth that philosophers talked about in my undergraduate anthropology class.

I lived with Raul and his family for a month, constructing fuel-saving ovens and lending a hand with house building and even small-scale silver mining. I noticed, amazingly, that folks only worked, on average, the equivalent of half a day. I learned a bit of Mam Mayan. But it was a small detail that impressed me, a child of suburbia, more than anything else: the footpaths.

Like the ones through the Pauls' property, the Mam footpaths wound through the woods with little allegiance to efficiency. They bent, looped, and curved playfully. The Maya considered the paths to be sacred, alive somehow, and imbued with greater life with the walking. Nobody had cars, and the bus I came in on only arrived about once a week. So we used our feet, onward to the outdoor market, the fields, the mine, the forest; untidy dirt paths, intersecting with other dirt paths. Often a rhythm would accompany our walk: a chanted tune, a kind of a Mayan-language mantra. We'd walk slowly, always, enjoying ourselves as much as getting anywhere.

Later, in Africa, I heard the story of a pair of African porters who were hired by a Belgian trader to walk with him deep into the forest towns in search of one commodity or another. After two days of brisk walking, the porters sat down on the ground and refused to budge. The trader first demanded they walk, then tried sweet-talking, and finally offered them an increase in salary — after all, time was money! No matter what he tried, they wouldn't move. Finally the porters explained: they'd been walking too fast, and they now had to stop to wait for their souls to catch up.

Along the Mayan footpaths, along No Name Creek, and along the Pauls' trails, I felt the way those porters did. That slow, considered pace allows your soul to walk with you. At the Pauls', I stopped on a footpath, their 12 x 12s barely visible through the foliage, to observe a cocoon on a twig. In the organic broth inside a cocoon, the organs of the new creature emerge with the pulse of a new heartbeat. Growth in nature happens not in a linear manner but rather through a series of pulsations. Growth is gentle; it reaches out tentatively into new terrain. This quote from Rumi captivates me: "Your hand opens and closes, opens and closes. If it were always a fist or always stretched open, you would be paralyzed. Your deepest presence is in every small contracting and expanding, the two as beautifully balanced and coordinated as birds' wings."

AFTER OUR WALK, I sat with the Pauls in the middle of a large circular garden beside their 12 x 12s. They had inlaid their garden, a full acre in size, with a Christian cross of grass, which split the round acre into four parts, Native American–style. Paul Sr. explained the interwoven religious tapestry and talked about Teilhard de Chardin's animistic idea that "consciousness shoots through everything" — even the rocks and river.

"It's not shooting through your plants anymore," I tried to joke, a reference to the storm-affected plants all around us.

"A disaster," Paul Jr. lamented. "It's the Greek god Deinos. Did you know the word itself, *Deinos*, is a combination of fear and love?"

"The literal translation is 'terrible lizard,'" his father noted.

Suddenly a deer, which looked incredibly vivid against the blue sky, turned and leapt away from us in a flash of brown and white tail. The Pauls got excited. It was the first time a deer had wandered so close to their circular acre. I imagined the deer munching up the remainder of their veggies, but they called it "a fortuitous sign from Deinos."

I couldn't help feeling, in that moment, that the Pauls seemed a tad naive. They had lived in urban environments for most of their lives, and their cerebral musings struck an ironic backdrop against the damaged crops in their field. They were trying, like Jackie, to build lives on the creative edge, in convergence with the earth. But if they were naive about the task they'd set for themselves, they certainly weren't being destructive. How often, in fact, did a desire for growth lead to destruction? I thought of Howard Schultz, chairman of Starbucks, who — when asked why it was so important to him that the company grow so rapidly — responded that if he didn't do it "Starbucks would be cannibalized by another chain that would wipe it out." Relentless growth was a more powerful force for him than his coffee. In a memo, he complained that his company's competitors were going after Starbucks customers. The startling words he used in that memo: "This must be eradicated."

"Eradicate" and "cannibalize" didn't figure into the Pauls' vocabulary, as they attempted to sculpt lives that, like the Maya's, blended with Gaia. But it is hard to escape our internal colonization, I thought, as I noticed the increasingly anxious looks on the Pauls' faces. They weren't unaware of their frost-bitten disaster. But more than that there was a vast, raw land around them. They wanted to do things! Build things! Cut trails, dam part of the river for a bigger swimming area, and as Paul Sr. said, "put a hundred sheep out here." A slightly horrific vision formed in my mind of their farm five years hence: not this perfectly raw, deer-filled, wild space, but a domesticated pastoral idyll with a summer camp feel. The Pauls would show people around and describe the present moment as those terrible days "when there was absolutely nothing here."

I recognized this as a symptom of that contagious, middle-class virus that causes addiction, anxiety, depression, and ennui: affluenza. The richer we get, the poorer we feel. To fill the void, we *do*. I know the feeling. Like the Pauls, I'm American, not indigenous Guatemalan. I am conditioned to equate my self-worth with being active, productive, useful.

"Oh my Lord," Paul Sr. said, a frown settling into his face. "I've got a hundred things on my list."

"A man is rich in proportion to the number of things he can afford to leave alone," I said, quoting Thoreau. At this, Paul Sr.'s face softened. Father and son both had a glint in their eyes as they reflected on this, their postures loose. Silence. The winds topping off the far trees. I got this acrid, almost gamey taste in my mouth just looking out into so much raw wilderness, and I said, "You could look at these thirty-two acres and think: 'What can I do with it today?' Or you could say, 'What can I leave alone today?'"

Paul Jr. had a growing smile on his face; Paul Sr. looked at me stoically.

"We could get up in the morning," Paul Jr. finally said, "and say: 'Let's not clear a forest for pasture today! Let's not extend that road. Oh, and I know what else we cannot do today: not build a bridge over the river.'"

He looked at his dad for approval but was met with a frown. Paul Jr. was undeterred: "'Let's not plant any more beds!' The less we do, the more time to be. To hunt mushrooms, watch beavers, hike..."

"...stargaze, compose poetry," I said. "All of which changes nothing and keeps the landscape nourishing you."

"But we *want* to do things," the elder Paul protested. "We get lost in our chores — could be working twelve hours and it flies by."

"But are we bringing our workaholism with us to the wilderness?" Paul Jr. asked of no one in particular. His dad shot him a searing look, and I sensed the tension between doing and nondoing, farming and philosophy. Whereas Jackie quite consciously farmed only perhaps 5 percent of her land — and that fed her just fine — leaving the rest of it a wild space for contemplation and animal habitat, these men were on the brink of developing a far larger swath of their land. There was work to be done, of course, but how much?

After a pause, Paul Jr. continued, "We don't need to go nuts out here. With our savings and my job..."

"Your job?" his dad said, "Your job is driving a truck."

"For an organic farmers' association."

"Ah, the benefits of a liberal arts education," Paul Sr. said, standing up into his full stooped posture. "And now," he said, turning to face the frost-bitten garden, "we have to get to *work.*"

SIMPLIFY

14. | THE IDLE MAJORITY

ON JANUARY 21, 1949, some two billion people woke up and got out of bed, still unaware of the terrible change that had taken place in their lives. Sip some tea, chat with a spouse or a neighbor, the sun tracing an arc into the sky; take winding paths to a farm field for a few hours of work. Lunch. Siesta. Maybe a little nooky. The day seemed the same as the one before for half the planet's people, but it wasn't. Whereas before they had been, well, regular people living regular lives, now they were something else, something ghastly: *underdeveloped*.

The day before, President Harry S. Truman, in his inauguration speech, declared that the era of "development" had begun, thereby minting a new terminology to conceive of the world:

> We must embark on a bold new program for making the benefits
> of our scientific advances and industrial progress available for the
> improvement and growth of *underdeveloped* areas. The old impe-
> rialism — exploitation for foreign profit — has no place in our
> plans. What we envision is a program of *development*.

Suddenly two billion people who had been doing all right — like my ambling Mayan friends in Guatemala — were no longer doing all right. They were underdeveloped. And in one of the most spectacular missionary efforts in history, the rich nations henceforth strove to lead the underdeveloped of the world to a paradise of development, where they too would be domesticated and tethered to a logic of Total Work.

Truman might have more accurately called these "underdeveloped" people the planet's Idle Majority, the billions who reject the Puritan work ethic and extol leisure. This "leisure ethic," as I've come to dub it, isn't laziness; it is an intelligent, holistic balance between doing and being. It is embodied by the Aymaran philosophy of "living well," which includes enough (and not more) food, shelter, fresh air, and friendship.

In international aid work, the philosophical chasm between living well and living better can lead to culture clash — as well as to serious marital problems. I know a French aid worker who married a woman from Burkina Faso. Their most difficult problem isn't money or in-laws but idleness. His wife, he confided to me one day, "has to have five or six hours a day of doing *absolutely nothing* in order to be happy." My friend is inclined to fill every available moment with work, hobbies, and travel, but his wife prefers to simply sit on the stoop watching the breeze in the trees, idly chatting and joking. If she doesn't get this idle time, she becomes grouchy.

On another occasion in the Gambia, a West African country, I found myself explaining to a local guy in a town called Gunjur, down the coast from Banjul, how workers in the United States and Europe waged decades of union battles to win an eight-hour workday.

He looked at me with complete amazement, as if I had just said that Papa Smurf lived on the moon and was waving down at us. "They fought," he finally said, grasping to comprehend, "to work *eight hours* a day?"

"Exactly!" I exclaimed, a little proud to have shared a bit of Western labor history that might help him in his struggles.

To my shock, the man burst out laughing. Amid guffaws he managed to get across that he and others in Gunjur worked three or four hours a day. It was absurd, he said, to fight all those decades to work more, especially in a rich country! It became a running joke with us. "Hey, Bill," he'd say whenever he saw me, "I think I'll work *eight* hours today," then collapse into a belly laugh.

At a certain point in my "development" career, I began to question the whole notion of who's impoverished. As the years passed abroad, I sensed that Truman had the thing turned on its head. Amazingly, most of the so-called impoverished beneficiaries of my programs were better off than me. That is to say, their cultures had come up with a way of living in the world that contributed more to happiness — in Dr. Seligman's sense of "general well-being" — than my culture. Throughout the Global South, people, by and large, had achieved higher levels of Seligman's three factors: they had bigger smiles; they were very often engaged in the moment; and through their kinship networks and close relationship with Mother Earth, they achieved a greater sense of meaning and purpose.

Thinking perhaps that my lived experience was too subjective, I decided to check the social science data. Holland's Erasmus University ranked Colombia — of all places — as the happiest nation on earth. Great Britain's *Journal of Happiness Studies* put Colombia at number four in the world. And the Happy Planet Index of the New Economy Foundation ranked Colombia second. These studies essentially ranked general well-being, or how people feel about their own lives.

The fact that folks in Colombia, a so-called underdeveloped country — which ranks below forty other countries in terms of GDP — is so darn happy is curious only when one equates higher material living standards with higher levels of well-being. In the Biswas-Diener survey, 96 percent of Colombians defined themselves as content with life. Most rich nations rank miles below Colombia and tend to have the planet's highest rates of divorce, child abuse, addiction, and suicide. Indeed, a recent Emory University study showed that just 17 percent of Americans were "flourishing" in mental health terms, while 26 percent were "languishing" in depression.

Eventually, it dawned on me that while, according to my job descriptions over the past decade, I had been working in underdeveloped nations, perhaps I'd actually been working most of the time in *developed* nations — and that I came from an unhealthily *overdeveloped* nation. Like a bodybuilder so loaded with steroids that he becomes impotent, America's hyper-consumerism came with unwanted environmental and psychological side effects.

I do not mean this to glorify material destitution. I make an important distinction: even in this revised conception, not every Global South country would qualify as "developed." I've accompanied some of the millions of people who cannot afford to live even 12 x 12. They live 0 x 0, with no lush organic gardens, no gently flowing creek, and no shelter at all overhead. They live in what you might call the Fourth World, those anarchic, failed spaces where community — the glue of enough — has been decimated by war, famine, and natural disaster, as well as by the great unnatural disaster, corporate economic globalization.

When discussing relatively "poorer" countries, we need to make a clear, explicit distinction between people living in a state of material destitution and people living healthy subsistence lifestyles. Terms like *poverty* and *Third World* mask this distinction and give license for modern professionals — of whom I've long been one — to undervalue, denigrate, and interfere with sustainable ways of life.

There's a point where one's material life is in balance: one has neither too much nor too little. Per my own analysis of GDP and global happiness studies, roughly one-fifth of humanity has too much and is overdeveloped; another fifth has too little and is underdeveloped. Neither of these groups experiences general well-being. The former, with materialism caked on like a million barnacles, can rarely experience the simple joy of being. The latter are so destitute that they can't sustain their bodies physically. Fortunately, the third group — those with enough — is by far the largest. It is what I call "developed," ranging from subsistence livelihoods like that of the Maya of Guatemala to the level of the average European circa 1990.

By this rough calculation, 60 percent of the world lives sustainably, in a global sense. In other words, if everyone lived as they did, one planet — the one we're on right now — would suffice to feed, clothe, shelter, and absorb the waste of everyone. (In contrast, if everyone lived at the level of the average American, we'd require the resources of four additional earth-sized planets.) One solution practically jumps out: The 20 percent with too much should share with the 20 percent with too little. Of course, there will always be inequalities, but isn't it in our best interests to lessen the grotesque differences of today's world? Social science research, spiritual traditions, and most of our personal experience tell us that neither too much nor too little leads to well-being.

Idleness has been under threat at least since we stamped "underdeveloped" on the majority of humankind, most of whom actually live in enough. In the past two or three generations, a significant portion of the Global South has flocked to cities from tiny rural villages, where they lived and worked in concert with nature and traditional values for centuries. Why is this? In part, it is the allure of modern life, of technology and industrialized affluence, leading to what you might call a voluntary flattening. This is exemplified by those highland Bolivian women (*cholitas*) who leave behind their mothers, still wrestling Pachamama for potatoes, and light out for the city to find jobs sewing underwear or selling cheap Chinese electronics — and then spend their hard-earned disposable income on neon-colored Chinese silk, wool Italian hats, and dangly earrings, becoming proud, flashy members of the Flat World. There's an undeniable seduction to individualism and consumption, especially when that seduction is sweetened by trillions of global marketing dollars.

However, there are trade-offs and often disillusionment: many *cholitas* end up living in the polluted, sprawling El Alto slums; Mexicans find themselves in cookie-cutter suburbs crowding the hills outside the Tijuana *maquilas*. Nor is this change wholly and truly "voluntary": *cholitas* sometimes cannot stay on the family farm because the potatoes are gone or nearly worthless. Crop failures fueled by climate change; price crashes caused by global agribusiness; and the sense, even in those small villages, that tending your local corn crop is a devalued, almost useless skill in the global economy.

Tough choices face both the Workaholic North and the Idle Majority. We're in the same ship, trying to navigate choppy twenty-first-century waters. Those in the Idle Majority who navigate it best seem to be the ones who don't exchange their entire culture for seductive consumption. In Bolivia, El Alto is an interesting example because many families living there go back and forth between that sprawling urban area and their traditional villages. They still maintain a connection with the land, including continuing to plant and harvest potatoes. They retain the best of what their grandparents knew, stewarding "vernacular culture" — a body of knowledge that has evolved over thousands of years in every corner of the globe. Vernacular culture is the enduring wisdom that sustains a spiritually rich life, so it is regenerative by nature of survival. Most such wisdom has a keen awareness of how to nurture dignified life in a certain locale with particular soils, climate, water, biodiversity, and cultural traditions. Nearly all vernacular cultures embrace abundant idleness, the "beingness" that binds humans and nature.

Could part of the solution to our ecological crisis be found in rediscovering ways to maintain a place for idleness? Instead of merely handing out "development aid," the North might also seek and receive "vernacular aid" from the Global South, gathering clues toward living more softly now.

AT THE 12 X 12, I NOTICED, part of wildcrafting involves re-claiming the right to be idle — a ratcheting down from overdevel-oped to developed, from too much to enough. Jackie expressed it to me once like this: part of the joy of simplifying one's material life is that you don't have to work long hours to buy and maintain a bunch of stuff. This leaves time for open-ended chats — like the kind I began to have with Paul Jr.

I found myself hanging out with him quite a bit. One day, shortly after we met on his farm, we engaged in a playful dharma chat at an outdoor table at Adams Marketplace, a food co-op and lunch joint twelve miles along the highway from Jackie's. He looked at me through his just-on-the-right-side-of-hip eyeglasses and asked, "Do you know Carlos Castaneda?"

I nodded.

"Okay. There's this moment in *The Teachings of Don Juan* where Castaneda is with the shaman, Don Juan, in this tiny house in the southwest desert. Don Juan asks Castaneda to look at one of the walls."

Paul Jr. paused melodramatically and looked at one of the co-op walls. "Castaneda studied the wall, taking comfort in the everyday objects in front of it: books, a lamp, vases, kitchenware..."

I pictured the wall of Jackie's kitchen, the spices and preserves, pots and kettle.

"And then," Paul continued, "Don Juan asked him to turn around and look at the opposite wall."

In my mind, I turned around in Jackie's, facing the wall with the windows looking out at the night sky, Venus in the window. Paul leaned closer to me and spoke more softly, "On the other side of the cabin, there was no wall, no comforting objects. Castaneda looked out into nothing but *deep, cold space*."

He looked at me, bright-eyed, appearing much younger than his thirty-seven years. "Do you get it? There's nothing. That's the point. We live in a cold, meaningless universe."

"What do you think?" I asked Paul.

"This is maybe the biggest question in my life. And I'm leaning..." — Paul shook his head, grinning — "I'm leaning toward
the cold void. Why do many people need a cuddly universe, loving
them? What do you think?"

Paul looked at me. I looked into the blue sky behind him, with
its wisps of cloud, as if for an answer. There's no answer, I thought.
Like nature, God is now you see her, now you don't. Is Castaneda
right, elsewhere, when he insists that "all paths are the same, they
lead nowhere," and that the only important thing is to choose a path
with heart? Castaneda found himself staring into Nietzsche's existential void. I was about to respond, when Paul said: "Oh look, that's
Jenny Jespersen coming our way."

"I'm on the tail end of my lunch break, so can't dally," Jenny
Jespersen told Paul in a staccato voice. "And do you work here, Paul?
Because I always see you sitting here."

"I'm an *ociologo*," said Paul with a grin. Jenny shook her head.
"A leisureologist," he translated.

Jenny was all business: she gave us a rundown of her agenda as
the senior finance committee chair for Adams County, and then, just
as quickly as she had arrived, she was gone. All around us, even in
the supposedly laid-back Adams Marketplace, everyone was in a
hurry, all the hip nonprofit people and biodiesel brewers and organic
farmers on the prowl for markets, for cash, for status, but Paul
hadn't stopped grinning. This was what I liked about him; he simply
loved the present moment. He never hurried, or hustled after money
or prestige; he just remained blissful in each moment. One time, I
accompanied Paul in his old pickup truck to the organic farmers' cooperative. His job was delivering produce around the state — but
he worked only one or two days a week, by his own choice. That
day we stopped to collect his paycheck for the past two weeks. Ten
dollars an hour times a couple of days didn't add up to much. But
Paul smiled, looking at the tiny amount on the check, shaking his

head in wonder at this bounty. He turned to me and said, "Bill, we're going to celebrate!"

I felt a rush of pleasure. The so-called enlightened master — the bodhisattva, the sage — has so much in common with the archetypal "fool," those blessed with Forrest Gump innocence and optimism. There was Paul Jr., a tiny paycheck, an enormous smile. He had a master's degree; he had every opportunity to find work that paid better than truck driving, but he valued time more than money. Slowing down, for him and others like him in Adams County, was a radical act in the context of an overscheduled America.

AS TIME PASSED, life in the 12 x 12 became a course in Leisureology 101. Embraced by a local subculture intent on joining the world's Idle Majority, I felt less guilty about the open days stretching out before me, with nothing on the agenda. Whenever the workaholism bug began to bite, I recalled Jackie's advice: For now, be, don't do. It occurred to me that the times when I slowed down — in the 12 x 12 and at other points in my life — were ironically the times when I got the most work done. Creativity flows smoothly out of nonaction, from deep wells of idleness. The creative self savors aimless wanderings where you slip into your own snug skin. It's what writer Brenda Ueland calls "moodling," or productively dawdling away the hours. When you moodle, your subconscious works out aesthetics and structure without the overactive rational mind's interference.

One day I flipped to a new card in Jackie's pile: DON'T BE SO PREDICTABLE. I smiled, picturing Jackie writing it and thinking about how "serious" science and spirituality, for her, intermingled with self-effacing humor. Her card said to me: Live uniquely in this unique moment. I must have subconsciously taken it to heart later that morning when I left the breakfast dishes unwashed and walked quite abruptly down the road — in my pajamas.

I didn't realize that I was wearing PJs — a faded T-shirt and paint-splashed sweatpants — until I was twenty minutes down the train tracks. I stopped, embarrassed for a second, but then laughed out loud at myself. I was on a train track in rural North Carolina. Who was I going to meet? I did twenty stretch-shouts — an energy-boosting technique I'd picked up at the wonderful Kripalu yoga center in Massachusetts — and then let my gaze fall into the distance, where four or five textured clouds staked a claim to the southern horizon. They were probably down in South Carolina someplace. All that space between the clouds and me! I smiled broadly and closed my eyes, imagining myself taking flight from the tracks and soaring over ponds flush from last night's storm, nose-diving through soft clouds.

The creek flashed below the railroad bridge, the fastest I'd seen it, thick with bubbles and pounding noisily against the bridge pillars. I found myself staring down into the creek, not thinking of a thing. Just listening. The sun climbed the sky. Still I sat there, listening to the creek. Eventually, when I felt like doing so, I got up and walked back along the abandoned train tracks toward the 12 x 12, realizing that my days were beginning to pass more like those of the Thompsons, the Pauls, Jackie, and so many others in the Idle Majority — in a blissfully subversive leisure. Jackie was shifting from overdevelopment to development. She is a talented physician who could have easily risen in wealth and status, and you could say she's instead chosen to live in poverty, but that's not entirely correct.

She lives in enough. She has abundant fresh food in her gardens, the music of a creek, a network of friends, neighbors, and family. She and other wildcrafters in Pine Bridge and throughout the rich world are choosing downward mobility — living well instead of forever striving to live better.

DON'T BE SO PREDICTABLE

15. | THE DRAGON

ONE DAY AS I WALKED by the Thompsons', a few of their younger kids ran up to me. They stopped and looked at me as if to ask, "What are we going to do?" So I picked up a handful of rocks and said, "I have ten rocks." They watched as I counted the gray gravel.

They each picked up rocks and started counting them. Brett held out two. "You've got two dollars!" I said.

"How much do I have?" asked Greg.

"You've got some pennies and quarters in there . . . six dollars and twenty-five cents."

"And me?"

"Five euros."

"Huh?"

"The money in Europe is called euros. And look, Greg, you have twelve Mexican pesos."

For an hour or more we explored the currencies of the world, and did a bunch of math to boot. The next day, Michele thanked me for homeschooling them.

"We were just playing."

"Exactly," she said, explaining that kids learn like adults learn —
by following their bliss instead of having the three Rs force-fed in
forty-minute blocks. She said she likes the traditional village concept
of education, where children spontaneously pick up knowledge while
working on the farm or interacting with neighbors like myself.

The Thompsons homeschooled five of their six kids using a
freely adapted version of the Mennonite homeschooling curriculum.
(Their eldest, Zach, attended a charter school because he was from
Michele's previous marriage, and her ex-husband insisted Zach receive a more traditional education.) There didn't seem to be any
rhyme or reason as to what or when they studied. I'd sometimes see
Kyle and Greg relaxing for an hour on the porch in front of their
pond, shirtless, their little tan bodies soaking up the morning sun:
Intro to Idleness. Other times they'd be feeding the hogs, out in the
forest, or biking. Then, for large spurts — once I saw Kyle at it for
an entire day — they'd read intensely.

"What ya reading?" I asked Kyle that day. He showed me.
Though he was only eleven, he was fully engrossed in an engineering text. I asked Michele about it, and she chuckled, saying, "That's
his gift. Kyle is always building things and it fascinates him. He wants
to be an engineer, so I focus his homeschooling around math and science. When he feels like it he reads entire novels, but I don't force it.
It comes from him."

As it turns out, there are some twenty-five hundred homeschooled kids in North Carolina's Research Triangle area alone, and
overall, homeschooled kids have admission rates into college equal
to those of traditionally schooled kids. Homeschooling isn't for
everyone. For starters, it means at least one parent must be home.
But it reflects a wider pedagogical trend, in which education is returning to the original Latin derivation of the word *education* —
meaning "to draw out." For example, new European models of
"holistic teaching" or "facilitation" consider the instructor to be a

coach in the child's own spontaneous exploration, particularly of the local communities and nature. Waldorf schools point in this direction, too. The factory education model that drives most US public schools, with its rigid time schedules and standardized testing, parallels the factory economy of twentieth-century workplaces. In the twenty-first century, the internet is softening the edges of that industrial way of working, providing the opportunity to invent more fluid ways of educating children.

Homeschooling blends well with wildcrafting — life on the creative edge of the system — because freeholders like the Thompsons have greater control of their time. Having escaped from the nine-to-five, they are free to live and educate themselves a bit like the world's Idle Majority does.

"WHY DON'T YOU RENT THAT HOUSE?" Kyle asked me one day while I was talking with his mom. He pointed to a two-story farmhouse that I'd hardly noticed until then. It lay in a clearing across the Thompsons' pond, right off Old Highway 117 South. Puzzled, I studied the house, and then looked to Michele.

"The thing is, they've gotten so attached to you," she said, "that they want you to rent that house when Jackie gets back."

The house wasn't particularly inviting. In fact, it looked a tad creepy. All the trees around it felled, too close to the highway. "Who owns it?" I asked.

"Bradley."

"Of course," I said. Bradley seemed to have a hand in everything. I wondered, momentarily, how someone so land- and property-rich could avoid the temptation to "sell out" his ecological values.

"Well, to be honest, we'd all love it if you'd rent it," Michele said.

"That's kind of you," I said.

"Will you deal drugs out of there?" six-year-old Greg asked.

"Greg!" Michele reprimanded. "I'm sorry. It's just that . . . well, the girl who'd been living there. Cops busted her with fifteen thousand dollars in crystal meth."

I shifted from one foot to the other. I knew crystal meth, cocaine's poorer cousin, was common in both urban and rural areas of North Carolina, since it was so cheap to make. It was so common, in fact, that people, when giving you a tour of their home, would routinely joke, "and this is the meth lab." But I never would have imagined it being produced one house over from the 12 x 12.

"We'd seen men coming in at all hours of the night," Michele continued, "and so we thought she was a . . . you know. But turns out the whole place was a giant meth factory."

The wind shifted direction. Cutting through the smell of the Thompsons' place — the smell of a farm — was a hint of the oppressive, dead scent of one of the nearby industrial chicken factories. *A giant meth factory?* Just through the woods from Jackie's beehives, heirloom teas, and honeysuckle; right on the banks of No Name Creek. I felt a little queasy.

Michele seemed to notice and went on, "We'd much rather you moved in than another Section Eighter. Just don't move in until after the 'meth-busters' get here. The squad that detoxifies the house."

I looked down at her the faces of her kids, the same ones who had recently been learning math and world currencies with me. I said, "As in, 'Who ya gonna call?' "

"Meth-busters! Exactly. It's in the police department. The drug is so toxic that it gets into the walls, floors, drains, everywhere. The 'meth-busters' use even stronger chemicals to get rid of it." My queasiness began to turn to nausea. "After that," she said cheerily, "it'll be ready for you to move on in!"

As if meth-next-door wasn't enough, a "cheeze" scare suddenly hit Adams County. It was headlined in the local paper after the drug — a cheap blend of heroin and Tylenol PM — killed several high school kids in Texas, and rumor had it that North Carolina dealers were adding it to their repertoire. I noticed the Thompsons eyeing José's and Graciela's kids, with their dark hair and skin and baggy pants, with even more mistrust, perhaps seeing possible cheeze dealers — the very ones they'd left the trailer parks to escape.

After that, on my walks and bike rides, I began seeing a different North Carolina. I noticed more despair on the porches of roadside trailers and run-down houses, heads hanging low, eyes staring blankly into the awakening landscape. Every day one hundred million Americans take drugs, and this statistic hit me viscerally, with a former meth factory next door and cheeze scaring my neighbors. The 12 x 12, perhaps because of the abundant energy I was absorbing from nature and the physical exercise of biking and walking, had inspired me to limit caffeine and alcohol in my diet. I had only the occasional coffee or glass of wine now. This made me even more sensitive to all the pain, anger, and estrangement being deadened by drugs.

"I AM A DRAGON / Fire is one of the things I favor / And sometimes acid."

I was reading aloud to Leah outside the 12 x 12.

"Now we know who 'the dragon' is," Leah said.

"Do we?"

This was Zach Thompson's poetry. The thirteen-year-old had passed me a copy of the poem along with a sixty-page novella called *Fallen Dragons* that he'd written for an English assignment. When Leah saw it in the 12 x 12 she said, "Ooh, I love reading thirteen-year-olds' fiction," and dug in. At one point she laughed and said, "Check this out: 'Two hundred feet and closing, the dragon spread his wings, and his two clawed feet spread. An innocent buck looked up, but too late. The dragon's massive claws wrapped around him like a soft taco wrapped the meat, lettuce, and hot sauce.'" She giggled, and continued, "His teacher — one Mr. L — took a red pen and crossed out 'like a soft taco wrapped the meat, lettuce, and hot sauce.'"

We read the rest of *Fallen Dragons* aloud, a tale of hatred, blood-shed, and destruction, in which the protagonist — a dragon curi-ously without a name — kills everything in sight. We wondered about the inspiration for this angry, violent persona. The poem "I am" gave clues.

"Start again," Leah said, and I read:

I am a dragon,
Fire is one of the things I favor
And sometimes acid.
I terrify people.
They just don't know,
Know who I am
I am a dragon.

I am the drums, loud and obnoxious,
But I help people with the anger
I talk to them when they beat me.

I am me,
This poem is me
So you think you knew me,
So what do you think of the real me?

We talked about who the dragon might be. It seemed to repre-sent blight. I only knew the Thompsons in their hopeful present phase, pursuing a dream of living as organic farmers. But Zach prob-ably still had the trailer park horrors vividly in mind, horrors that now seemed to be following his family into Pine Bridge. Just beneath the dream was the flattening, the deadening; the nameless dragon.

I BIKED TO THE QUICK-N-EASY in Smithsville to call Leah on the pay phone. Fluorescent lights; the hot dogs rolling in a glassed-in oven; a dozen types of malt liquor; a bounty of chewing tobacco. I was studying the drink selection when an African American woman, maybe early thirties, came up beside me with two daughters. "You want the blue one?" she asked her toddler. Her older daughter grabbed a Coke, and she a king-sized Dr. Pepper. "You from around here?" she asked me.

I told her I was staying at a friend's up the road for a while.

"I know everyone here, and I said to myself, 'Who's that guy?' "

We introduced ourselves. She was Pam. She said, "Me, I've never lived outside of Adams County, only traveled once to Myrtle Beach."

Her older girl jumped in: "You've been to Busch Gardens!"

"Oh yeah, there too."

"These your kids?"

"Nicole . . . and Darleen," she said, beaming. "Darleen's thirteen, going to the eighth-grade prom, but they treat it like a high school prom. You should see her in her dress. She's like, like a beauty queen."

"*What* was ninety-nine cents?" A customer was complaining loudly about his receipt to the cashier.

"This," the cashier said, pulling a beef jerky out of his bag.

"Says sixty-nine. The bigger one is ninety-nine."

"Oh."

"I know, I'll just trade it for the bigger one."

"I'm always tryin' to shit somebody," said the attendant.

Pam turned away from me and joined their conversation, saying with a friendly grin: "She did it on purpose!"

"Yeah, I know she did. Ninety-nine! Now we're square."

The customer left with his purchase, and Pam looked back at me and said conspiratorially, "You know I went into Ashboro, you know Ashboro? No, well, you can get there in twenty minutes on the back roads if you ever want to go somewhere more exciting than here, but anyway I went to Belk's there and got her a prom dress that was $250 for $24.99. Don't tell her."

"I promise," I said.

"And I got the shoes for $19.99. They look like Cinderella slippers on her." She looked over at Darleen, her pride obvious. "You know a lot of folks think she's my sister," she said. "Soon she'll be off to college. But I've still got her. At that prom, she's going to be a real Ms. America..."

Pam stopped speaking; she was the only one in the Quick-N-Easy still talking. Someone turned the radio up. Something terrible was happening across the state line at a place called Virginia Tech.

THAT EVENING, LEAH CAME OVER to the 12 x 12, still in her work clothes: a long brown suede skirt and a cream sweater. She got out of her car, her hair falling in a flop over one shoulder, and hugged me, whispering, "How horrible." We went straight over to José's, to see how he and Hector were taking it, talking as we walked about the "why" of the Virginia Tech slaying: earlier that day, over the course of several hours, a Virginia Tech student had shot and killed thirty-two people, wounding scores more, before committing suicide. Part of it must have been plain mental illness, but that couldn't have been everything. Does our culture sometimes value production over life and alienate people to the point where mental illnesses deepen and going postal becomes routine?

At José's, an enormous fire blazed in the backyard. The thirteen-year-old Hector, his back to us, was burning garbage. Though the fire burned just fine, Hector threw additional gasoline on it, sending the flames up so high that they singed the treetops and licked his hands and arms.

"Hector!" I called out.

He spun around, equally surprised and self-conscious. Had he been thinking of the kids killed a hundred miles away, across the border in Virginia?

"Quemando basura" — "Burning garbage" — he finally said,

turning his back to us again. He put the gasoline can down. Leah and I stared into the flames. The fire dwarfed Hector's small silhouette. No Name Creek rushed by reflecting the flames.

The fire made me think of America's early pioneers, not Mexicans and Hondurans settling twenty-first-century North Carolina, but the European immigrants who arrived long before José and Hector. As they caravaned through the American heartland, they sometimes lit the prairie on fire to announce they'd found water. A poetic gesture, but also an overly extravagant one that captures something of America's ethos, where ebullience over one beautiful thing leads to destruction of a greater one.

In the firelight I regarded the rest of José's property. Not yet a year since he'd cut the red ribbon to his new house — the neighbors and Habitat for Humanity volunteers applauding — and the place was already beginning to suffer from neglect. The back doorknob lay rusting on the porch right where it had fallen off. Several screens were ripped and one window cracked. Bicycles lay rusting outside, and — though José's prized carpentry shed was immaculate — his tool shed's roof panels were starting to cave in. Perhaps his carpentry shed was immaculate only because he'd just finished it two months before. It stood sturdy, padlocked, but had not been treated.

"My dad's inside," Hector said into the fire, a single military plane zooming overhead. Graciela's dog rounded the house, looked surprised to see us, and changed course, limping in a slow arc around the fire, and disappeared into the woods. Yellow and white-headed dandelions and other weeds made their way through the mess of a poorly mowed crabgrass lawn.

Inside, José told us, "I sent Hector to burn garbage so he wouldn't see any more of the terrible news." There was no place to sit on the messy sofa, so José busily moved aside a jacket, a newspaper, some component parts of furniture he was making. The TV was too loud. Leah's face scrunched up a bit over the volume and the images of dead bodies on the campus. Unenthusiastically, José bit into a fish stick. He offered to make us some, but we weren't hungry and declined.

A reporter interviewed a Virginia Tech professor who'd hid in his office as the students were slain. The journalist asked the professor how the students would deal with all of this the next day, and the professor's voice caught, as he held back tears.

"*Got him,*" Leah whispered, and then: "Christ! This is what I hate about journalism. Everyone at the station was itching for that: someone whose voice would catch dramatically."

Hector came in from the back, his arms soot covered, and slumped onto the couch. José scrambled for the remote to change channels. But Hector saw the bodies. He sighed and started playing video games on a laptop next to Leah as his dad flipped to the telenovela *La Fea Más Bella.*

To lighten the mood, José began talking in Spanish about the lives of the soap stars now on the screen: "That actor is from Mexico, but his parents are Dominican, and the other guy was *born* in Mexico but his parents are from Spain. The female actress, La Fea, her mom was a Mexican beauty queen far prettier than her daughter..."

Eventually I asked Hector in Spanish, "How are your grades?"

"Huh?" He was engrossed in his game, killing chickens with a shotgun and pitchfork.

I repeated the question in English. Still just a blank look. José shifted in his seat and was about to say something when I went on, "Do you get As, Bs, Cs?"

"Cs, Ds," Hector said, looking back at the soap, frowning, and then back at his screen. "I need more chicken bones. You see" — he showed the screen to Leah — "I've got a record now, but I need more bones."

I slept poorly that night and woke up just after sunrise thinking of Weimar, Germany. I hadn't thought of it for a long time, but in the summer I was nineteen, I spent several weeks digging through the former Buchenwald concentration camp garbage dump near Weimar.

It probably wasn't the wisest choice for a sensitive teenager like me, but I signed up for an East-West peace exchange in which twenty Soviets, Americans, East Germans, and West Germans — it was the summer of 1990; the Berlin Wall had fallen, but the USSR was still a country — got together in the Buchenwald trash heap and dug for personal items to return to the victims' families, almost fifty years after the Holocaust. If the families were not found, the items would go to a museum in Buchenwald to educate the youth of the newly uniting Germany about the dangers of fascism.

I unearthed prisoners' spectacles, coins, cups, and belt buckles. Almost none of it could be linked to specific people, so it ended up in the museum, next to the human skin lampshades and light switches made out of mummified thumbs — items that Ilse Koch, the wife of the camp commandant, ordered to be made from gassed Jews. Next to the museum was the oven chamber, with people-sized ovens, where tens of thousands of prisoners were incinerated after being worked, flogged, or shot to death. At night, I collapsed, sometimes in tears, onto a cot in my bedroom: a former SS barracks.

When I got back to Brown to begin my sophomore year, I signed up for Professor Volker Berghahn's Modern German History course, and I read everything I could on National Socialism. I thought that if I could understand Hitler, and the millions who willingly followed him, on an intellectual level, I might be able to fight similar evils in our world today. During a college recess on Long Island, I once asked my parents over dinner: Didn't they see the parallels between our society and that of Nazi Germany? The Germans killed Jews, but we were killing the planet with acid rain and global warming. Then it was genocide; now it's ecocide. Why were we collaborating?

Just five miles up the road from Buchenwald is the town of

Weimar, where, while the ovens burned tens of thousands, life went on as usual with weddings, church on Sundays, and kids going to school. How can we understand and explain such docility at the gateway to the Holocaust? Hitler's internal policing explains part of it, but there was also a certain amount of denial — there are films of Weimar residents brought to Buchenwald right after the defeat of the Nazis. They were truly shocked and many fainted. After the Virginia Tech slayings, down by No Name Creek, I smelled the light stench of the chicken factories: Was there a similar floating stench from the Buchenwald ovens? Like Weimar's citizenry during World War Two, we twenty-first-century Americans don't want to know exactly what kind of animal torture takes place in the factories, nor how undocumented Mexican labor is being exploited, nor, in a larger sense, what kind of effect our overconsuming lifestyles have on the planet.

A big orange sunrise burned right into a No Name Creek that blazed more strongly than I'd ever seen. Down deep, rich lacquer and satin. These deeper lights interacted with surface textures, dimpled, shingled, wavy, calm, and streaky. I looked away from the glare, back toward the 12 x 12 up the hill. The previous day — the day of the Virginia Tech massacre — 171 people died in bombings in Iraq, and in the ten previous days thirty-two Americans had been killed — the same number killed at Virginia Tech. With all this violence at home and abroad, is it any wonder our kids lose themselves in chicken-slaying video games, cheeze, and dragons, and that the number of emotionally disturbed children in America has tripled since the early 1990s? At what point does the blight become too deep?

16. HOLDING HANDS WITH EXTINCTION

EACH DAY, AS I WALKED THE TRACKS or the creek's edge, I'd hear my father's words from his hospital bed, *You're a man without a country*. The words rang truer every day.

Paul Jr. stopped by the 12 x 12 two days after the Virginia Tech massacre. As we sipped some of Jackie's rosebud tea outside, we talked about it for a while and then lapsed into silence, staring out at the ever-taller winter wheat and the thickening forest.

Finally Paul said, "We're at that age where we have to ask ourselves: Am I going to start a family, or remain a bachelor?"

I shifted uncomfortably in my chair. No Name Creek sounded especially loud that morning, flush with the previous day's showers; it flowed accusingly over its stones.

"I'm not sure I want a family," Paul continued. "I'm thirty-seven. I feel like not having kids is a way of fighting."

"Fighting what?"

Paul went into a head-tilted, toe-tapping, thinking smile and finally said, "Fighting against... Help me out here, *amigo*."

I only vaguely glimpsed what Paul was driving at. Then he lit up and said, "It's when they really get you!"

"They?"

"The advertisers, the marketers, the culture. They kinda-sorta have you when it is the stuff *you* have to have. But they've got you by the balls when it's the stuff your vulnerable *kids* just have to have."

He squinted toward the woods, as if listening to the creek, and continued: "I've got a friend, about forty, who's got two kids. He says to me, 'Paul, if you don't have kids, you're not in the game.' Not in the game? *What* game? You go from comparing jobs and salaries to comparing what school your kids got into."

He talked about how having kids in any society, anywhere in the world, is a way of saying that society is good. Or at least good enough. Worth perpetuating. He wasn't sure whether he felt ours was.

"But what about you?" he finally said. "Are you going to get married, have kids? What about Leah?"

I looked away from Paul and at the 12 x 12. It stood there staring at me, silently, simply. A fixed point in a swirling universe.

So I told Paul that I had a two-and-a-half-year-old daughter, Amaya.

He looked a little startled. After a moment, he shifted position in his chair and said with a kind expression: "Talk to me, my friend. We've got time."

I hesitated. My daughter was in Bolivia, with her mom, and this was the longest I'd been away from her. I thought about her every day, saw her expressions in Allison Thompson's face, and kissed her photo each night before going to bed. I didn't like to talk about it. I kept my love for her close to my chest because talking about her was like reopening a wound. Just as I had been repressing my anger toward the three gangs that had attacked me, I'd been repressing a confusion of feelings about my fatherhood. Beyond the wound of physical separation was a sense of failure: I hadn't lived up to the ideal my Catholic parents and I had of what a father, a family should look like.

Deeper still, the stakes of a flattening world had gone up exponentially since her birth. What had before been my life's work was now a question of what kind of world my daughter would inhabit, a world whose future appeared bleaker by the day.

The wind whistled a little in the trees; No Name Creek lowered its voice. I started talking.

MY DAUGHTER, Amaya Powers Cortez, emerged from her mom's womb in Bolivia. Amaya ("beloved first daughter" in Quechua and "spirit" in Aymara) took her first breath in a hospital surrounded by palm trees whipping and swaying furiously in an angry *sur* that had blown up from Antarctica, slicing a chill through the tropical heat. One of the four doctors attending my daughter's birth handed the newborn to her mom, Ingrid, who then passed her to me. I felt the purest love imaginable stir inside, things I had absolutely never felt before.

But I wasn't to dally. In Bolivia the baby belongs not only to Mommy and Daddy but to a web of extended family. I passed Amaya to Mama Martha, her maternal grandmother, who passed her to Papa Mike. Then she was passed to Tio Eduardo, Tia Alison, and Tia Melissa. Each person kissing her pure white forehead, her red hair, looking into her gray-green eyes — she was a carbon copy of me, looking nothing like any of them, but nobody minded a bit. She was part of *la familia*. We then ate quail eggs and drank champagne, pouring the first few drops onto the floor as a gift to Pachamama, Mother Earth.

My own parents became "Mama Anna" and "Pop Bill," and despite the initial shock to their values, they played those roles with genuine love and grace. So, essentially, my daughter was born with three mothers and three fathers, and that was just the beginning:

today, I can't count the number of her Bolivian relatives, and of the many neighbors and friends who love her as much as any relative.

"*¿Dónde está nuestra Amaya?*" — "Where's our Amaya?" — the neighbors would say when Amaya was a year old. Ingrid or Mama Martha would pass her over the little fence and she'd disappear into their house for hours. I'd hear my daughter squealing with laughter.

Little red-haired Amaya grew up with her mom, extended family, and a slew of neighbors in a kind of *kunda* household. My mother came down to Bolivia several times and joined in with the clan. Amaya's hands and feet hardly touched the ground that first year — she was always in somebody's arms. I lived in my own house and visited her all the time and was accepted as part of the family.

From a Western perspective the whole arrangement was extraordinarily nontraditional, but it worked beautifully. Ingrid — a strongly independent twenty-six-year-old Bolivian biologist — and I decided from the beginning on two things, both grounded in that peculiarly Latin idea of destiny: First, for a variety of interwoven reasons, we decided that our fate was not to remain together as a couple, whether in a traditional marriage or not. And second, we considered without question that we had been destined to bring Amaya into the world, and though we would likely live on different continents at various points in our daughter's life, we would do everything in our power to give her the best possible life.

During the first two years of Amaya's life, we took her all around Bolivia, which is to say into places of great natural beauty. Bolivia is three times the size of the UK and has only nine million people. It's a world without edges, one of V. S. Naipaul's "half-made societies." This is not a bad thing. It means the other half still belongs to Pachamama and still breathes. It means that the other half might still be left alone, instead of slashed and mined, produced, packaged, marketed, and sold. It means it's still soft.

Amaya wandered among the giant fern trees of Amboro National Park, in the shadow of a jaguar-shaped Inca temple, as I scribbled away in the artist's retreat where I was on a fellowship finishing my book *Whispering in the Giant's Ear*. On the other side of Bolivia, in the famous Madidi National Park, rare monkeys came down from the trees into our canoe and scurried over to the eighteen-month-old Amaya. Fearlessly she reached out her tiny hand, and one of the smaller monkeys grabbed it. Amaya spoke to the monkeys, gesturing with her other hand to the trees, and then pointed at herself and said "Amaya." They listened and then responded. Amaya argued with them about something but then broke out in a grin and took their hands in hers.

Around Bolivia we traveled, Amaya making friends with humans and other species. Ingrid and I were constantly awed by the way our daughter brought joy into so many people's lives, just by her very presence. And everywhere we went, the rainforests, cloud forests, raging rivers, and Andean peaks seemed a perfectly natural, fresh world to grow up in. Bolivia seemed insulated, protected by low human population density, strong indigenous traditions, and geography, with the seemingly impenetrable Amazon on one side and the towering Andes on the other. Yet, as was happening around the world, the rainforest, that strange green beast, was being slain. It got worse each year. The very monkeys that befriended Amaya began fleeing into the last remnants of their reserves. I knew that unless the global economic system causing this destruction was fundamentally changed, Amaya's children would not have any at all left to enjoy.

I BEGAN TO SEE MORE CLEARLY in my work that, along with the forests, the Flat World was eliminating the people who live in them, rapidly spreading across the globe, the pulses on the earth's heart monitor ceasing. Flatlining. Of the sixty-eight hundred languages spoken now, half will be dead in fifty years — about a tongue per week. When languages are forgotten, the culture itself soon follows, as if the memory of what it means to be of a certain people can be expressed only in that language. Next on the wait list for oblivion are the Amungme of Indonesia, Paraguay's Enxet, and Kenya's Ogiek. Within Bolivia, tribes like the Pacahuara, Araona, Uru-Chipaya, and Weenhayek are also on the way out. The villain most often cited is the spread of global capitalism, including the impact of television.

As a father, I now felt the stakes of my work had sharply increased. I loved Amaya deeply and wanted the world she would live in to be kind and fair. I felt, in an increasingly personal way, how the Flat World virus, by destroying nature, also destroys those societies living in harmony with nature, hundreds of them. In Amaya's Bolivia, this was epitomized by a remarkable woman named Kusasu.

In my two years of work in Noel Kempff National Park, in the remote east of Bolivia, I befriended Kusasu — the very last speaker of Guarasug'wé. I went to Kusasu's village, Bella Vista, deep inside the park with the desire to help save her tribe from extinction. My project team and I had written it as an activity in our workplan as part of a much bigger aid and conservation project covering that region. The activity: "Cultural survival: Guarasug'wé." Through reclaiming language and handicrafts and securing land for the final Guarasug'wé, perhaps we could apply defibrillators to bring the culture's heartbeat back, to tease a stubborn blip from the flat line on the monitor.

The trip to Bella Vista was magical. With a skinny park ranger named Misael, I raced up the Iténez River in a motorized canoe to the Guarasug'wé area. Light shimmered on the immense, beautiful river. The water reflected the sky and the thick forest around us. We sliced through the water, into a candy store of multicolored birds: wading in the shallows, soaring above, fleeing just ahead of us.

I'd stayed up late the night before, poring over everything ever written about the Guarasug'wé — a grand total of one book, anthropologist Jurgen Riester's *Guarasug'wé: Chronicles of Their Last*

Days. Candles and incense ablaze, and Andean music on my stereo — charangos and walaychos strummed to the rhythm of wancara drums, overlaid with zampoña cane panpipes — my imagination followed Riester's account into the Indian Territory under the Amazon's seven skies, heading toward the Guarasug'wé Ivirehi Ahae, or "the land without evil." I had also met in person with Dr. Riester, and he told me that for the Guarasug'wé, a canoe carries a person to the next world after death. Your soul travels up an Amazon River tributary like the one Misael and I traversed, toward a hole in the sky, finally slipping forever into the seven skies.

For several hours, the sameness of the jungle wall seemed to be luring us toward that eventual hole in the sky. I pulled my green park ranger–issue rain jacket tight around me and closed my eyes, imagining the fish, caimans, and eels below and the jaguars and foxes lurking just out of sight. Finally we passed a structure. Then another. Huts made of thatch, with the roofs caved in; Misael told me that these were the places where Guarasug'wé used to live.

We arrived in Bella Vista, climbing the embankment and heading to the schoolhouse. There we convened a meeting with the local community, to brainstorm strategies for cultural rebirth. *"Yo soy Guarasug'wé!"* — "I am Guarasug'wé!" — an old woman said. I realized who she was: Kusasu. She must have been eighty and had a long gray braid hanging over each shoulder. She sat with her spine straight, her firm jaw set, and her attractive, softly wrinkled face held high. Though she said this in Spanish, she quickly repeated the same thing in Guarasug'wé, which caused the dozen teenagers present to break into embarrassed giggling.

Staying strong, answering the teenagers without scorn or raised voice, Kusasu said, "Why do you laugh? How can you remember your language if you do not speak it?" She then shifted her gaze to me, "You can call me *sarí* — grandmother."

With this, the teenagers laughed outright at her. The Guarasug'wé teens, in their shorts and T-shirts, had adopted the style of their adolescent counterparts in neighboring Brazil. Misael and I continued this ruse of a meeting, our presence revealing itself for what it was: a fool's errand. Kusasu was the only one who spoke a decent smattering of the language. This wasn't a culture; it was a hospice of full-blown AIDS patients on their last T cells.

Still, Kusasu had a vitality about her, inviting us back to her home after the failed meeting. Her nephew had hunted a tapir in the forest, and the large animal was roasting on a spit. She pointed to a leafy plant that she said cures rheumatism; she pressed my palm against a tree and said their mattresses used to be made of this bark. Like the few words of Guarasug'wé she still spoke, Kusasu offered these things up to me proudly. Even under the direct barrage of mocking teenagers, she had been unwavering, certain of the language and customs she held tight to her chest.

While eating later with Kusasu and several relatives in the open-air kitchen next to their hut, I asked the old woman about Ivirehi Ahae, the Amazon's seven skies, and the canoe ride to the hole in the first sky. She told me that was what "the ancestors believed," but real emotion broke only through when she said, "Sometimes I miss Mother."

She chewed a piece of tapir, staring off toward the river and the disappearing forest over the river, in Brazil. "It's nice to have a mother," she finally continued. "We would work all day, talking Guarasug'wé." Her eyes closed, the rounded lids like moons, imagining the past.

"Who can I speak the dialect with now?" she asked. "My children don't want to speak it, and my aunts and cousins are dead. Dead! *Sí, estamos perdiendo la cultura un poco*" — "Yes, we're losing a little bit of our culture."

With this understatement I completely lost my appetite. Excusing myself I walked down to the river and sat there in silence until well after sunset. That night I slept fitfully, getting up at dawn to a sunrise over the river and marshlands, pink freshwater dolphins surfacing, and a hawk flapping to the other side of the river with a large fish in its claws. The tragic story of Kusasu's people wasn't unlike that of the Amungme, the Enxet, and the Ogiek: a story of twenty-first-century races falling off the flat edge of the world.

For centuries the Guarasug'wé lived in communal longhouses where everything was shared. Their simple houses were easily abandoned as they migrated through the Chiquitania into the Amazon on the parallel trail of good hunting grounds, the Ivirehi Ahae, or "land without evil." The Guarasug'wé believed that our physical life formed part of a reenactment of the archetypal journey to Ivirehi Ahae. The prominence of Ivirehi Ahae in the Guarasug'wé worldview was magnified as Portuguese and Spanish colonists — and later the Brazilian and Bolivian governments — penned them into an ever-narrower area. Remarkably, the Guarasug'wé eluded these opponents right into contemporary times, as they continued their search, now with time running out, for the land without evil.

But industrial capitalism dealt the coup de grâce in the mid-twentieth century. Massive quantities of rubber were needed for a growing fleet of motor vehicles in the United States and Europe, and some of that rubber was found in Guarasug'wé lands. Bolivian and Brazilian rubber tappers on the payroll of wealthy barons invaded, enslaving the Guarasug'wé. They were also given license to kill those who resisted.

A few held on, abandoning one shelter after the next as they fled deeper into what is today Noel Kempff National Park. But soon there was nowhere else to go. The rubber tappers were everywhere, and all that was left was to surrender or fight. The last Guarasug'wé chief died in a standoff with well-armed and rubber-hungry invaders; their final shaman fell in a pool of blood soon after. The spine of their political and spiritual leadership cracked, and the last fifty or so

Guarasug'wé, including a younger Kusasu, disbanded and huddled together in the homes Misael and I saw along the banks of the river — to die.

Before I left Bella Vista, Kusasu took my lightly freckled Irish hand in her wrinkled, bony one. The sound of our canoe's motor overpowered the swish of the river's eddies. I knew, as Kusasu did, that there was really nothing to say, so I just held her hand in mine for a very long moment — and then let it go.

LIKE JACKIE, KUSASU IS A WISDOMKEEPER. Against odds, she has fought the good fight by simply being who and what she is, rather than letting herself be melted into an endless homogeny. Sometimes now, when I hold my daughter's hand, I can feel Kusasu's in the other. Amaya's hand is tiny but growing, pink and soft; Kusasu's is dark, calloused, thick with heavy veins. Amaya takes my hand loosely, telling me about her day. Kusasu's grip is steadfast, insistent, and sometimes feels like a vise.

I gave my daughter an indigenous name. Her mom and I kept up the tradition of letting her hair grow without a single haircut for her first two years and then cut it in a *ruthuchiku*, or traditional community haircutting ceremony. I teach Amaya about indigenous values of love of nature (about Pachamama). I even authored a children's book titled *Kusasu and the Tree of Life* that portrays a Chiquitano girl who learns from the Guarasug'wé to integrate ecological consciousness into her Western university studies, bringing her skills back to her people. Is all of this enough? Amaya is a Flat World child who now lives in Santa Cruz, a globalizing city of two million inhabitants in Bolivia. She attends prekindergarten at Cambridge College, an English-speaking school.

I look down at my hands: Amaya holds one, Kusasu the other, the creative edge being born and dying as the Flat World crushes in on us from all sides. For a moment, it seems possible that if we find more hands to hold, we can walk with strength into the flattening world, planting seeds of the old cultures for the young to cultivate. It is not that we want the world to remain static, unchanging forever. Change is inevitable, but is there a way to change without destroying cultural and ecological diversity? If we connect to others who want this new paradigm shift, it might be possible to bend the Flat World in enough isolated places and communities that they eventually push out and touch at their fragile, diverse edges.

17. | SUCHNESS

SITTING ALONE ON LEAH'S FIRE ESCAPE, I can hear her inside cooking breakfast, the smell of bacon frying, and find myself reflecting on the Buddhist concept of "suchness." Suchness suggests that things are exactly as they are, and not otherwise — "such" as they are. Much of our unhappiness comes from missing the true essence of things. Take Leah's tree — it towers over us whenever we're in her white citadel of a house. Its "suchness" has to do with size. It wraps its arms around the house, folding everything into a hug. Once, during a storm, its enormous leafy branches drenched in water slapped at windows, the walls, and caused the back door to fly open.

The fire escape door swings open and there is Leah, her eyes clear blue as the sky behind her, her blonde hair blowing in the same direction as the giant tree's branches. She hands me a plate of eggs from the Thompson farm, scrambled the way I like them, along with some of the Thompsons' bacon and a slice of thick-crusted bread she's baked. The food's glorious smell fills my nostrils as she bends down, pushing her hair aside, and sits. Such as she is.

Leah and I had talked about my daughter before we became lovers, but at the time I didn't wanted to dwell on the topic. But once I'd opened up to Paul Jr. about it, I for some reason felt the need to talk about it more with Leah. She now picked up our previous conversation, saying, "I admire you for taking responsibility for Amaya."

"How could I not?"

"Do you know how many millions of men wipe their hands of that responsibility completely?"

"Yes, but how many millions more form a family."

"Is that possible? I mean in this case?"

I'd been over that question so many times in my life. Though Ingrid and I agreed from the beginning we wouldn't form a traditional family, we hedged on that once we both fell deeply in love with our daughter; we wanted to give her as much of a sense of security as possible. We discussed what it would be like to live together as a family, but luckily both of us had the maturity to know, down deep, that we were far too different in our perspectives and interests to make it work. We knew that if we married we'd likely end up as half of US marriages do, in divorce. What would be better for Amaya? Defining our own clear, respectful co-parenting arrangement from the beginning? Or forming a false togetherness with the likelihood of it later ripping apart, causing much greater pain? To us, the answer was obvious.

Leah took a bite of bacon, and I felt that the tree — hovering heavily over us, over the entire fire escape and house, casting a light green glow around Leah — seemed to be listening to our conversation. I opened up to Leah about something I rarely shared, from my childhood: I'm Bill now, but in grade school I was B-B-Billy. I had a stutter. And this in addition to being a carrot-topped, four-eyed smart kid. "Where ya g-g-going?" kids would call from down the hall, shooting spitballs at the back of my neck. Knowing how awful it feels to be the outcast, to be marginalized, was part of what drew me into helping others and nature through aid work.

My parents' love got me through the stutter. They wisely went against my teachers' advice and refused to stick me in speech therapy. Instead of seeing me as damaged goods, they accepted my suchness, stutter and all, until my speech defect healed. Most healing, of ourselves, of our society, is really just holding a space for things to come into alignment.

"Not being a household dad," I told Leah, "feels like that stutter felt. It was a piece of me that shouldn't be there." Even though Ingrid and I took the best course of action given our circumstances, something in me still couldn't accept the suchness of it. I *should* be in a nuclear family like my parents; I *should* be there with Amaya, every single day.

We sat on Leah's porch, under the gigantic tree, for a long time in silence. Finally, Leah asked: "What's love?"

I felt blood rush into my chest. I pictured my daughter as an infant, the first time I held her. I said, "You first."

"It's something you can't help. It's literally 'falling' in love. It's gravity."

She bit into a strawberry. "I like this," she said, opening Jonathan Safran Foer's *Everything Is Illuminated*, which she'd brought out. "This is love...isn't it? When you notice someone's absence and hate that absence more than anything? More even, than you love his presence?"

I replied with my own quote from the book: "From space, astronauts can see people making love as a tiny speck of light."

"You've read it."

"Have you ever been in love?" I asked.

Leah thought for a moment. The other day she'd said to me: "Not a lot of women will tell you this, but the desire to *be pregnant* is like the desire to eat when you're starving. And it's distinct from sexual desire; a physical craving to carry that weight." She looked at me as she said this, and I had to look away. I felt choked up. We had so much in common, Leah and I, but did I — did we — want more than *anam cara*, a soul friendship? All I could imagine was this: another child, another continent, loves scattered around the globe. I thought of Paul's question, about whether I wanted to marry and have more children. A side of me could imagine it, but I hesitated.

"Yes," Leah finally said, "I've been in love. I've had my heart broken, and now it's got these tiny cracks."

Everything, just then, was illuminated. A squirrel on the brick patio below did little pushups and then froze in the down position, belly to the ground, legs splayed to the sides, absurd. Then it leapt back to life, darting through a yellow-white pattern of insects. The begonias gleamed, and I could smell the white pollen that was fluttering down from the trees, swept up and down in soft air currents, and settling on my jeans. Across the street, teenagers cajoled drivers to hang a left into their benefit carwash. A bird screeched.

"Those cracks," Leah said. "Light streams out of them."

"THIS IS MY DAUGHTER," José said. We were at his house, and he passed me a photo.

La Fea Más Bella was on the TV in the background. Hector played RuneScape on the computer, killing chickens as usual. José told me that Hector was not his only child. His daughter, Ofelia, age eight, had gone back to Mexico with her mom. They'd separated several years ago and split the kids. José showed me a photo of Ofelia in her first communion dress, saying he hadn't seen her in two years.

I took a photo out of my wallet — Amaya at age two — and handed it to him. He looked at it for a long while. Light filled the room to the muted sounds of video carnage. "She's an angel," José finally said.

Somehow there wasn't much more to say. José changed the

channel. Hector came in and sat next to me on the couch, and we watched TV together. Later, I biked into Smithville and called Bolivia on a pay phone.

"Estoy triste" — "I'm sad" — Amaya said. I asked her why. She replied: *"Te extraño"* — "I miss you." It's a parent's natural instinct to cheer his child up, so I told Amaya how much I missed her and then quickly changed topics. I asked about her preschool, about her kittens and dog (named Skip, after a card in the game Uno). She talked about her simple world for a while. When I finally hung up the phone and gazed across the Quick-N-Easy's island of gas pumps, I felt a dull, deep ache to be back in Bolivia, close to Amaya.

The next day my Honduran neighbor, Graciela, pulled up to me in a red sports car. She flung open her door — *"Hola!"* — and launched into a stream of quick Honduran Spanish, heavy on the *rr*. She cut the engine. All the time in the world. I loved this: instead of rolling down her window, she had her whole door wide open. It seemed so Latin, so open. Her grin was joyous; she'd passed her McDonald's SafeServe test with a 90 percent score.

"I'm not that literate," she said, "even in Spanish. And the test was in English. I stayed up until one and got up again at four. Studying!"

"How did you understand the test if you are illiterate?" I asked.

"I can read some of it. And the rest — *¡el diccionario!*" she said, flipping invisible pages. She boasted that only one in ten passed the test; even many of "the Americans" failed. For passing, she'd get a dollar raise.

"What was on the test?"

"Health stuff. Like bacteria."

"Now you can forget it all," I said.

"Oh no!" she said, suddenly serious. "I won't forget."

We talked for a long while. At one point a pickup I'd not seen before drove around her car, picked up something in front of her house, and then pulled out past us again and onto Old 117 South. Her mechanic, Graciela said. Their car was in the shop; this red one was her aunt's.

She has *an aunt* around here? How lovely that cars circulate freely through the Honduran extended family. It got me nostalgic for Latin America. Now Graciela had an arm and leg dangling casually out of the side of the car. We laughed some more, and then she closed the door and drove along, as casually as when she'd stopped a full forty-five minutes earlier.

ALONE, 12 X 12.

No visitors on the agenda, just an overcast day stretching out all around me, the *New Yorker* insufficient company. David Sedaris buying pot in a trailer park. I laughed at a sardonic *Onion* news article Leah had left. The headline read, "Seven Percent of World's Resources Still Unconsumed":

> A report released Monday by the U.S. Department of the Interior indicates that 7 percent of the natural resources that existed before the dawn of the Industrial Age still remain unconsumed.
>
> "The global environmental crisis has been greatly exaggerated, as there are still plenty of resources to go around," Deputy Secretary of the Interior Russell Kohl said. "In addition to more than 30 tons of fossil fuel, the planet has literally hundreds of acres of tropical rainforest."
>
> Exxon celebrated the announcement by spilling the contents of a supertanker.

Then I flipped to a *New Yorker* cartoon in which a woman was saying to her husband: "Don't judge me until you've walked a mile on my medication." I laughed dryly, but then felt a pang of sadness. Leah and I had spoken the other day about healing. I told her the term comes from a word meaning "entire" or "complete," adding that Sartre said that Che Guevara was our era's "most complete human being."

"Because Che overcame his own inner shit," Leah said. "He

linked his life to the fate of the poor. And do you know the root of the word *therapy?* It's 'to support' or 'to hold up.'"

Over the next several days, as I continued my daily walks on the tracks, through the forest, I felt sensitive all over, like skin blistering. The wound of my separation from Amaya was now exposed. I realized that on one subtle level I was playing the victim: I'd somehow been deprived of a stable, traditional family, of togetherness with Amaya. *What nonsense*, I realized, as these feelings surfaced during meditation one afternoon. Didn't all of my life belong?

Later, I watched a spider down by No Name Creek. This clever little spider, I noticed, never built its web between two rocks. A strong wind might then take the web right out. Instead, it always constructed its web between two reeds or blades of grass. That way when the wind gusted through, the web naturally bent with the plant, ducking beneath the breeze and rising back up when it was calm. We can construct our characters in the same way: with definite structure but flexible moorings.

The wind was blowing hard through my life. I had a choice. I could choose to resist, to create a victimhood or other drama out of my separation from my daughter, maybe even going so far as to flee the 12 x 12 and return immediately to Bolivia to feel her love in the flesh and blood. Or, on the other hand, I could accept the imperfection of life, such as it is; like that spider, I could allow the difficult times to blow over and then come back up in the calm. Did it have to be either-or: with Amaya all of the time or none? Could we create a rhythm of togetherness that rose and fell regularly, gracefully?

In an ideal world, Amaya would have Daddy by her side all the time. How did she feel about our separation? I talked about this with Leah, a child of divorced parents who grew up with her mom. Leah said the *most* important part, for her and for her friends in similar situations, was not the constant presence of both parents, but the feeling that Daddy loves you no matter what, supports you, calls you regularly, and that you sense that he's got you in his heart. She added that I certainly made the grade in all of those categories. I knew Amaya missed me and wanted to spend more time with me, but I took comfort in the fact that she was secure and healthy and surrounded by love in Bolivia.

While reflecting on this, I received a letter from Jackie. "I've made a decision," she wrote from her desert pilgrimage. "After thirty years I've decided to move on from being a physician. I'm giving up the last of the image of me-as-doctor."

I was astonished to read this. It seemed a radical step. She then wrote a little cryptically that "faithfulness to the path given is the way to learn to love":

> I have been pulled into peace walks, how they blend a passion for being in the natural world with the silence, the discipline of putting one foot in front of another. It's something in my most activist days I would have made great fun of: "What's the good of it?"
>
> It's a big decision. But by leaving work, leaving medicine, I will be free to respond to what is presented in a way not possible before. My sister is moving to a retirement place; I can go down and spend two months helping her transition. I will spend two weeks doing deep cleaning at the Catholic Worker in Birmingham on the way to my sister's. A humble path seems to open. I'm no longer seeking "high drama." Like the notion of pilgrimage, I'll go out of familiar places into what is not known. Follow the path.

FAITHFULNESS TO THE PATH GIVEN

18. ∥ SOLITUDE

WHEN I WAS BY MYSELF, I'd sometimes pause to look at the inner walls of the 12 x 12 by candlelight, or regard it from outside as the evening sun warmed its wood siding. The house looked like a sculpture of solitude, art shining through utility. Jackie's honest choice. She had chipped and carved away the clutter, releasing something essential.

A 12 x 12 doesn't distract. I recalled my reaction the first time I saw it, the horror of the small. How I craved something that proclaimed the glory of the human, ten thousand square feet in which to lose myself. Jackie, I believe, went into solitude so that her outward life would contain more presence. I already knew about this process from meditation practice. In meditation you sit and allow thoughts to surface, like bubbles in a glass of champagne — and then allow them to float away. A deep well might open up, coal black and filled with dragons. But you maintain presence.

At the 12 x 12 I sometimes thought of Kusasu's solitude in the Bolivian Amazon. The last speaker of Guarasug'wé, she once said to me that she had no one left to speak her language with. On the surface it's axiomatic: she's the last speaker, hence no one else to speak with. My first emotion was pity. Which chamber of hell is that, where the Flat World has eliminated everyone who speaks your language? Not only are your parents and grandparents and siblings gone — leaving you with only the memories of meals and hanging laundry and trading jokes, all of it still fresh in your mind — but so too is every person you might share those memories with in the language in which they were created.

My pity for Kusasu didn't last. The light in her eyes dissolved it. I didn't see any self-pity there, nor any rage against the world that had eliminated her race. She reached out her skinny hand, veined like the air-roots of a cambara, and touched my hand, telling me something through her touch: *I'm complete. I may be incomplete as the member of something, but as Kusasu there is nothing missing.* Before heading into the Amazon's seven skies — and, considering her age, it might be soon — she seemed to have found the radically present place of her own solitude.

When you pray, who hears your prayer? You do. Prayer is a concentration of positive thoughts. Once, at the end of an exhausting eight-day yoga retreat, the instructor asked our group: "Do you feel the energy around you?" I did. Muscles burning, joints oiled, tendons warm and light, I felt an overflowing reservoir of what the Chinese call *chi*, or vital energy. "That's your protection," he said. "Nothing else."

IN THE SUMMER OF 1996, on a break from teaching Native American seventh graders in New Mexico, I volunteered as a human shield in a remote hamlet in the Lacondon jungles of Chiapas, Mexico. It was one of my first experiences with solitude. The previous year, the Mexican military had flown bombing sorties over the Lacondon and killed a thousand people, aiming for Zapatistas and their sympathizers. I was part of a hundreds-strong volunteer team of international observers to simply *be* in Zapatista villages. The thinking was that the Mexican military would not hesitate to kill innocent Chiapan peasants, but they would not risk the terrible global publicity of slaughtering Italians, French, and Americans. Our presence was "official," part of the San Andres Peace Accords, but the military refused to recognize us, so Mexican NGO workers had to smuggle me past military checkpoints in the dead of night. Then I had to walk for a full day, deep into the jungle near the Guatemalan border, before finally arriving at my designated village.

All went smoothly to that point. But soon the reality of my role set in. For weeks on end, I had absolutely nothing to do but "be" in the village. My Spanish was terrible back then, so I could hardly communicate. Because Zapatista guerrillas were camped in a secret location right beyond the hamlet, I wasn't even allowed the pleasure of a hike. So I spent a lot of time on the straw bed in my mud hut reading, thinking, staring at the walls. After a week, I began to go stir-crazy. I wanted to at least explore the jungle. I wanted out. After all, I was using my vacation time to do this; I could have been exploring the pyramids at Chichén Itzá, Palenque, and Tikal or scuba diving in Honduras. My vacation time was precious; was I spending it uselessly, in the solitude of a mud hut?

Amid these doubts, something happened. I was making rudimentary coffee one morning over a wood fire when I looked up and drew a quick breath of shock. Towering over me was a beautiful Zapatista woman, in full camouflage, her black hair pulled back in a ponytail, rounds of ammo slung around her shoulder, an antique machine gun held across her chest. She was so iconic she looked surreal. Up to that point I hadn't seen any of the actual Zapatista *guerreros* — they kept to their hidden camps in the forest, where the villagers brought them food. But here she was!

I mumbled something. She just stood silently, unsmiling, hand on her weapon. I didn't agree with violence then, and I still don't. But

I understood and admired the Zapatistas. These are Mexico's most neglected people, the disenfranchised descendants of the ancient Maya. Like Kusasu's Guarasug'wé they are nearing the precipice of extinction, being pushed off the flat edge of the world — but not without a fight. Symbolically and practically, their uprising began on January 1, 1994, the first day of the North American Free Trade Agreement, or NAFTA. At the time, respected economists, since proven right, said that NAFTA would flood Mexico with cheap American corn, thereby undercutting the livelihoods of millions of Mexican corn farmers and turning them into the urban poor, forced off their land and into Mexico City's dangerous slums to work at whatever they could. To make matters worse, corn remains a potent mythological symbol. Traditional Maya believe that corn represents the perpetual circle of life. They imagine God with corn in the blood and consider themselves to be children of the corn. They decided to resist.

Today, the Zapatistas continue to wage what has been called the first postmodern war, using tools of media and global sympathy much more than actual weapons. When they captured Chiapas's capital, San Cristobal de Las Casas, many Zapatistas had only wooden guns, a powerful symbol as CNN's cameras rolled. Others had real guns, of course, including the *mujer Zapatista* who stood in front of me. I poured a cup of coffee and held it out to her and also indicated some corn tortillas I had on a wooden plate. She refused. But before she left, she shared a heartfelt smile with me, which I took to mean *"gracias"* for being present in the village. For the remainder of my service in the Lacondon, I relaxed into the solitude, knowing it was tied to a larger purpose.

Solitude in service of being a human shield is clearly pragmatism in action. The silent force of a hundred European and North American people in Chiapas kept actual bombs from dropping. But conscious solitude is always pragmatic, always active. How else to learn to honestly look into the dark, infinite well within, to see those foreign lands that no one else can ever know?

IN MYTHOLOGICAL STORIES, heroes face demons and thereby grow as people. In solitude you find the warmth and glow of the hearth — the deep bliss of the unity — but you must first go straight through the fire.

I had a terrible, vivid dream one night at Jackie's. An ugly old man, somehow connected to the Nazis, maybe earlier in his life during Hitler's reign, lived in a deep woods. A younger man visited him, and something hateful was planned. The younger man had a contingent of a half dozen other young men along with him; they milled around outside. Inside, the old Nazi and the younger man laughed, and then the young man left with the others. The old man was once again alone.

Until that point in the dream, I saw events from a distance, as if from the perspective of the forest itself. The scene seemed vague, the humans tiny against the deep forest. Then my perspective flipped. I was no longer looking at this as if perched on a distant branch in a tree. I was right next to the old man. I could see the black moles on his cheek, hear him breathing, even smell his sour breath as he sat alone. Not alone in a luminous solitude, but rather utterly lonely, the very definition of loneliness: avoiding the well. He wasn't angry; he'd already resented and hated the world so much it had charred him into deadness itself. He had no feelings at all.

I awoke from the dream and grabbed my bedside marbled notebook to scribble down the details. In my semiconscious state, I realized to my horror that I was writing the dream down *in the first person*, as if I were the old Nazi. Here is how I started to write, directly from the journal: "A younger man came to visit me, and we made a hateful plan, and then we laughed..."

Tibetan Buddhist art is replete with horrifying statues, their grotesque faces displaying every kind of negativity, from bitterness and resentment to anger and outright murderous hatred. Western missionaries misunderstood these to be idols of gods and devils; they are not. They represent our own inner states that we "meet" when we go deeply into silence and solitude. After the Nazi dream, I biked into Smithsville and called Leah. "What's sin?" I asked her.

"For me," she finally replied, "sin is when I'm at the center."

We often turn away from or ignore the darkness within, whether it's labeled Christian "sin," Jung's "dark side," or Eckhart Tolle's "unconsciousness." But I am glad when I meet the dark places on the shadowy borders of solitude. *The black moles and sour breath, the deadness.* On the surface, my dream arose from my time living in the SS barracks in Buchenwald. Sleeping each night beside the ovens made National Socialism very visceral for me. But the dream hinted at the lifeless, the flat inside of me. *A younger man came to visit me, and we made a hateful plan, and then we laughed.* Kusasu's death is in me. The destruction of the Bolivian rainforests is in me. Buchenwald is in there, too. I'm complicit.

"So what do we do?" Leah said, days later down by No Name Creek. We'd been talking about our inner flatness, how we were habituated to a central evil of our own time, what the late Susan Sontag called "an American-style consumer society that spreads itself across the globe, destroying the past, and enclosing all horizons within a selfish materialism."

Leah and I talked about Sontag, who in one of her last speeches warned of "the mercantilist biases of American culture."

But it isn't enough to replace Thomas Friedman with Susan Sontag. Too many of us do this, if unconsciously; we think other people's thoughts. Solitude's richest gift is allowing one's own thoughts to flow, and not through mental aqueducts built by others. That engineering is ecocide's infrastructure. There's so much mind control, more now in our hyper-mediated world than ever, and truly thinking for ourselves may be the hardest thing to do. Yet could this, ultimately, be the only way our society will achieve the necessary basis of change, a paradigm shift?

DURING LEAH'S VISITS TO THE 12 X 12, we usually spent some of our time in solitude. Once we decided to spend the morning in the woods, separately. She plopped down on the banks of the creek, a hundred yards from the 12 x 12, dangling her feet in the water, her fingers stroking the mossy bank as if it were a drowsy cat. Meanwhile, I walked down the creek, as far as I ever had, until No Name Creek finally came to an end. It liquidated itself into a larger river.

In the place where the creek disappeared, I stuck in a toe and then eased in my body. The chilly water cooled me, and the current massaged out tensions. I came out dripping and sat on the bank. An hour passed, two hours. A blade of rock sliced the water and the creek's lacquered flow touched the edge and sent off caviar dimples of water that instantly grew into quarter-sized whirlpools. Another moment and twelve inches later they swirled into silver dollars reflecting the branches of the tree above. That reflection on the circle of water looked just like a dragonfly. And the water's motion made it appear to be flapping its wings. Furiously. Earnestly flailing for its life, as if wanting to break free of two dimensions. Flapping like that, it actually became a live dragonfly to me. I focused on the spot where they were biggest, and they zoomed by, hundreds of them with their long thoraxes, heads, antennae, and translucent wings, to be killed in their prime, and by not very much: a nub of falling water slaughtered them.

Watching all those dragonflies die, I thought of how thoughtlessly I'd squashed a fly the day before. I noticed it upturned, buzzing away on its back by Jackie's front door. The buzzing sound annoyed me mildly. It would stop, but every ten seconds there'd be another burst of buzzing. Its dying gasps. Hardly thinking, I got up, took one

step, and the next one crushed its tiny body underfoot with a crackle
of insect parts against cement. I sat back down, laptop in lap — but.
But a single point, like a black magic marker dot, caught my periph-
eral vision, and I knew I couldn't write another word with the corpse
in full view. So I ripped off a square of toilet paper, scooped up the
fly, and deposited it in my little trash bag, feeling better without an
accusing corpse in plain sight.

Then — seemingly out of nowhere — Kusasu came to mind.
Her people used to live in the rainforest. But over the years, logging
and rubber operations — and big soy plantations — took over much
of the land, destroying the forests and corraling Kusasu's people into
ever tinier areas. Others fled into far-off cities to become "pavement
Indians," unable to assimilate, begging for scraps on street corners.
I thought of how the Amazon's indigenous people are now "environmental refugees," forced to migrate into Third World urban
sprawl. And suddenly, that fly felt like a metaphor. I squashed it almost unconsciously; it was the evidence of that unconsciousness staring me in the face that bothered me. *Bring it to light.* Is it really a
stretch to suggest that our civilization crushed Kusasu, the Guarasug'wé, and their rainforest home with its boot heel but quickly hid
the evidence? *Bring it into the light.* Genocide is part of me; ecocide
is part of me. *Don't repress it. Make it conscious.* I walked quickly back
up along the creek toward Leah, the ripples shining like blades. I
stepped with splashes, then up onto the bank through the tangle,
building up a sweat, feeling the sun burning my forehead. Rounding
a bend I finally saw Leah.

She sat in the same spot she'd been hours earlier, feeling the
water with her feet. I stopped. She didn't see me. There was no journal on the bank beside her, and she'd long since finished *My Name
Is Chellis and I'm in Recovery from Western Civilization.* In fact, she
seemed to read less and less. There is a point where we must let the
feel of water on bare feet replace books and spiritual practices. They

can be very helpful as guides, as structures, as inspiration, but can also, if we hold on to them too tightly, obstruct the most important thing: an unmediated facing of the world as it is, which is to say, as we shape it.

I walked through the gleaming water up to Leah and asked: "What's the shape of the world?"

She looked directly at the earth. Splashed water with her feet, sank her fingers into the supple moss. "It's not flat," she said, squinting up at me.

I looked into No Name Creek. No more suicidal dragonflies; here the water was woodcut, carefully etched with a sharp metal tool. But those neat streaks suddenly jumbled into a rutty swirl, like pasta loosening in boiling water. "The world is everything *but* flat," she said, standing up. "Feel the smooth river rocks, the spongy banks."

Colors tangled together in the creek: light purple, red, and orange. "The world curves," I said.

"It spins."

"It's sandy."

"There's clay."

"There's jellyfish."

"Rainforests full of animals."

"Slithering anacondas."

"Giant pandas."

"Six-toed sloths."

I'd look back on this moment as transformative: Leah and I groping for softer language concealed the flat, proclaiming the immediacy of smells, sounds, and textures. The beauty of the earth grew as we chose its beauty as the focus of our attention. The world is wet, Leah said, getting into the creek.

It's cold! I said, following her in.

Deep canyons.

Snowy peaks.

A million people die today.

A million are born.

The world is divine! The world is mine. *It's yours.* No, it's ours. *It's . . .*

Leah opened her mouth as if to say something else, but all that came out was a puff of air. Emptied of words, she collapsed onto No Name Creek's yielding bank and pulled me down next to her. We listened. Trees shimmered; water flowed, and a hawk called out, urgently, thick in the south.

19. | SOFT ECONOMY

LEAH HUGGED A GOAT and then paid the farmer for its cheese.

Durham's farmers market, a few blocks from Leah's house, was alive that morning. Fifty farmers had come in from the surrounding counties with meat and veggies, and a thousand of us gathered to take those organic products off their hands.

After paying, Leah and I lingered with Jim and Keisha, a farming couple in their midtwenties who had just bought thirty acres for fifty-six thousand dollars. "We love it!" Keisha told Leah while giving another customer change. "We're now in a yurt on our land, but we'll slowly sell enough goat cheese and vegetables to build a house. But there's no rush." Leah didn't want to leave their presence. I could feel the tug, too. Both of them were so vital, full of zest and health.

We went from table to table, filling our canvas bags. Leah floated through the place with an irrepressible smile, greeting the farmers, their kids, their dogs. She pressed a fresh blueberry between my lips; we sampled all kinds of cheeses, crusty breads, fruits that gushed juice onto our cheeks. Produce smells blended together. I felt joyful.

This was a far cry from a supermarket or the Gold Kist factory. No heavy packaging, no corporate logos. Natural colors merged gracefully with the faded old pickups, the farmers' tie-dyed Ts, the bustle of the place. It evoked a Bolivian or African market.

Farmers markets are like an emerging social contract between twenty-first-century *polis* and *dumos*; country folks produce healthy foods in an earth-friendly way and townspeople pay a little more. The number of farmers markets in the United States has more than doubled, from 1,755 in 1994 to 4,385 in 2006. They provide a lot more than food. Leah and the rest of us were there, you might say, to heal. Farmers markets, I began to realize, heal the edges of our über-industrialized economy, allowing a less chemical- and fossil fuel–intensive economy to flourish. They heal our relationships with each other as we reconfigure the buying and selling of food around fresh air and community. Most importantly, they heal our spirits, because if something pays, it stays, and those of us at the market that morning sensed we were voting with our dollars for a kind of independence: the right to farm.

"Leah!" said Jack at the next stand, his T-shirt reading, "Fix Marriage Not Gays." "You need some pork?" As he handed her a pound of meat, freshly slaughtered the night before on his farm, he asked me about myself. I told him where I was living.

"Your neighbors are *who*? Mike and Michele Thompson?!"

"Yes."

He silently shook his head, lips pursed. "They, how should I put this, are libertarian. Now I'm libertarian, too, and so is my partner, but we're libertarians on the left. The Thompsons are libertarians on the *right*."

I said I thought they were good people.

He laughed and said, "I wish them well with their farming. Just that I don't know if they have it together. I hear their whole operation, what there is of it, may go on the skids. Hopefully it won't be welfare for them again."

Our canvas bags full, we took a spin past an iron foundry and watched sculptors create. On the walk back to her house we passed the restaurant Piedmont, an art deco place that serves only local and organic food. All of this flourished within walking distance of her little white apartment.

"This could be the new economy," I said. "Healthy, community-centered."

"Eerie. That's exactly what I was just going to say." This was another change in myself I noticed. Since coming to Jackie's I'd become more intuitive. Several times I knew exactly what Leah was going to say a couple of seconds before she said it. While part of this was simply our getting to know each other better, I also discovered how mindfulness — being fully in the roomy present moment — enhanced a natural sixth sense. Goethe talked about this, how he became so sensitive to his surroundings that he could predict the weather with precision just by opening a window.

As we walked, Leah told me about her evolving dream. For years she'd fantasized about having a farm. Buy land, homestead, live with two chickens and goats and vegetables. Now it was economically viable to be an organic farmer. She could still be a journalist on a freelance basis, perhaps blend the two in some creative way. How empowering to discover that, if the culture around us was not working, we could join others who were creating a new culture.

That night Leah and I went to the Full Frame documentary film festival in Durham. Out of nowhere I heard, "Billy. *Billy!*" Suddenly, my mom's warm arms were hugging me.

Billy, she kept repeating. Childlike. Happy and present, in all her sixty-eight years of glory. She wore an earth-toned outfit and a necklace I'd gotten her as a gift while in the Ivory Coast a couple of years before. She hugged me again and took me over to introduce me to three of her friends from their activist group, The Raging Grannies, liberal-looking gals, good Americans. I asked my mom, "How about we have lunch tomorrow?"

She immediately agreed, as I knew she would. Leah came over. Introductions and hugs. Leah got a little stiff, as she always did when meeting new people, her "I'm-a-producer" mode, a professional young woman keeping a bit of distance. Mom's three friends asked for Leah's business card; all the while Mom's face beamed love toward me.

Then Leah and I disappeared into the film festival. What a pleasure to be in a place where your parents live, spontaneously bumping into them, setting up a lunch. To have a friend I adore at my side. To be at a film festival, in a smallish town in America, in spring. I wondered: *Could I stop being a man without a country? Could this be home?*

AT THE 12 X 12 I STARTED DREAMING about a soft economy.

Being with Jackie, being alone in her tiny house, provoked a question: How might personal economy and the leisure ethic come together as rebellion? Jackie's lifestyle is a twenty-first-century Boston Tea Party, but she hasn't thrown just one product overboard; rather, she's tossed the whole lot of planet-killing junk. Today it's not the British Empire colonizing us, but a pervasive corporate globalism. We resist through our vote, and I don't mean for this political candidate or that, though that's certainly part of it. We cast powerful votes for the kind of world we want to live in whenever we fish out a twenty or click BUY on the Web.

After Jackie's tea party, here's what remains on her permaculture ship: a tiny car that she runs on biodiesel; delicious local and organic food, 90 percent of it produced by herself or her neighbors; fresh drinking water she collects herself at a local spring; solar flashlights (she doesn't use disposable batteries for anything); a slight house, with building materials so minimal that the forests can live; and not a cent into federal war coffers.

She's part of a larger rebellion that includes wildcrafters like Bradley, the Thompsons, and the Pauls, who are reshaping Adams County; the Slow Food and farmers market movements in the larger

Raleigh–Durham–Chapel Hill area; and the budding national renewable energy, natural foods, and national TV-turn-off subculture. There are intriguing trends like the Compact (groups of citizens who join together and buy nothing new for one year), national Buy Nothing Day (no purchases for a day), and Boulder Bucks (cities like Boulder, Colorado, create a parallel currency that circulates only locally, therefore encouraging the local economy). But even if no such efforts existed, each of us possesses an incredibly powerful tool of resistance: our household economy.

It's been said that only little ideas need patents because the most transformative ideas are protected by public incredulity. Household economy as protest is one of those big ideas. Being at the 12 x 12 reminded me that I can examine with acute interest every single penny that goes out of my accounts. Is that penny helping create a vital farmers market or McWorld? The Thompsons' free chickens or Gold Kist's beakless chickens? A simple elegance that coexists with Bolivia's rainforests, or a decadence that fosters comfort but destroys a far greater beauty? Ideas like warrior presence, the Idle Majority, and the creative edge, I realized, can be crystallized in my life by becoming aware of personal economy's radical effects — and changing the direction of pennies.

LEAH AND I ATE OUR WAY into Jackie's soft economy. We gathered from the garden the herbs we used for baking with Mike's chicken. Leah pulled from her hair a bright red ponytail holder and used it to bunch basil. She had me smell each herb on the farm individually with my eyes closed. We sometimes brewed dark coffee — and once Leah rooted around until she found a special chocolate spice Jackie had ground herself. She added a little bit to her coffee, and I sampled it — even richer and more luxurious! I added a bit to mine, too.

I bought the coffee at the Adams Marketplace, the community-owned natural supermarket halfway between Pine Bridge and Durham where Paul Jr. and I had talked. The coffee was organic, shade-grown Bolivian, from the same Andean farmers cooperative I'd supported while working there. With each sip I felt a visceral connection between the work I'd been doing over the past decade in the Global South and choices I was now making in the States. For years, I gave technical assistance to cacao and coffee farmers in South America, so they might gain access to these very markets. The sense of coming full circle in that way — being able to picture Don Ernesto and Dona Celistina maintaining their local rainforests to produce coffee in an ecological fashion as I sipped that very product outside the 12 x 12 — warmed me to the core.

Leah and I would go to Adams Marketplace together. The food and other products in Leah's home were increasingly organic and fair trade, as our consciousness deepened. At Adams Marketplace I learned about Slow Food USA, which per its website "promotes the pleasure of good food and the integrity of local cultures that grow it" and "envisions a region with local markets, restaurants, and small farms overflowing with fresh food and food choices." The movement began in Italy at the foot of the Spanish Steps as a protest against McDonald's and the homogenized, fast-food culture it represents. It now has eighty-five thousand members worldwide, including twelve thousand in the United States, and six chapters in North Carolina.

During my stay in the 12 x 12, both Barbara Kingsolver and Bill McKibben passed through the Research Triangle; they were on separate speaking tours, but both focused on transitioning from our industrial food economy to something more local, organic, and "durable." Leah bumped into Kingsolver at Adams Marketplace, joining her, her daughter, and her husband for a bite of free-range egg omelet and *tertulia*, a relaxed conversation about her family's year of eating only local foods in their native Kentucky.

DECOLONIZING OUR CONSUMPTION PATTERNS is about more than shopping differently or shopping less. Food can be the simplest way to vote with one's wallet because it tastes so good. Trickier are all the ways our relationships and emotions are entangled with the corporate economy, such as how we give gifts. Consider that the average American spends $900 on Christmas gifts, not counting the shocking $120 per person for dog and cat gifts.

We were passing a large store in a mall in Chapel Hill called A Southern Season, and Leah said this was where she bought gifts for her parents, her colleagues, everyone. It was, she admitted, her addiction.

We got into the delicate issue of personal finance, and it turned out Leah lived from paycheck to paycheck. Right on the edge. Her December gift splurge alone set her back the better part of an entire paycheck. As a society, we are raised to express love with our wallets; suggesting we "spend less" can be almost like asking someone to "love less." It's such a sensitive topic that merely raising it can be enough to cause offense.

I remember feeling anxious when my mother, several years back, proposed the idea of a no-buy Christmas in our family. We'd make things for each other or figure out other ways to express love and gratefulness. *Wouldn't it feel stingy?* I thought. After all, we'd typically had dozens of wrapped gifts piled under the tree. Then Christmas morning arrived, and I gathered around the tree with my parents, my sister, her husband, and their son. There were few gifts underneath it, making each one more special. My father gave my sister and me excerpts from his journal around the time of our birth, where he reflected on the joy we brought him. I gave my parents and sister each a beautiful shell I'd found in a village on the Gambian coast, sharing with them the story of a day without money, and what it taught me about the importance of belonging, not belongings. They still have those shells prominently displayed in their homes, as bells — or rather shells — of mindfulness. My sister, tapping into her talents, painted us beautiful wall hangings with inspirational words on them. It was a meaningful, deeply joyous Christmas. Though we have not kept up a strict no-buy Christmas practice, the experiment woke us up to an empowering fact: We can create our own culture around gift-giving. Since then we've reduced gifts to a fraction of what they were while still experiencing an abundance of love and togetherness.

JACKIE MINED THESE ISSUES DEEPER STILL. She used her household economy as radical rebellion. I have spent years exploring ways to weave a softer economy into my life, and her example pushed me further.

Declare independence from the corporate global economy, Jackie seemed to say. Doing so has two synergetic positive effects. First, by simplifying her life and working less, she creates less garbage on the planet. Second, the time and space she liberates nourish her. We exchange something very precious for money: our life energy. Do we want to spend our time and energy earning money and contributing to the market economy, or fostering creative pursuits, our relationships, and community, and contributing love?

One way I've tried to do this is to take regular "sabbaticals" (what Tim Ferris, in his book *The Four-Hour Workweek*, calls "mini-retirements" interspersed throughout your life). I have found them to be the absolute richest parts of my life; they create time and space for my creativity to flourish. During the sabbaticals — the time in the 12 x 12 turned out to be one of them — I followed my bliss instead of the necessity to pay bills. I found my voice as a writer during such periods of "moodling": walking along abandoned railroad tracks, bathing in creeks and rivers, listening to crickets and macaws, meditating, reading hundreds of books, and growing flowers and food. These activities and nonactivities require little money but abundant time.

My father taught me an important lesson when I was a teenager:

live within — or below — your means. He taught me this by putting me to work. Even though he had money to spare, he had me bus tables at a restaurant starting at age sixteen so that I'd earn my own spending money. I also worked through college, first in a pizza restaurant and then at one of Brown's libraries, and also through graduate school, by then in part-time professional positions at the World Bank and World Conservation Union, earning enough to pay off all my Stafford Loans on graduation day. He instilled in me the connection between life energy — my sweat — and dollars; this can also be understood as the interconnection of the material and the spiritual.

Unfortunately, I forgot my Dad's lesson after undergraduate university. Suddenly I had debt on two credit cards and lived from paycheck to paycheck. A good friend handed me Vicki Robin and Joe Dominguez's *Your Money or Your Life*, which argues that we trade our precious hours of life for money, then use that money for things that bring little satisfaction. Their idea is to ratchet down personal expenses and grow savings in order to have less need to work for money and, thus, more free time to focus on what we really love.

This new take on voluntary simplicity was dubbed post-capitalist. People from modern, industrial societies were for the first time consciously scaling back consumption instead of trying to increase it. One PBS documentary showed professional couples in Holland, a hotbed of post-capitalism, selling their cars and riding only bikes. They also scaled back to the bare minimum of household products. As one Dutchman explained, "With shampoo, I start by using half my normal amount. If that still lathers, I use half of that half. I keep halving it each time until it has no effect, and then I increase the amount slightly every day until I find the perfect quantity."

Influenced by these ideas, I began tracking every penny that went out of my life in an account book each evening, and I was amazed to find that some 30 percent of my expenses were on things that, in the end, I decided weren't worth the exchange of my life energy. I graphed it over the months, watching the line of expenses go down without any drop in the quality of my lifestyle. I paid off the debts and took a pair of scissors to my credit cards and have since used only debit cards. I never made a bundle as a junior high school teacher at a Native American school, nor later as an aid worker, but I always "paid myself first" before paying the other bills, depositing 10 percent of every paycheck into investments. I taught myself financial planning for free on the helpful Motley Fool website. Over time, I found myself living well below my means with enough of a buffer to fund those creativity sabbaticals.

Ironically, the more I treated my life energy as sacred and lived frugally, the more I was able to indulge myself; I could gush generously where it counted. I learned this during my decade among the world's Idle Majority, the leisureologists of the Global South. Subsistence cultures have a forest instead of a supermarket; board games and guitars on stoops instead of minigolf and other paid entertainment. They aren't materially rich, yet I found myself continually amazed by their generosity — in the form of a meal, a bed, and all the time in the world to be with you. In that spirit I support the Sierra Club and other worthy causes, especially those that spontaneously arise in my daily life. And I don't cringe over a fifty-dollar bag of organic and local groceries because that's the actual cost of producing food in a healthy world. That same bag at Safeway is cheap because the costs to the environment — of pesticides, soil erosion, cultural erosion, and genetic modification of life forms — are not included in the price. Can we look beyond the sticker price to see the true cost of our goods, and our economy?

FOSTER A SOFT ECONOMY

20. | HUMILITY

THE SOLITUDE, THE SPACE, the time by the creek, all of it helped break the skin of the cocoon I'd been in. As spring emerged into full-ness, I felt the structure of my cellular tissue dissolve and re-form, and something new begin to emerge.

During those days I felt that if a hummingbird were to fly into me, I'd break out in tears. Inside this softer world the trellises filled in with greenery, the bones of plants found their leaves, the canopy cast fuller shadows. I ate olive caper bread with cheese from a local farm, chewing each bite thirty times to fully appreciate it. As I chewed — and chewed — I noticed the new lettuce rows, garlic, the walking onions, asparagus, shiitake mushrooms, larger on their logs. This lives.

Next to this flourishing garden was my bike, just waiting, an on-going invitation to pedal into air and silence. I sometimes biked alone, other times with Kyle, and I hung out with Hector when José was at work. Sometimes I gardened with the Thompson kids. They taught me new things about permaculture, things Jackie had taught them. She would have them over all the time, they told me, and teach them about her garden. Greg used a push mower to cut the grassy parts around the 12 x 12, while Kyle and I weeded the lettuce, onions, and asparagus. Afternoons passed in banter and work, and before we knew it the chores were done.

But something about my mood those days bothered me. At one point I read a news story about a general census in Great Britain, in which four hundred thousand people identified their religion as "Jedi," or among the lightsaber-wielding characters in *Star Wars*. Okay, I thought, that's an ironic statement for some, but there must be plenty among those hundreds of thousands who all too seriously think of themselves as enlightened crusaders battling the Dark Side of the Force.

The story about UK Jedis woke me up to something that was happening, unconsciously, in me. As I learned about wildcrafting, warrior presence, and compassion, and began to reduce my carbon footprint, consume more responsibly, and eat fair, organic, and local food, my ego grew attached to the idea that I was becoming "more enlightened." Walking the aisles of the organic Adams Market, I looked around and saw what I might become: a holier-than-thou progressive, carving an identity niche out of being so darn responsible. I was actually, in many ways, trying to eliminate my individual ego identity through warrior presence. The trap, I was discovering, was that the fiction of the ego is replaced by an even heavier fiction: that of being a Jedi, a spiritual warrior, an enlightened being — and therefore better than those miserable people who are not. This is why so many supposed spiritual teachers have such big egos; they've fallen into this very trap of specialness and are therefore not real teachers at all. It's high irony: building an ego out of the notion of having conquered it.

Afterward, I was looking at the 12 x 12 one day, and I suddenly saw it differently. The luster it held for me vanished, and for an instant, it was a mere shack. You could easily view it that way. Likewise, Jackie — if you bumped into her walking along the railroad

tracks and Old Highway 117 South in central North Carolina —
might not appear particularly noteworthy. Her oversized navy blue
jacket, the salt-and-pepper hair, small frame, slightly off-white teeth,
mild Southern drawl. She certainly wouldn't identify herself as a
doctor (she never uses the title Dr. Benton) or try to impress you as
a Wise One. She might seem a jolly lady out for a stroll.

And that's what she is. Jackie is wise, spiritual, and inspiring,
but she's completely unattached to any of this. That is to say, she's
humble. Like the classic Tao master, she is an ordinary person.

IN LEAH'S WHITE APARTMENT, the giant tree hovered above, its
now leafier branches brushing lightly on the windows. I smelled
herbs from Jackie's and spotted a dozen of the Thompsons' eggs on
her counter. We'd begun reading less and viscerally experiencing
more, but we maintained our habits of juggling several books at once.
She dipped into the play *Homebody/Kabul* (she was interviewing
playwright Tony Kushner the next day) and Thich Nhat Hahn; I was
reading *The Solace of Open Spaces* and a volume of Galway Kinnell's
poetry. We'd occasionally look up from our books and exchange
glances. I read aloud to her Kinnell's poem about a little boy who
sleeps soundly through a litany of alarmingly loud household noises:

> *but let there be that heavy breathing*
> *or a stifled come-cry anywhere in the house*
> *and he will wrench himself awake*
> *. . . he appears — in his baseball pajamas, it happens,*
> *the neck opening so small he has to screw them on.*

The tree swayed above us, and I told her one of my most frightening memories. When my daughter was three months old, she suddenly stopped breathing. Her mom and I rushed her by taxi to a
Bolivian hospital. I tried desperately to rouse Amaya, to feel some
sign of life, but there was nothing. Amaya's mom couldn't even

touch our daughter; she let out these primal wails as we skidded to a stop at the emergency room.

As soon as Amaya landed on the gurney, she woke up, blinked once, and began to bawl. The doctor told us this happens. The infant has such a long day that it goes into a coma-like sleep where it can't be roused.

Leah put a hand on my shoulder. I looked out the window, wanting to hold my daughter. We sat there for a long time. Finally, Leah took Kinnell out of my hand and read his short poem "Prayer":

> *Whatever happens. Whatever*
> what is *is is what*
> *I want. Only that. But that.*

I looked through an open window at algae green plants, heard birds, and felt the breeze, and these senses became one, whipped together into a batter of silence. Presence began to grow. We talked about the poem, untangling those three lovely *is*'s, the strong full stop ("But that."). Leah said that the "what is" in the poem was her idea of God. Whatever *what is* is, is what she wants. Her old cowboy boots stood at attention next to my sneakers by the back door. *Only that. But that.*

DOWN BY NO NAME CREEK ONE DAY, I noticed how, in the present light, it looked so ordinary. A creek, one of a hundred in the area. There's a Zen saying that goes like this: When I was young, mountains were just mountains. As I matured, I realized that they were so much more than mountains. And now that I am older, I realize that they are just mountains.

This is the vital step between the wet, still flightless thing that emerges from the cocoon and a soaring butterfly: giving up the idea of being a butterfly. I noticed that writings about humility abounded in the 12 x 12, as if when Jackie reached certain levels of success as a physician, an activist, and an "enlightened" human being, she had to fortify herself with ordinariness to maintain simplicity, joy, stewardship, and compassion.

Gandhi knew this peril. When he felt even a shred of pride over his accomplishments, he stopped and imagined himself as a speck of dust that is crushed underfoot. And when he was that piece of dust, he didn't stop. "I imagine myself," he wrote, "as so small that even that piece of dust would crush me." Gandhi went to such extremes for humility because he was in such a perilous position. The leader of a movement that would free hundreds of millions from colonialism: hearty fare for the ego. He could have had all the money, power, and self-sufficiency in the world, but he figured out a secret: we must remain atomically connected to others to feel truly happy, and we don't feel that way when we're on top; we feel separate. So he gave all of his money away. He cleaned toilets, wove and washed his own clothes, and lived in voluntary poverty in an ashram.

In one of his diaries, Thomas Merton writes of humility: "The proud man loves his own illusion of self-sufficiency. The spiritually poor man loves his very insufficiency." By stripping myself, at the 12 x 12, of some of the manifestations of independence — a car, a phone, electricity, piped water, a home — I'd come to "love my very insufficiency." In 12 x 12 simplicity, I discovered my nothingness and began to love it.

I looked into No Name Creek. The sun was setting, the water in gleaming flux. The creek's beauty took me further out of myself into the country murmurs around me, to the soft new leaves on the breeze sounding like paint going on. To frogs that sounded like crickets. To the voice in my head, now just a whisper, and then silent as the waters calmed momentarily and I saw my muted reflection below. It was no longer sharp edged, as it had been when I arrived. Half of my face was clear, but the other half was who I really was: nothing concrete. I laughed a little, and then laughed deeply, right from the belly, at that fluid person, edges loosening on the water's surface. The gloriously softening boundaries of the ego. Jackie, silently, was taking me by the hand and walking me through the gate of humility, which leads to the deepest, most lasting source of joy: simply being.

THEN ONE DAY, just as I was discovering the joy of ordinariness, as I felt the smallness of ego identity loosen its hold on me, I was yanked out of my bliss as I walked into the Smithsville public library.

"You're William Powers," the librarian said to me. She was flanked by another librarian. They were staring at me with dewy eyes and a little apprehension. A silence stretched out. I shifted from one foot to another.

The other librarian clarified: "You're an author."

"I read *Blue Clay People* a couple years ago," said the first, still gawking. "I still think about it. It's so . . . Can you . . ."

The other librarian finished, "Can you autograph our copy?"

As I signed, I noticed my ego expanding slightly and said to myself: *I am a piece of dust.* One woman said, "We'd love to invite you to speak at the central library. But here we are taking your precious time."

Then, checking my email on a library computer, I found a letter from a reader in Australia. "You don't know me, but I know you. I've read both your beautiful books." *Be so small that even a piece of dust can crush me.*

Soon half of Pine Bridge was reading my books, the Thompsons included, as the librarians spread the word. Gone was the pleasant ordinariness I'd felt, the joy of being. I'd been an obscure nobody, and suddenly the people around me were telling me I was "special." It became increasingly difficult to practice what I was learning about humility. Specialness and its close cousin, competition, are a kind of disease. We make this up as an American culture, taught since childhood enough one-upmanship and hyper-individuality to make Ayn

Rand look socialist. The ego is the fountainhead of your worth; I think — and do — therefore I am.

When this disease begins to invade, I consult Rule Number Six. It's something a manager-friend would use in his humanitarian aid projects. Whenever ego wars, slights, and offenses would surface, someone on the team would say, "Rule Number Six," and amazingly, harmony would return to the situation.

I asked him what Rule Number Six was, and he told me: "Don't take yourself so damn seriously."

We both laughed, and I asked him, "What are the other five rules?"

"They're all the same," he said. "See Rule Number Six."

I consider humility as closely tied to gratefulness. Thus, if someone praises me, I'm grateful; if they don't, I'm also grateful. Even when I'm criticized, it's an opportunity to be grateful for the breath I draw in that moment, for the sunshine and breeze, and for whatever lesson there is to learn. By being grateful, appreciating all we have instead of focusing on what is lacking, we allow more of the same to flow toward us. When I focus on missing Amaya, for example, I create a drama out of lack, of not-enough, and that becomes my reality. Instead I can focus on how much I love her, how grateful I am that she's my daughter.

Jackie talked about this — the mystery of being grateful and "allowing" — in a letter she sent me after my time in the 12 x 12. She spoke of the first days of her walk to the Nevada Atomic Test Site, sending a line from John O'Donahue — "At its heart, each human life is a pilgrimage, through unforeseen sacred places that enlarge and enrich the soul." She wrote:

> Been walking in the desert's emptiness, in silence. On the third night, a priest talked with us. We are all on pilgrimage, he said, a literal one to the Atomic Test Site, and also on an inner one. Using the stories of Moses and Abraham, he talked about being "called out of our captivities into unknown places... not able to see where we are going."... Transformation. I am grateful for the

gift of going into this pilgrimage with no expectations, open to take what comes. And it is a gift, not something I've been able to achieve.

A few days later, I looked into No Name Creek. Before, half of me had been blurred, half clear. Now the clear part was blurred, too. "I" had completely vanished.

But this was not the dull facelessness of my reflection in the Durham industrial park lake on the day of the 5K race. This "me" was full of color and leap, a dynamic jumble. Two frogs, on either side of me: one, lime green with patches of beige, its feet twice the size of its head; the other, a big old bullfrog that suddenly splashed into No Name Creek. *Like the creek, I don't have a name.* I felt a surge of gratefulness for this feeling body, this thinking mind, this heart, and for my precious Amaya.

"*Hola* Daddy!" Amaya said cheerfully on the phone, when I called her the next day.

"*Hola Amaya,* how's my *hijita preciosa?* "

She told me a story in half baby talk about Mama Martha and Tio Eduardo, about her kittens and puppies, about a world where she had little consciousness of herself as separate from the One Life, a natural humility.

CALLED OUT OF OUR CAPTIVITIES,
INTO UNKNOWN PLACES

21. NOISE AND WAR

WHILE I WAS SITTING IN JACKIE'S ROCKING CHAIR, a sonic boom crashed above the 12 x 12: military planes flew overhead, reminding me that America was at war.

Test flights from North Carolina bases like Fort Bragg, Pope Air Force, and Camp Lejeune regularly sent down a thunder that caused the surface of No Name Creek to fluster. At the time, North Carolina citizens had already spent $12.3 billion in state taxes to keep state bases running — to say nothing of the hundred billion and more in federal taxes Americans had paid to fund the war. These were the taxes Jackie was resisting. Body bags came back to North Carolina, particularly from poorer families: Brian Anderson (Durham); Patrick Barolow (Greensboro); Leonard Adams and Mark Adams (Morrisville); Darrel Boatman and Charles Buehring (Fayetteville); Larry Bowman (Granite Falls). Fifty-three North Carolinians, who had been stationed at Fort Bragg alone, died in Iraq while I was in the 12 x 12, just a few of the thousands of Americans and hundreds of thousands of Iraqis who had perished.

Not a half mile from the 12 x 12, by the railroad track stoplight, stood a US Army recruitment billboard with a GI Joe–type fighter, a blond young American, against a comic book background of war. The caption: FIGHTING FOR FREEDOM. One time I biked past a girl kneeling beside a dented old car, a camouflaged leg coming out of it. I looked away just as she looked up and saw me. I guessed that he was about to head off from Fort Bragg to Iraq.

As a relief worker, I've seen war up close. I've seen the front lines in the former Yugoslavia, and the wounded shipped back to Zagreb. I've ministered to war-affected youth in Sierra Leone, including those who had had limbs amputated by rebels trying to terrorize areas. During Liberia's civil war, I had to hunker down in the bush as a skirmish broke out in the capital, and I was at another point evacuated from my home to a compound closer to the airport and the US embassy as rebels advanced toward Monrovia. I've seen enough to know that war is disgusting business.

The day Jackie had nearly reached the end of her pilgrimage across the desert, she wrote me a letter. Reading it, I was struck forcefully that while I was in her 12 x 12 cultivating peace in silence, she was, in her own way, making noise about war:

> It is a bit of a ragtag band, one could say — or one could say, it's a bit of a nomadic beloved community of pilgrims called into the desert. Imperfect humans in imperfect community — what else could it be? We bring ourselves, our broken-nesses — and we bring hearts bursting with a yearning for peace, to love better, to go deeper into compassion.
>
> The outer pilgrimage of this nomad band is the Sacred Peace Walk — six days walking deeper into the desert, walking to the Nevada Atomic Test Site calling for an end to all nuclear weapons.
>
> Mornings — we drum till the sun rises over the mountaintop, circle, plan, and are smudged with sacred sage by Willie of the Western Shoshone, whose tribal lands are illegally occupied by the Test Site. Willie brings his willow staff and his wisdom. Every morning, he tells us again: remember, every step is a prayer for peace.

And then we walk. Just keep putting one foot in front of another. Right foot, left foot, right foot, breathe. Beside us mountains, before us mountains, behind us mountains. The desert enfolds us. We startle a rabbit, little birds in the brush. An inch of rainfall last year, we are told — yet the desert lives — branches of creosote bushes bend gracefully, as a dance. . . . The desert makes its way into your heart and soul as the dust makes its way into your evening soup bowl.

We've dived deep into many ways of naming Spirit: sharing Muslim evening prayer, Friday evening Shabbat, bathing the Baby Buddha, re-hearing the Christian and Hebrew stories of pilgrimage, of our ancestors who were called to leave captivity, leave the familiar, and strike out into the desert, to places unknown.

Today's last full day of walking — carrying our banner and flags — brought us here, very near the enormous gates of the Test Site. We walked and shared the fourteen nuclear stations of the cross, graphic images of the horrors of war, the threat of nuclear annihilation and the daily death-dealing of resources poured into the nuclear arsenal. Palm Sunday mass was celebrated by Fr. Louie Vitale and Fr. Jerry Zawada, who've spent months and years of their lives in prisons for nonviolent resistance to war. The setting was a gravel lot at the edge of the desert, against a van covered with a banner to ABOLISH NUCLEAR WEAPONS.

And now — we are spread out across the desert's edge — the sun just set in unspeakable splendor behind the western mountains and the wind has died down. The moon is almost full and Orion hangs in the southern sky. Early in the morning we'll walk to the Test Site to keep saying *No, not in our name, not ever.* It is good to be in this place.

I read her letter several times, moved by it, but unable to see the beauty she saw. I read some of the books and articles on warfare Jackie had on the 12 x 12 bookshelves, becoming all the more horrified the more I learned. Humans have slaughtered one hundred *million* of our own species in twentieth-century wars. And the twenty-first century has the seeds of something worse. Political scientist Chalmers Johnson, in his *Blowback* trilogy, says societies have had to historically choose between democracy and empire — but you can't have both. He writes of "the last days of the American republic," in which an entrenched military-industrial complex sinks the vestiges of democracy. The United States, according to the State Department, has 721 military bases in foreign countries (unofficially, it's over one thousand) and continues to build new ones. In terms of its nuclear capability, America's current plan, called Complex 2030, is to build a new generation of weapons, including a first-strike arsenal that could theoretically destroy an entire continent and intercept incoming nukes through a protective shield.

Against the peaceful backdrop of the cabin, I read a refresher on the destructive effects of nuclear weapons. There are immediate, instantaneous effects — the blast itself, thermal radiation, prompt ionizing radiation. And there are delayed effects — radioactive fallout and other environmental impacts — that inflict damage over a period ranging from hours to centuries. Despite this, and despite the world having constructed 67,500 nuclear weapons from 1951 to the present, the United States continues to invest billions in tax money toward more.

Is this the world, I often reflect, that my daughter is to inherit? "All within me weeps." This was the refrain of a Native American woman at another anti-nuclear rally in 2007. Hundreds of Americans gathered at the gates of the Los Alamos National Lab, an annual event. Along with the politicians and celebrities, a Native American woman rose to speak: her family came from the area, which was taken from her people by the US government to create the Los Alamos nuclear complex, the place where the bombs dropped on Hiroshima and Nagasaki were put together. She described the destruction and suffering caused by those nuclear devices, the higher levels of cancer in her people, and the government's plans for Complex

2030. When she finished, the protestors sat for a thirty-minute meditation, and they ended the day with the floating of Japanese lanterns,
a tradition they follow every year in Hiroshima to remember loved
ones lost in the nuclear holocaust. "All within me weeps," she repeated.

Even more than protesting, Jackie suggests that if we wish to
lessen the nuclear threat, we must first look inward and take responsibility for our interior space. Are the conditions — the anger, resentment, and fear — that cause humans to go to war and support
violence inside of us? Can we regain faith in the goodness of human
beings, including, most importantly, of ourselves? Then, can we express this faithfulness in action and love, perhaps by joining a peace
study group or participating in nonviolent action? As the plaque on
the Pettus Bridge in Selma proclaims: "When you pray, move your
feet."

Jackie's brave response to darkness inspires me. So many of us
get clobbered by the system and end up living what Thoreau called
"lives of quiet desperation," living, you might say, in Weimar and
pretending that Buchenwald is not up the road. Social psychologist
Eric Fromm astutely observed that the main reason people perpetu-
ate evil systems is remarkably simple: they don't love life. Sometimes
I see it clearly in myself: a going-through-the-motions, an acquies-
cence, a living-with-it — but without the vital pulse of love. Jackie's
courage in the Nevada Desert arises out of a deep love for life.

ONE NIGHT I SAT WITH PAUL JR. at his bonfire, in silence for a
long while, thunder sounding in the distance. The candle went out in
Paul Sr.'s 12 x 12, and then he came out and joined us. The flames cast
a jagged glow on the left side of the old professor's face, the right
side in near blackness. "The neighbors turned us in," he finally said.
"They told the police we're living in small houses."

"That's a crime?" I said.

"A misdemeanor. The inspectors came after the tip-off. You're only officially allowed to live in a 12 x 12 if it's for part of the year, not year-round. And we couldn't prove a permanent address elsewhere. Because we don't have any other address."

According to that rule, Jackie wasn't legal, either, and could be forced to move out of her 12 x 12.

Paul Jr. chimed in: "And they said our front and back porches made the houses 'effectively bigger than twelve by twelve,' so we have to install toilets, pay various taxes..."

"They're also trying to make us install electricity," Paul Sr. said. "Do you know it's not legal to live without electricity in North Carolina? It's not a choice you may make. It'll cost us a fortune, and could sink us. Just like legal costs to defend an ecological vision are sinking Bradley."

Paul Sr. got up, saying he was going to bed. The entire right side of his body was now illuminated by firelight, his left side fading into oblivion. "Hell is other people!" he blurted out. "What does it matter to them if we live simply? It makes me all tense inside. I believe in community, but..."

He paused. Paul Jr. was staring down at the beer in his hand, perhaps trying to think up a Carlos Castaneda rejoinder. His dad finally went on: "Do you know what? I can't get beyond me. Do you think I haven't tried group living? I've tried for so long to diminish my ego. It doesn't happen. I'm Descartes's child; I only exist at all because I think." He hit his palm against his head. "With *this* brain!"

I thought of what Leah said: *Sin is when I'm at the center.* Paul Sr. looked off, to an invisible point out in the forest someplace. "Individualism is part of our cultural DNA. We'll never escape it."

I FELT AS IF A DARK CLOUD WERE PASSING OVER the Thompsons as well. One day, after waiting for a booming military jet to fly over, I asked little Kyle if he wanted to go biking. He shook his head and said no.

This surprised me, even hurt a little. One of my great joys at the 12 x 12 was biking the dirt roads with Kyle, his Joycean flop of hair pressed back by the wind, flying along in silence to the post office. He always asked me to do things with him: fish, walk to the creek, bike. We'd tear down the dirt road together and lay down long, curving skids, then compare them. We'd laugh and exchange out-of-breath jokes.

There was an awkward pause. Finally, I said: "Some other time then?"

"Maybe," the eleven-year-old replied, looking suddenly older. "But probably not. I'll be riding *that* from now on."

He pointed up toward the disheveled woodpile, where the first fourteen ducklings of the season had cracked through their shells. Beside it was the first all-terrain vehicle, or ATV, I'd seen in Pine Bridge. He told me excitedly that it was the first of two ATVs their grandma was sending them from Florida. She'd traded a Bobcat — evidently another kind of machine — for the ATVs.

Later that day, while I watched the pink puff of a lime green chameleon's chin on the side of the 12 x 12, something began to drill a hole in the blessed silence. Just a little prick at first, a distant whine that turned into a motorized anti-*om* as a screaming red ATV ripped through the greenery into my line of vision, not two feet from the deer fence. Mike was at the helm, his long goatee sailing back into the wind, little Allison in his lap, both giddy with fossil-fueled fun.

After Allison came Brett, Greg, and Kyle, each riding with their dad, roaring past the 12 x 12, my nostrils assaulted by the blue-black smoke spewing out of the ATV's tailpipe. Coughing and covering my ears to muffle the motor noise, I fled deep into the woods, my inner struggle flaring up, thinking of Paul Sr. saying that "Hell is other people." The enemy now was Mike. *You're flattening the world for them*, I told him in my mind. *Why not let them ride quiet, pollution-free, exercise-promoting bikes? They look up to you, adore you. Why teach them motors are better than pedals?*

I viscerally react to too-much-of-the-human, too much loud, intrusive, tacky technology. It's connected to guilt — my own complicity in the use of technology, which increases human reach and power while also causing forests to be felled worldwide and the climate to cook. Not to mention my own blatant hypocrisy through enjoying the fruits of it all. When I heard the whine of those motors I flashed back to my ecotourism project in that Bolivian cloud forest. The slash-and-burn. The global economy coming over the hill. I felt as if the harmony I'd seen so clearly in Pine Bridge's wildcrafting community actually rested on a rather fragile foundation: everyone making somewhat similar, compatible choices with how to use their part of the land. The ATV motors roared right past the 12 x 12 all that day and the next, erasing the peace.

Just when the ATVs stopped, I heard something else. *Rrrr-rrrr*, came the sound. It definitely wasn't an ATV. Less whiny, deeper. Must be out on Old Highway 117 South, I figured, continuing to stare into the creek, just down the embankment from the 12 x 12, and thinking about the neighbors who turned the Pauls in to the authorities for living in small houses. But the sound increased.

I looked up. Nothing.

Then, a flash of mustard yellow, and the rusty scoop of a bulldozer, fifty meters or so through the woods. *RRR-rr-rr!* stuttered the machine, and a tree came crashing down. It seemed surreal. I pictured rainforest trees falling a continent away, the Andean bears, monkeys, and jaguars retreating deeper into their disappearing nature reserves. I ran through Jackie's woods toward the machine. There were two men, one manning the bulldozer, the other on the ground. I waved my arms. The bulldozer lurched farther and knocked down another set of small trees, the forest falling. It was aimed directly at the 12 x 12.

22. | ALLOWING

"STOP!" I CRIED OUT, stepping in front of the bulldozer.

The engine roared even louder. The man in the bulldozer removed his helmet, a big frown etched into his brow, and he waved vigorously for me to move. I realized, suddenly, that I'd been hearing the machine each day, between lulls in the ATV noise, but I had apparently been in denial. Now, facing that large, rumbling yellow machine, which was turning beautiful trees into stumps and ripping out the forest on a direct line toward Jackie's 12 x 12, I had no choice but to accept that Bradley must have made new plans.

The scowling man finally turned off the bulldozer. "Hi," I said. No response. A mustached good ol' boy. Below him, a Latino man was chainsawing the brush; he turned off his chainsaw as well.

"I'm living over there," I said, nodding toward the 12 x 12, which from our angle was completely concealed by trees.

This concept sank in: property owner. "Howdy," the mustached guy said.

"You all work for Bradley?" I asked.

"Uh huh," he said, even friendlier now at the sound of his boss's name.

"What's the plan?"

"The plan?" the man said, squinting his eyes, suddenly suspicious. What was Bradley doing? I knew he was trying to bring wildcrafting to scale, going against the powers-that-be to create innovative eco-communities. But what was this bulldozer for? I also knew that Siler City legal efforts to stop Bradley from building cooperative housing were sinking him financially, so perhaps, to cover his debt, he was now planning to develop additional lots in the thirty acres surrounding Jackie's.

"Ya'll cutting a road all the way to the creek?" I asked.

"I don't know. Bradley just gives the orders for a day at a time."

"I see," I said. Just what they need to know.

"But I believe this here is meant to be a walking path," he added.

Sure, I thought. *A walking path as wide as an interstate.* I walked away, along the creek to the railroad track bridge and along those abandoned tracks, wondering if there was anywhere at all beyond the Flat.

I began having nightmares. Once again the aging former Nazi man living in the woods was visited by a younger man. I saw it all as if from the trees, and then that quick zoom and I'm looking right at the old Nazi; I am him. He has (I have) the same warts, wrinkles, and odor; it's now the stench of chicken factories.

I woke up soaked in sweat, lit a candle up in the loft. That absurd 12 x 12 slab of bare cement below. I imagined falling down onto it from the loft, with a thud. Despite all the inner progress I'd made, I wondered if it could stand up to the ATVs and the bulldozers racing toward the 12 x 12. *They'll give No Name Creek a name*, I thought, my spirits sinking further. Storybook Creek they'll call it, and Jackie's nameless road will be Cinderella Lane. The loop into the Thompson farm: King Arthur's Court. In the forest beyond José's, new roads, Mark Twain Lane and Robin Hood Road, this soft place domesticated into a thematic suburb: into the no-place I'm from.

At the same time that as I was witnessing this destruction, I met Julie and Yvonne at the Thompson farm. They'd rolled up in their old van to drop off a few Muscovy ducks for Mike. They were both heavyset, with fat rolling off of every joint, and they had bravado about farming. Julie said they were partners and lived in a shed with no electricity, "but we have Netflix"; a solar battery pack powered their DVD and TV. I told them I might bike over sometime to visit.

They didn't tell me not to stop by, but — come to think of it — they didn't agree either, and when I arrived I figured out why. Theirs wasn't a farm at all; it was a garbage dump. The carcasses of a half dozen vehicles rusted away, plastic wrappers caught on the edges. "Not for Human Habitation" was stamped all over their home. Actually, it wasn't a house at all; it was a shed. They'd bought it for three thousand dollars at Shed Depot.

The animal smell was terrible. If the Thompson farm was a pleasant chaos of goats and fowl, this was an anarchic mess, a cacophony of Narragansetts scraping the hard ground with their feathers, geese honking, ducks quacking, hogs grunting, four dogs in a barking frenzy. Julie emerged from the shed.

We talked amid the drone of animals. "I was going to clean that up," she said of the trash around us. "We're still getting set up here." It had been two years.

Tea wasn't an option. They had nowhere to sit down, just their bed and an overflowing table in their Shed Depot abode. So we stood and talked. "We don't exist as far as *they* are concerned," Julie said, gesturing out toward the powers-that-be. "We tried living in the system, tried to change it. But the blight's too deep."

By "not existing" she meant they paid no taxes, weren't on any census list. They managed a hardscrabble existence from the eggs and meat of their animals. It was a kind of anarchist, lesbian-punk, fuck-you to all of society. To the empire. To complicity. Suddenly I pictured Jackie, and a thought crossed my mind: *She's naive.* She's now finishing a walk across the Nevada desert to a US nuclear test site. Could anything be more absurd? Why bother with useless little meditative pilgrimages across a desert?

If there was a rock bottom of cynicism and despair for me at Jackie's, I'd reached it.

Sitting in that garbage dump of a yard, I felt the cumulative weight of Kusasu's extinction, the elimination of the world's rainforests, the military jets booming overhead on their way to Iraq, Complex 2030's new generation of nukes, and the bulldozers about to flatten the forest around No Name Creek. And things were worsening for José and other local Latinos. The Easter anti-immigration protests turned out to be mercifully small that year, but they had new worries: AgroMart, an industrial agriculture conglomerate, was spraying North Carolina crops with pesticides so haphazardly that its Mexican field laborers were being exposed, allegedly causing Latino babies to be born without limbs. Because the workers were undocumented, they had little leverage to protest. What's more, the state's industrial hog industry was growing by the day, and the number of industrially produced hogs in North Carolina had surpassed the number of people. Could warrior presence stop a blight this deep? Wildcrafting on the creative edge? It all began to seem hopelessly quixotic.

Then I noticed something at Julie and Yvonne's, the chicken factory smell. To my horror, beyond a line of trees and over some barbed wire, maybe thirty yards away from where I stood with Julie — rose a chicken factory, white and windowless. It spewed the smell of suffering, the beakless-featherless-boneless chickens dwelling in darkness right beside her shed of a home.

I felt faint and found my way to a rusty chair and sat down. This was how bad it could get. Yvonne and Julie had tried to live in the

system and been defeated, instead creating out of their lives a dark
contemporary art piece, throwing society's blight right back in its
face. Is this what would happen to the likes of the Thompsons, the
Pauls, even Jackie? Perhaps trying to live on the edge in America is
so difficult that eventually, one day, you just free-fall into nihilism.

ABANDON ALL HOPE OF FRUITION.

This was one of the cards in Jackie's stack that I always found
incongruous with the rest. It seemed far too negative for Jackie. A
chicken jumped into my lap, and I petted its stiff feathers. Another
jumped up next to it for a little love. And amid the despair I was feeling I began, vaguely at first, to *get* something key to Jackie's philosophy that had eluded me up until then. Abandoning all hope of
fruition suddenly began to make sense, a necessary puzzle piece.

"They lay eggs in our laundry basket," Julie was saying about
the chickens, but her voice drifted to me as if in slow motion. I'd become absorbed by the beauty of their animals. The friendliness of the
angora goats and even the hogs; such a profusion of birds and they
were constantly at our feet. They lived along with Yvonne and Julie
inside the shed — as well as outside, as they wished — and expressed
a "suchness," their proud animal simplicity forming a fierce contrast
with the domestication of the chicken factory right next door, where
tens of thousands of birds lived in crippled, deformed, genetically
modified imprisonment. Three Narragansetts, ablaze in color, pressed
against my thighs; Julie petted a goat under the chin, and it pressed
tighter up against her huge breasts as if to suckle. Guinea hens at her
ankles, along with a cat and a beagle. She stroked a chicken. I stared
at the Gold Kist factory, lost in an unusual texture of thought, the
swirling sense of a profound growing realization.

Later that evening I lay on the grass under the stars at Jackie's.
Abandon all hope of fruition. Just give up and accept the world, factory
farms and all? No, that couldn't be what it means. As I considered
this, two airplanes soared above, just an inch apart. No big deal,

planes are common, even out here, little more than heavenly static. These two planes, though, were inching forward *along the exact same line*. Suddenly a shooting star appeared, white hot, and threaded right through those two planes. Of all places in that vast sky, nature's light blazed between the two dots of human-made light. I sat up in wonder, the shooting star's trail fading to black.

As if an afterthought, one of Pine Bridge's ubiquitous fireflies illuminated the shooting star's tail, tracing a bit of its fading glory before turning itself off amid some heirloom tea bushes.

Just as I thought the show was over, a satellite — an even fainter afterthought than the firefly — followed the airplanes, in triangular tow behind them. Just a dot, trailing across the screen of the sky like a period.

What did it mean, "artificial" light streaking in one direction, "natural" light plying the opposite route? Airplane versus firefly, industry versus nature, Man versus God? Heavens no. I stood up from the hammock, walked down to No Name Creek, which cupped starlight in its eddies, and I knew that there really isn't any opposition at all. It was a mystical feeling, even deeper than the one I'd experienced that night with Leah, when I felt the house slip inside me. Looking into that sky, I wondered if *all* of those lights were part of the same One Life, and the apparent duality an illusion.

THE FOLLOWING WEEKEND, Leah and I danced at the Shakori Hills summer music festival. At one point we stopped, out of breath, to eat bowls of curry, and then jumped back up for a band from Mali playing kora harps, negoni lutes, and a balafon-style xylophone. The crowd swelled as the melodies did. Black, white, some Latinos, all kinds of colors, a spring gathering. It was Earth Day. The wordless music spoke of birth and death, light and dark in the same breath, and my body moved, the hips loosening, ankles and neck more rubbery, shoulders straightening and falling, torso, hands, fingers — each part of my body found a different piece of that layered rhythm.

"It's like the blues. Malian music," Leah said.

"It's got this pulse of joy."

"And sadness."

Leah kept dancing, while I went to the side of the lawn and sat down for a moment. As the sun set in brilliant orange, present in that seamless moment, I felt what Jackie had years ago: I must go beyond shame and blame, not just with myself and my personal imperfections, but in relation to the impact my species is having on the planet. I have to let go of my Nazi dreams, my guilt over ecocide, and all of the rest of the negativity that keeps me in a cramped, dim self. This means allowing myself, and the world, to be. When I see unworthiness, *anywhere*, I'm to trace it. To allow doesn't mean to condone. Jackie had found a more precious jewel still on the other side of allowing, which spoke clearly to me about the nature of resistance to injustice — transform the enemy, not by fighting head-on with blame and anger; this just makes the enemy more powerful. Instead, be so present in the reality that you manifest an entirely different reality. The question is how to transform our anger into the energy of compassion, so that we can see the true cause of suffering. Then we can see more clearly how to root out that suffering.

Allowing is the way to experience the other world inside of this one. It lets us accept all of life's complexities so that we can come from a place of love at all times, even in a chicken factory, at a nuclear test site, and even, as psychologist and former concentration camp prisoner Victor Frankl observes, in Auschwitz and Buchenwald. It's essential to peaceful, creative resistance and transformation.

On the drive back to the 12 x 12, Leah at the wheel, we passed new subdivisions with enormous, energy-consuming houses in a space that used to be forest. I watched my inner reaction. Neither of my "normal" reactions was present anymore, no rage, no guilt. Still, I remarked aloud to Leah about the destruction.

"Are you sure?" Leah said.

"What do you mean?"

"Are you sure?"

"Of *what?*" I'd forgotten that ARE YOU SURE? was one of Jackie's cards — the one, in fact, I'd put out that very morning.

Leah stopped the car at the edge of a ridge, cut the engine, took my cheeks in her hands, and pointed my eyes forward, saying slowly, forcefully: *"Are you sure?"*

From our now slightly higher vantage point, I looked out over a green forest canopy, stretching to the horizon. Just beyond the development hugging the road were rolling hills, forested smack down to South Carolina. We looked at each other for a moment and then back over this natural scene, which still contained so much green. Couldn't this, at least possibly, emerge as the face of globalization? Our consciousness grows and wildcrafter farms and forests fill the old slave plantations?

I took Leah's hand loosely, feeling a little dizzy. Patterns of light streaked across my mind: airplanes and comets, satellites and fireflies, the message in the sky coming through more clearly. I had the questions wrong. My questions implied a good and bad, a right and wrong. I thought of Lao-tzu: "Do you want to change the world? I do not think it can be done. The world is perfect and cannot be changed."

I looked out over a suddenly perfect landscape, saw the Soft within the Flat within the Soft. My greatest teachers are my sufferings. Global warming, hyper-individualism, rainforest destruction, and racism, these things had led me to Jackie's place, forced me to struggle. The Buddhists put it eloquently: "no illusion, no enlightenment." I momentarily grasped nonduality, that at the deepest level everything is exactly as it should be at any given moment — including one's own gradual awakening through the force of apparent evils.

I've since found this is a difficult concept to convey. Atheist or agnostic friends and colleagues furrow their brows, exactly as I used to do before I experienced it directly. Words are mere connotations, pointers at something that must ultimately be lived, felt, breathed. It's helpful to think of persons who embody it — Gandhi, Mandela, Martin Luther King Jr. They come from a nondualistic perspective, from a sense of One Life, while still accepting the existence of oppression and racism *on the level of form*. Instead of dualistically opposing these "evils," they trace them through compassion and act through love — in other words, the enlightened master's resistance.

Allowing is the foundation, not the house. As I would soon discover, it is the necessary basis to achieve an even more sublime insight.

ABANDON ALL HOPE OF FRUITION

23. | GOD'S FEET

AS HUMAN BEINGS, we are suspended between spirit and clay. Spirit is the stuff of allowing, of detachment, of transcending the world. This is Buddha "overcoming the world" or Jesus "transcending the world." Through spirit, we discover the level at which the supposed dichotomy between the world and ourselves is smashed, giving a sense of fearlessness and joy.

But we are clay as well as spirit. We exist, earth bound, for some seventy or eighty years. The problem I have always had with any overly "spiritual" path is that it sometimes denies life. We have an eternity to exist in the soup of universal energy, but just a few precious decades to savor rich coffee, whether it's bad for us or not. To plant zucchini; to people-watch in a subway car; to love jazz. To love others, even if it gets messy.

If we take "allowing" to the extreme — detach from our creature-hood, and exalt only our spirit-hood — we may feel blissful for a while, as I did during mystical moments at the 12 x 12 — but we'll miss out on half of what makes life meaningful: the portion of us that is clay. To me, the tension between spirit and clay is exemplified in a

Raphael painting I saw in the Uffizi gallery in Florence, Italy. The Renaissance artist shows Jesus rising out of this world — but with his feet still hanging down into this one. Why doesn't Christ rise completely, detaching from the suffering of the world to become pure blissful spirit?

The first time I saw it, I lingered in the Uffizi and gazed at Jesus' feet, about to leave this world. After a while his feet seemed to be wiggling in the painting's fresh air, then tapping to music. I listened. No, it wasn't celestial harps. Perhaps Jesus likes jazz. He doesn't ascend — *not quite yet, those gorgeous earthly riffs*.

I wonder if it was jazz Jackie heard as she walked across the vast Nevada desert to a nuclear test site to utter the word *No*. A person has to love messy, soulful, heartbreaking life to march across a desert to oppose the weapons that could eliminate it. Not too tight, but neither too loose; clay and spirit like to dance. Loving-kindness is the goal, not a disembodied detachment. But we can't get to loving-kindness through ego-driven love. We can only authentically inhabit ourselves as clay after rising first into spirit.

One of Jackie's favorite writers and teachers, Thich Nhat Hahn, embraces loving-kindness in the way he names the source of the problem, which is different from blaming, which can be a way of displacing one's own anger and frustration onto another. Nor does Thich Nhat Hahn refrain from suggesting concrete action for personal and societal transformation. At Jackie's, I discovered his reinterpretation of the five precepts of Buddhism, in order to cultivate compassion in a way that keeps with the changes in society: "Aware of the suffering caused by the destruction of life, I vow to cultivate compassion and learn ways to protect the lives of people, animals, plants, and minerals."

I read this one morning at six A.M. in Jackie's loft, the silence gathering. I let my feet dangle down from the loft, toward the 12 x 12 cement floor below. My toes tapped to the improvisation of morning birds, and I was seized with an urge to descend. Down the ladder, mindfully, feeling my big toe touch bare cement. Walk out into the gardens, and into the woods barefoot, the soil now loamy with spring life. How good it is to be clay! To be alive, and to be free to choose a wildly ethical path.

God's feet linger here because of the human heart. It's never fully born. *Amaya*, I think, and then feel something catch in my chest. As hot as the blood is the missing of her. God, how I want her little hand in mine. Only another parent can fully get this. It's completely different from separation from a parent or lover. The clay in me wants to touch that part of myself — my blood flowing through another heart — touch the memories of her birth. The first time I held her, she was the length of my forearm. Her mother's ecstatic smile over this perfect form that's come out of her, laced with the courage of giving birth to someone she knows will someday die. Kathleen Norris captured this:

> *her water breaking,*
> *her crying out,*
> *the downward draw of blood and bone.* . . .
>
> *Now the new mother, that leaky vessel,*
> *begins to nurse her child,*
> *beginning the long goodbye.*

Not long after leaving the 12 x 12, I finally got to see Amaya, if only for five days. Her mother, Ingrid, came to Little Rock, Arkansas, to visit her high school exchange host family from years before. On a walk through the suburban neighborhood where her host family lived, Ingrid pointed at a nursery school, the Growing Tree, which stood directly adjacent to a funeral home.

"Next to the Dying Tree," I said.

On my last night with Amaya I look into her light eyes, kiss her cheek, and say her name out loud. She says mine: "Daddy."

"Amaya," I repeat.

"Daddy," she says. The moon overhead waxes oblique, like a beach stone, and the trees blow in the wind, and I feel warm and shivery at the same time. A plane crosses the moon, its tail of smoke gray on the moon's white.

"Amaya."

"Daddy."

"Amaya," I repeat. "Daddy," she says. "Amaya." "Daddy," this time smiling big and leaning over to kiss me. "Amaya," I say, kissing her. "Daddy," more serious now. "Amaya." "Daddy." We're memorizing each other.

"Amaya."

"Daddy."

I rise above Little Rock, looking out over what really is a little rock, a tiny airport, those couple-of-skyscrapers enveloped by the big curve of the Arkansas River, and all the dead, soy-scarred land stretching north toward St. Louis, where I will connect to New York, and I think: I might never be in Little Rock again. Might never land in St. Louis, I think, later, as we hit turbulence and the plane sighs deeply, the woman next to me mumbling something. I'm aware of the irony — here I am, on a plane again — and consider for a moment how incredibly hard it is to live sustainably, particularly when I want to see my daughter.

The plane banks toward the St. Louis Arch, an upside-down smile, a piece of twisted tin against the treeless plain, and lands. With a long layover, I decide to leave the airport, walking out beyond all the asphalt to a patch of green, an empty lot filled with overgrown grass and wildflowers. The sun sets, painting itself in fiery crimson. I miss Amaya.

There are two types of problems we face in life: convergent and divergent. Convergent problems are like engineering problems or jigsaw puzzles, putting pieces together to arrive at a definite answer. Divergent problems are those of the heart and spirit, diverging into greater mystery the more we try to untangle them. Perhaps a lot of the modern dilemma is that we try to solve divergent problems with convergent logic — instead of disengaging the mind and getting to the subtler levels that guide people like Jackie. Here's this moment's dichotomy: I miss my daughter, and at the same I watch a softening world with joy. Instead of creating an inner drama out of paradox, I sit with it, allowing a butterfly to land on my arm. It's black with flecks of ginger, and its wings beat slowly. In an instant, it's gone, lost to me in the sunset.

A moment later the butterfly flutters back. Lands on a flower beside me, as the day ends, finding nourishment in what's right here.

IT WAS MY LAST DAY AT THE 12 X 12.

Leah came out to help me clean and pack. Jackie was coming back in a few days, and it was time for me to depart for New York. Just as we finished — the bare cement floor swept, my bags in her car — a train horn sounded, low and solemn to the south. It was one of the only times I heard a train pass on that lonely stretch of track across No Name Creek. Leah took my hand and said in a childlike voice: "Let's try to catch it."

We ran, side by side onto Old Highway 117 South, narrowing in on the train. It sounded again, and this time we were so close to the machine that it vibrated all the way through me. We ran harder. I looked over at Leah at one point and her face was pink and sweaty and serious, as if she were putting all of her soul into this one thing. We ran, the train right ahead, its bell still ringing, but alas, we arrived just as the caboose swept by.

But we kept on running, along the track now, laughing and slowing down, those familiar railroad ties under my feet, the heat of the train on our faces and chests, the widening gap between that old train and us.

Then, eventually, silence. We continued to walk, onto a path into the woods, along No Name Creek, and we began to talk about us. We felt love for each other but both knew at our cores that we weren't meant to form a couple. There are some people who touch your life for a month, others for a season, and still others for a life-time. We had touched each other for that spring, grown together in the light of Jackie's lessons, and now we let go of each other.

It was not easy, or completely clear. We stopped by the creek and held hands and kissed, and talked about seeing each other again — when I came down to visit my parents, when she came up North for a visit. And we would see each other again, in the future, but it would be as friends. An hour passed with Leah, in silence. We watched the creek's flow, and I knew that there's no greater gift to the world and to others than being true to your deepest self. So many times, out of fear of loneliness or other negative emotions, we form relationships that are good enough, but untrue to our uniqueness. Doing so risks flattening ourselves.

That's when one of Jackie's most important secrets bubbled up to me from the creek. A revelation (*re-velar*: veil again) that came up in full clarity and then concealed itself. I understood what the 12 x 12 really is.

Its floor, the bare slab of white cement that Jackie steps down onto from the loft every morning. What's under it? According to physicists, our bodies and the earth itself are 99.99 percent empty space, more a wave of energy than anything solid. That floor is Jackie's integrity: a 12 x 12 rock over nothing.

We are God's feet, and it is out of a place of total emptiness, a place beyond "the world" that we must create our lives. We sculpt our characters out of wildness. Leah and I held hands for one last moment beside No Name Creek, and then we let each other go.

ON MY LAST DAY AT THE 12 X 12, the Thompsons' two ATVs sputtered out and died. The second failed right in front of the 12 x 12.

It took three of the brothers to push the lifeless machine up to their woodpile, where it now lay belly-up.

"You want to ride bikes?" Kyle asked me.

"Sure, Kyle, let's ride bikes."

The other kids came running down to us. "Hey, you all been swimming?" I asked them, as they shook the water off their bodies, having just emerged from their makeshift kiddy pool — one of the hog's water basins.

The four-year-old mumbled: "Bradley's got a bush hog."

"He does?" I said, picturing the mammals I'd seen in Africa. "Like from the *Lion King*?"

Kyle, in a teacher-like tone, explained the obvious to me. "It's for clearing bushes. It takes down the rough stuff."

"Those are our new pigs!" Greg said, pointing to a black one and two pink ones, new arrivals.

"That's right," Mike said, walking all macho toward us down his drive. "I'm getting heavily into hogs."

"Wanna know their names?" Greg said. "Bacon-for-Breakfast, Sausage-for-Lunch, and Ham-for-Dinner!" The other kids squealed with delight.

"Bacon!" said tiny Allison, grabbing my pant leg for attention.

Kyle and I rode down to the post office and back, and when we got back to the Thompsons' driveway a kind of spontaneous party seemed to be forming. All six kids, including the baby in Zach's arms, were there, along with Leah, Michele, and Mike. And remarkably, for the first time ever, José's son, Hector, was there, playing with the other kids, real evidence of a cultural and racial healing at work.

Animals honked, bayed, scurried, and flew around us — indeed, the Thompsons were "getting heavily into hogs" and other animals. The farmers market rumors seemed unfounded; perhaps this family had a chance of making it. New pens and the number of animals had grown since I'd arrived. Mike had enrolled in the community college sustainable agriculture program. As I'd seen in Durham, there was demand for organic, local produce, and room for creativity for this new-old American Dream of being a Jeffersonian-style freeholder.

Later that afternoon at the Thompson farm, I saw Julie and Yvonne, the ones living in a shed in the shadow of the chicken factory. Their van clunked along toward us, as Leah, myself, the Thompsons, and Hector and José chatted and joked among all those animals, the setting sun causing their duck pond to positively sparkle, the woods rising in deep green down by No Name Creek. The van pulled up and both women climbed out, huge smiles on their faces, their hair going every which way, and Yvonne — without saying a word — opened the sliding back door.

A long pause stretched out over the farm.

Even before it happened, before the rush of sound and color, it occurred to me that I could be looking at a piece of the New We. This ragtag bunch in Adams County, inspired by Jackie and their hearts, were living according to their loves. If the aborigines have it right that the twenty-first century is dreaming the wrong dream, perhaps these particular Americans were dreaming a more inspired one.

All of a sudden: *WHOOSH!* Dozens of Muscovy ducks alit from the van and fluttered crazily out toward us. Mike had purchased a fresh batch of ducks from Julie and Yvonne, and they were making the delivery. "Muscovys!" Julie cried out.

"Woo-hoo!" Mike yelped. "We're going heavily into ducks, too!"

What followed, in the sunset at the Thompsons', made little rational sense. I'd look back on it later as a kind of ecstatic play. Adults, kids, and animals alike began running in circles, whooping, doing a jig. The animals didn't try to flee, and at times they seemed to be chasing us as we laughed, skipped, and danced up onto the Thompsons' porch, the sky now fantastically aglow. I found myself twirling with Leah and with Mike, receiving a duck handoff from Kyle, and suddenly, completely out of breath, I stopped.

I stopped, but the dance continued: *Leela*, divine play, the song of the Tao. By doing this, deeply, we were doing everything at once. It smelled like a farm, sounded like an out-of-control symphony, and moved with the swoosh of wings against my arms and cheeks. Cackle, whoop, yaw; the howl of a dog. I looked into that soft blur. I couldn't smell the chicken factories, but Gold Kist still worked up the road, and the stench would return tomorrow. The box stores would open their doors, inviting us to consume. The nuclear arms complex would puzzle over ways to destroy the planet five hundred times over. The planet would continue to heat up as many of us feel nothing but flatness both inside and out and shrug.

But thousands, perhaps millions would discover the kind of wild-crafting afoot in Adams County and send out feelers along the creative edge. The primal swirl of human and wild continued around me, but I remained still, sensing a truth. The 12 x 12 is a space of integrity, and also a symbol of a larger, growing resistance to standardization. A No — and a Yes. There's life at the heart of empire. The world can be freer if we allow our inner lives to be vast national parks. We are wilderness. Jackie's integrity is more than that 12 x 12 slab of concrete over nothing. It's the ten thousand 12 x 12 squares of wild space that she's liberated from the Flat World.

Suddenly, through the swirl of people and animals, I noticed something attached to the woodpile: a detail that stood out precisely because of its stillness and smallness. I walked over, leaning in to take a better look: the black casing of a cocoon, broken open, the butterfly gone.

24. | TOUPEE'S SONG

THREE MONTHS AFTER I LEFT the 12 x 12, the nonprofit World Conservation Union sent me on a three-month assignment to postwar Liberia. There, I was to help that fragile country negotiate a sustainable timber agreement with the European Union. I knew that, to be truly transformative, warrior presence must withstand even the most difficult situations — even a hell on earth. Going to Liberia would be the first real test of my 12 x 12 rebirth, but the experience proved to be more than I bargained for. Jackie's whole philosophy was about to come under assault.

Liberia shocked me. I'd worked there for two years during the civil war, from 1999 to 2001, as an aid worker, an experience that led to my book *Blue Clay People*. In 2003, the war ended, and the blood diamond–smuggling, child soldier–commanding Charles Taylor was driven into exile. It was now 2008, and I expected to find a country on the rise. Instead, Liberia was in many ways worse.

There was still no electricity or piped water, even in the capital city, Monrovia. Malnutrition was so bad that, according to a UN report, "stunting" of people's bodies from malnourishment was costing the economy some $400 million, offsetting all foreign aid. Malaria, TB, and HIV/AIDS were spiking. And there were the young girls. I'd seen some of them in Monrovia's poorer markets, as young as thirteen, often very beautiful, sometimes dressed in their school uniforms, selling their bodies for about a dollar.

One afternoon, I found myself walking along Monrovia's Poo Poo Beach. The city's residents dubbed their central beach with this sardonic, affectionate name because it acts as both bathing spot and public latrine. I stepped carefully to avoid the fecal land mines. Meanwhile, a few blocks away, the government had just completed a mini-Berlin Wall around the city cemetery to keep former child soldiers from sleeping in the graves. *A place where they have to build walls to keep people from living in graves?* I thought to myself.

This wasn't confined to the capital. Up-country, ArcelorMittal, the world's biggest steel conglomerate, had a team of Brazilian miners on alternating twelve-hour shifts to extract the best of Liberia's iron ore rapidly while the postwar government was still weak. Mittal had cut a dream deal with the corrupt interim president Gyude Bryant that created a virtual nation within a nation — a nation called Mittal, inside Liberia, that had sovereignty over the Nimba Mountains, the Buchanan port, and a prewar railroad line linking the two. A nation of greed. The global price of minerals was shooting up as the Flat World demanded ever more — and ArcelorMittal stepped up to do the dirty work.

I journeyed by rough road into the Nimba Mountains to see what was happening. Schmoozing my way into the mining area and befriending some of the Brazilian mine workers with my awkward Portuguese and love of Brazil, I saw firsthand how Mittal pollutes the water supply, exploits the Brazilians with low wages and few rights, and leaves behind scant technical capacity to prevent Liberians from eventually running their own mines.

Moreover, ArcelorMittal is owned by London-based Indian billionaire Lakshmi Mittal. At the time, he was considered the world's fourth-richest man, and the richest in Europe, with a net worth, according to *Forbes*, of $45 billion, after Americans Bill Gates and Warren Buffet and Mexico's Carlos Slim. Perhaps to compensate for being just fourth on the list, he created new superlatives for himself. He paid $60 million to host his daughter Vanisha Mittal's wedding at the Palace of Versailles, making it the most expensive wedding ever. And he dished out $128 million for his residence at 18–19 Kensington Palace Gardens in London, the world's most expensive house. He even decorated it with marble from the same quarry that supplied the Taj Mahal, dubbing his palace the Taj Mittal.

As I watched Lakshmi Mittal's air-conditioned trucks zoom right through the markets in Monrovia where Liberian schoolgirls were selling their bodies for a dollar a day, I pictured his pillaging of Nimba's beautiful mountains. As I walked along Poo Poo Beach, I felt uncertain. *Warrior presence?* Was it just a useless concept? I couldn't hear the murmur of No Name Creek anymore. Liberia's problems nipped away at my inner reserves, and I spiraled downward. I stopped doing yoga, practically stopped meditating, and had almost no contact with the kind of pristine nature that buoyed my spirit at the 12 x 12. And I began to drink.

There, at the bar at Monrovia's Royal Hotel, I had plenty of company. A disillusioned and cynical colony of expatriates was ready to receive me into their circle. Along with UN peacekeepers, Western embassy staffers, NGO workers, and businesspeople, I drank one whisky after another and blocked out the hell around me.

Get up in the morning. Drink coffee. Look on the positive side. At least my work was having an effect. Amazingly, half the country is still covered in primary rainforest, and Liberia had canceled without compensation all of the concessions to arms-for-timber lumber companies engaging in uncontrolled logging — including the Oriental Timber Company, which as I documented in *Blue Clay People*, colluded with dictator Charles Taylor to ransack enormous swaths of the Krahn Bassa and Sinoe wildernesses. I spent long days helping to set up a multimillion-dollar monitoring system to ensure that only "legal timber" could be exported to the European Union; only one of every thirty trees would be cut, leaving the forest intact and bringing cash to local people instead of corrupt politicians. Warrior presence helped there; the reserves of strength I'd built up at Jackie's helped me focus on the job at hand without being overtaken by cynicism and dread.

Then I noticed a change in the national forest ministry, where my office was housed. Along with the usual crowd of colleagues — Liberian government and NGO officials — were new faces. Asians. Once a week at first, but then at least one group a day — Da Cheng Ltd., China-Liberia Holding, and a dozen other mostly Chinese companies — were arriving or quickly set up to erase Liberia's virgin forests and thereby supply China's coastal factories with the wood needed to send cheap furniture to Ikeas in the West. Unfortunately, China was not subject to the supposedly airtight legal timber policies we were putting in place.

I met with the Chinese chancellor — China was at the time busy building its biggest embassy in West Africa in Liberia — to try to persuade them to commit to legal-timber standards, but he used every diplomatic sleight of hand imaginable: deflection, flattery, even feigning ignorance of the presence of Chinese logging companies in Liberia. Flat World economic globalization, it seemed, would in the end be far stronger than any legal-timber shield we might construct.

Physically exhausted one day after banging my head against Chinese diplomatic walls, and then getting sideswiped by a Mittal SUV racing into the interior as I left my office, I beelined to the Royal for a whisky. I sat at a table with some tipsy UN peacekeepers, embassy staffers, and an NGO worker or two and placed my order. One of the UN guys, already fairly loaded, joked about getting some "underage pussy for about a buck," but he was only half kidding;

another couple of drinks and it would probably tempt him. Just as my drink arrived, my cell phone rang.

It was Toupee, the friend of a Liberian colleague from my civil war work in Liberia. I didn't know her that well, but that didn't stop her from asking a big favor. Could I drive a full hour from the Royal into a dangerous neighborhood, at night, to pick her up at a clinic and take her home?

The whisky in my glass was positively glistening in its ice. Despite the sleazy banter, the cozy cynicism at the Royal was better than what lay outside in the Monrovian night.

"Now?" I said, weakly.

"I have plus-two malaria," Toupee said. Then the phone connection cut.

Plus-two malaria, I thought, fingering my glass. *So what?* Malaria is as common as a cold in Liberia. I hardly knew this person. I'd already worked a twelve-hour day. I wanted out of the terrible reality around me, not more of it. Did I really want to drive into a neighborhood full of ex–child soldiers, into a rat-infested clinic in miserable Barnersville? I didn't need more contact with a world where one person hoards $45 billion while kids die of preventable diseases like malaria, where the kids dying are the same ones being exploited to amass more money for those on top.

How can we live together on the same planet and bear the psychological strain of such vast inequality? Through denial, of course, but that's tough in a place like Liberia, where it's in your face every day. No, I was allowed a little denial. I'd earned it. I lifted my glass.

Then, under the din of the bar, beneath the tasteless comments and drone of CNN International, I heard it: the murmur of No Name Creek and Jackie's voice — *see, be, do.* I visualized Toupee in the clinic, blazing hot with malaria. She was, what, twenty-two? Though Toupee was in college now, how many steps away from prostitution was she? I closed my eyes, and in my mind I beat a narrowing path into the darkest part of the woods. "The narrow gate that leads to life," as Jesus beautifully put it. It is narrow indeed, just this: these tiny eyes, ears, and fingers touching the present moment.

I put the glass down, the whisky untouched, and drove into the humid Monrovian night. The slums got progressively dodgier, but I finally found Toupee's clinic. I helped her sister shoulder Toupee's feverish body into my car and drove Toupee and her sister back across the city to her room, on my side of town, stopping on the way to buy them groceries. I gave Toupee money for medicine and sat there with them for a long time in her mildew-covered room, a fifteen-dollar-a-month rental. Its dimensions were almost the same as Jackie's, about 12 x 12. Like 99 percent of Liberians — like Jackie — Toupee had no electricity. We talked for a while but then slipped into silence, the moonlight streaming in through the single window into her tiny square room.

There I rediscovered something I'd lost: warrior presence, a way of being in the world that slices through negative energy. Instead of letting myself drift into cynical disengagement, I allowed the gift of Jackie's wisdom to lift me to a different frequency where those negative energies passed right through me, like moonlight through a window. Through this, I learned that warrior presence isn't a shield that repels fear, greed, and other forms of negativity. These emotions entered me, but when I let go of my narrow ego-consciousness, these emotions had nowhere to lodge.

After that night helping Toupee, I resolved, as a kind of mindfulness practice, to perform at least one selfless action a day. One of my organization's drivers needed a thousand-dollar loan to meet a payment; I had the money and gave it to him. A Liberian friend's son needed a job and skills; I created a paid internship for him, and in my spare time I taught him how to use the internet and make spreadsheets. Each of these actions flowed naturally from the warrior presence I'd developed in the 12 x 12, a state in which I felt love for myself, for others, for the world.

The day before I left Liberia, at my going-away party, I was surprised to find the love flowing back in my direction, as those same people I'd helped showered me with beautiful African clothing, long heartfelt speeches, and even an African name. It had been only three months, but what does that matter? I'd spent two full years in Liberia the previous time and did not receive a fraction of that warmth and love at my going-away party.

One more quite remarkable moment occurred before I left Liberia. Toupee sang to me. She'd recovered from her malaria, and we met for lunch at Sam's Barbeque on 16th Street in Monrovia. She looked so much better. Her hair was tied back in a bunch of thick braids, and her eyes were aglow over our now-finished plates of jollaf rice. I don't know exactly when she started, but I slowly became conscious that she was humming, something wordless, staring out into the busy street.

A Mittal truck raced by on the road the Chinese were paving into the interior; the rainforest and minerals needed to feed the global economy. Probably one of five people walking by Sam's Barbeque had AIDS. Toupee herself was a war child, having grown up in refugee camps in Guinea and the Ivory Coast as two hundred thousand people died in her country's civil war. Something was tipping in me. I balanced between negativity and peace on that humid early afternoon: a full stomach, the walk-and-jive of the passersby, Toupee humming next to me. The details smashed together, and suddenly I was living one of those atmospheric moments in a Geoff Dyer or Murakami novel, where an expansive, breathing setting transports you beyond plot. A hum, now a song, as smooth as the 12 x 12 creek's flow.

I've rarely heard more beautiful sounds, part slightly off-key

African pulse, part North Carolina gospel. Liberia was settled by freed US slaves in the early nineteenth century, and many elements of antebellum plantation culture, including gospel music, mixed with Kpelle, Mano, and Grebo culture; Pine Bridge flowed into her song. The lyrics touched on greed and exploitation — AIDS walks by, ecocide rolls by — but the refrain kept coming back to love. "Praise," she sang, each time more beautifully. "Praise confuses the enemy."

A post-malaria war child hummed, but someone else now sang: a third-year sociology student, who went to school in refugee camps and was home again, in a changing Liberia. The international community had just canceled Liberia's national debt. Many Liberians were coming back from a global exodus to help their country heal. These details, Toupee sang, were the correct objects of our attention. Her song, at a plastic table at Sam's Barbeque, reinforced the lesson I learned on the banks of No Name Creek. The lesson that kept slipping, that I kept rediscovering, in the most unlikely of places. *Praise confuses the enemy*, Toupee sang. Don't let the enemy into your glorious inner space.

PRAISE CONFUSES THE ENEMY

POSTSCRIPT

"DADDY, *HAY LUZ*." — "There's light."

It's a year after my time in the 12 x 12, and I wake up in Bolivia, next to Amaya. She's become interested in transitions, like the one between night and day. We cuddle for a while, I kiss her cheek, and it's time to start the day.

I'm living in the village of Samaipata near Santa Cruz, where I've been for six months. My mother is here for a two-week visit, and she and Amaya spend the morning together while I finish a free-lance essay. They sing and pantomime songs ("The Wheels on the Bus" and "Barnyard Dance"), and then Amaya shows her grand-mother, her Mama Anna, the garden she and I have been cultivating together: squash, green onions, and flowers. A Quechua neighbor joins them. He tells them about how his ancestors farmed, suggests some changes, and then reaches into his pocket and passes some seeds into Amaya's cupped hands.

Finishing my work, I notice the peace around me. I look down from a bougainvillea and passion fruit terrace toward the village, a couple hundred modest, whitewashed adobe homes with clay-tiled roofs. Above them, on the cliffs at the far side of the valley, crouches a jaguar-shaped Inca temple.

I reflect on how profoundly the 12 x 12 experience has changed me. When abroad, I used to live in large homes or apartments. Now I live in a rustic two-bedroom bungalow without a television or any other appliance besides a refrigerator. I've put my secular mission-ary days behind me — no more converting the Idle Majority to a Western idea of Progress. Now I try to join the Idlers as much as possible, thereby freeing up time to grow my own food and be with my daughter, who is with me on the weekends. I don't own a car anymore. Instead I walk, bike, or take public transport.

These external changes flow from inner change. I've released most negativity: no more Nazi dreams, no more anger toward the people who physically assaulted me or guilt over the shape of my fa-therhood. I realized that such negativity does no good and I grad-ually let it go. Above all, the 12 x 12 experience catalyzed more mindfulness in everything I do. I've come to increasingly inhabit "the other world inside of this one," that state of consciousness that Jung and Einstein talked about, where durable change happens. It's not about "me," but rather about overcoming the dim, narrow space of ego — and humbly dedicating my life energy toward a broader process. I find myself listening to my intuition every day, and it tells me, very clearly, about my place in the whole.

I walk over to my daughter and mother. On a large sheet of paper, they're now painting the idyllic village below, a place where corporate globalization touches lightly. Samaipata has little adver-tising, absolutely no chain stores, the town's three thousand people surrounded by some three million acres of nature. Inca culture goes back to 1500 BC and is still present in the village's robust way of liv-ing with instead of against the earth. Amaya and my mom paint some of that: the neighbors spinning raw wool into yarn and gathering medicinal herbs.

A side of me wishes to freeze this scene. But can we? Amaya, for one, doesn't seem to think so. She's added something to the painting, above the brush-stroked circular garden and the Inca temple: a rainbow-colored airplane with butterfly wings.

In the past this might have saddened me: "globalization" in the form of noisy 747s roaring over this traditional village; my daughter, disconnected from place. Now I'm less fearful of change. There's a suchness in that detail, something to be traced to its source and transformed. Jackie doesn't suggest that we constrain ourselves to cookie-cutter eco-austerity, copying her. Quite the contrary; she suggests we be still, look deeply inward, and then act.

Change will come; it is coming. For me personally, Amaya's mom may accept a master's scholarship in the United States, and she would bring our daughter there for a time. And a think tank in New York has asked me to use my years of field experience to help shape US global warming legislation aimed at conserving the world's last rainforests because of their role absorbing greenhouse gasses — in other words, work toward a paradigm shift.

There are trade-offs. I admire my expatriate friends who have come to settle in Samaipata for good — one runs an organic café, Tierra Libre (the Free Earth); another manages a sustainable farm, La Vispera (the Eve) — and I aspire toward a more physically rooted life. But I know that my place in the whole, for now, remains global.

Even in large cities, it is possible to maintain warrior presence and scale back from overdevelopment to enough. By planting a windowsill or community garden; doing yoga; walking and biking; and carrying out at least one positive action for others every day. Nor do we need to live 12 x 12 to experience the subtle joy of being. Whether in the city or the country, leave your cell phone, books, and other distractions behind and sit or walk — very slowly. Pay attention to your senses; feel the breeze, notice smells and sounds. Try the meditation three-times-ten: Breathe in to a slow count of ten, drawing in light and gratitude. Hold that abundance for another count of ten. Then let your breath out slowly, counting to ten, exhaling any fears, negativity, or resentment, all that inner charcoal. Doing this during a busy day, I find myself much more patient and relaxed with myself and with others. We decide what gets globalized — consumption or compassion; selfishness or solidarity — by how we cultivate the most valuable place of all, our inner acre.

As I cultivate that acre, it naturally links with others. There is enormous hope for more mindful internationalism. One million community groups, NGOs, and other grassroots efforts have sprung to life around the world, the biggest upswell of people power ever. Thinking of this, I feel new questions bubble up: If we are globalizing, why not globalize a reverence for the still, the small? Can we globalize planes with "butterfly wings": ones that run clean? Can we globalize maladjustment to empire by linking those one million soft spots within the flat — Samaipata and Pine Bridge; Quechua culture and permaculture? While the current global economic downturn might challenge these NGOs in the short term, in the long term it might get people living on less and closer to the earth, and turning away from a life of excess. Because of the financial crisis, even some of the captains of industry I've talked with are finally understanding that another kind of globalization is necessary. The current world — built on a shaky platform of blinding wealth and grinding destitution — is not in their interest, either, because it makes the whole system unstable.

As Amaya and my mom put the last touch on their painting — a bright red and orange sun over the whole scene — I'm reminded of the quality of light at Jackie's on my final visit there: eight months after I'd left Pine Bridge, and right before I came to the Bolivian village.

I spent the night in the Pauls' 12 x 12 guesthouse. Jackie came over to their place for dinner, and we all caught up by candlelight.

The Pauls were doing remarkably well. They had negotiated a don't-ask, don't-tell arrangement with the state inspector; they eventually signed a statement saying they did not live in their 12 x 12 year-round so as not to have to install electricity, plumbing, and so on. But — wink-wink, nod-nod — they still live there year-round.

To my dismay, the Thompsons' freeholder experiment had failed. Their trailer park background hadn't prepared them to farm. Under financial pressure, they had sold their animals and purchased a Rent-a-Center franchise to try to generate enough income to keep their land. When I went to visit them, they and all the animals were gone. Only a lifeless silence hung over their place.

I also learned some hopeful things. José had just made a sale in Siler City — and he would continue crafting his beautiful furniture. Graciela got her raise at McDonald's and would continue to work there for a few years before retiring in her native Honduras. And Bradley had just completed a new eco-community; dozens of home-steads for wildcrafters-to-be were about to go on sale. And the 12 x 12s he'd built for the Pauls demonstrated the kind of fruition possible. When I woke up the next morning in their 12 x 12, I felt the peaceful absence of electricity. Paul Sr. wrote poetry longhand on his porch across the way; Paul Jr. smoked a pipe, staring out toward the curving paths that led to the creek.

That afternoon I went to Jackie's, and I noticed that day's card on her tiny stand. Hidden in the stack behind it were the ones I'd puzzled over, like ARE YOU SURE? and ABANDON ALL HOPE OF FRUITION. But this one was the simplest yet. It read: MINDFULNESS.

Something clicked. I recalled that this was the very title of the Mary Oliver poem Jackie had sent me in her letter, inviting me to stay in the 12 x 12. I looked over at Jackie, in the late afternoon sun-light, and asked her, "What do you think it means, that line in the poem about 'this soft world'?"

Jackie didn't respond. The light streamed in, illuminating her

bottles of homemade wine. It illuminated the cedar wall, the translucent rainwater catchment tanks outside, and the Sun Shower bladder hanging from a branch. As the silence stretched out, I knew this
nonanswer was her answer. Ultimately, we must figure it out for ourselves, whispering alone into the well, attentive to what comes back
up. Through the window, a radiant No Name Creek shimmered, and
the sunlight gathered in brilliant intensity around Jackie.

This is the same light that infuses my bedroom in Bolivia.
Amaya is the first to notice it, and she nudges me awake. *"Hay luz,"*
she says. I mutter something about "ten more minutes" and hug her
close. She's quiet for a moment but then insists: *"Ya no es noche. Es
dia."* — "It's not night anymore. It's day now."

We walk outside into a new place — the same one. The home
I've been searching for, I now know, has always been millimeters
away. Home is the luminous everyplace where spirit meets clay.
Change is coming, but I hold Amaya's hand. A dozen butterflies flutter over the garden, inviting us to grab tools and press seeds into this
soft world.

MINDFULNESS

APPENDIX: RESOURCES, CULTURE, COMMUNITY

HERE ARE A FEW SUGGESTIONS on continuing the journey. This brief appendix is a condensation of the much wider network of resources on my website, www.williampowersbooks.com.

PERMACULTURE AND WILDCRAFTING

- *World Wide Opportunities on Organic Farms* (www.wwoof.org): Help out on a family organic farm during your next vacation, in exchange for room, board, and sustainability skills.
- *El Bosque Organic Garlic Farm* (www.vrbo.com/118083): Stan and Rose Mary Crawford have turned a circular stone cabin in their garlic fields into a B&B guesthouse; harvest with them in their revolutionary fields.
- *The Permaculture Research Institute of Australia* (http://perma culture.org.au): Study the things our grandparents knew but our parents forgot with Bill Mollison, or check out his book, *Permaculture: A Designer's Manual*.

- *Being Self Sufficient-ish* (www.selfsufficientish.com): Twins Andy and Dave Hamilton give practical advice on extracting oneself from the corporate economy — even without taking an all-out permaculture plunge.

SOFT ECONOMY

- *Find a farmers market* near your home by visiting the US Department of Agriculture website: http://apps.ams.usda.gov/ FarmersMarkets.
- *Slow Food USA* (http://slowfoodusa.org): Support good, clean, and fair food through a local chapter of the nonprofit Slow Food group.
- *Socially responsible investing* can be done through Social Funds (http://socialfunds.com). For financial advice and help cutting up your credit cards, visit Motley Fool (www.fool.com).
- *New American Dream* (www.newdream.org): Ideas for shifting American culture from overdeveloped to enough.
- *CouchSurfing* (www.couchsurfing.org): Find places to stay for free worldwide through the nonprofit organization Couch-Surfing.
- *Buy fairly traded goods* from the Bolivian coffee cooperatives with whom I worked and from others on the creative edge of the Global South through the Fair Trade Federation (www.fair tradefederation.org).
- *Calculate your carbon footprint.* Input information about your lifestyle, and the Carbon Footprint website (www.carbonfoot print.com) will compare your carbon footprint to other averages around the world.

WARRIOR PRESENCE

- *Healthy, Happy, Holy Organization* (http://3HO.org): This nonprofit kundalini yoga institute holds solstice yoga retreats and a White Tantric Yoga event. Their challenging eight-day retreat in New Mexico was one of the most rewarding weeks I've had.

- *Thich Nhat Hahn Plum Village retreats* (http://plumvillage .org): Attend spiritual retreats at Thich Nhat Hahn's retreat center in Plum Village, France.
- *Alternative children's education* includes homeschooling and the Steiner Waldorf Schools (steinerwaldorf.org).

FURTHER READING AND (NON)DOING

- *A Garlic Testament: Seasons on a Small New Mexico Farm* by Stan Crawford: Stan's masterpiece, as discussed in chapter 8.
- *Your Money or Your Life* by Vicki Robin and Joe Dominguez: This book provided many of the ideas for chapter 19; it helps to reshape household economy as rebellion.
- *How to Be Idle* by Tom Hodgkinson: This is a witty manifesto on working less.
- *Anam Cara* by John O'Donohue: This exquisite book contributed to the ideas in chapter 23.
- *The End of Nature* by Bill McKibben: McKibben continues to be an intelligent voice for sustainability in American culture. Other recommended books include *Enough*; *Hope, Human and Wild*; and *Deep Economy*.
- *Yes!* (www.yesmagazine.org): *Yes!* is a positive, nonprofit news magazine with up-to-date happenings on the creative edge.

ACKNOWLEDGMENTS

I AM DEEPLY GRATEFUL to the many people who have helped with the creation of this book over the past three years.

Thank you to the friends who have read and given feedback on earlier drafts of *Twelve by Twelve*: Carolyn Burns Bass, Juliette Beck, Nick Buxton, Laurel Corona, Stan Crawford, Melissa Draper, Bethany Hensel, Dan Keane, Jessica Keener, Faith Krinsky, Karen Powers Liebhaber, Peter Manseau, Drew McMorrow, Evan Meyer, and Pamela Russ. Your ideas flow through these pages.

I am grateful to the World Policy Institute for its generous support for the book. WPI's executive director, Michele Wucker, and director of development, Kate Maloff, have assisted the book and its ideas in innumerable ways.

New World Library's extraordinary team has been wonderful to work with. A special thank you to Jason Gardner, my skilled and compassionate editor, as well as my dynamo publicist, Monique Muhlenkamp, and the imaginative, supportive Munro Magruder.

Copy editor Jeff Campbell went beyond the call of duty, providing *Twelve by Twelve* with deft line and structural editing.

I am very thankful to my agent, Michael Bourret, whose friendliness and professionalism make him a pleasure to work with.

Three interns, Tanushree Isaacman, Jonathan Kime, and Morgan Lehman, provided outstanding research assistance, editing, and outreach around the book.

For writing retreats, thanks to Jacques Schillings (Amsterdam), Sat Gurprasad Kaur (Espanola, NM), Walter of the Circle A Ranch (Cuba, NM), and also to Amy and Andrew Powers for inspiration at the Vermont dome.

And thank you to my mother and father, as always, for your love and encouragement.

Finally, a resounding, embracing thank you to everyone who appears in the book. I am incredibly grateful that you are part of my life and of this story.

INDEX

ABOUT THE AUTHOR

WILLIAM POWERS is the author of two critically acclaimed books. His Liberia memoir, *Blue Clay People: Seasons on Africa's Fragile Edge* (2005) received a *Publishers Weekly* starred review, and *Whispering in the Giant's Ear: A Frontline Chronicle from Bolivia's War on Globalization* (2006) has been featured on NPR's *Fresh Air* with Terry Gross and in *Newsweek*. For over a decade Powers has led development aid and conservation initiatives in Latin America, Africa, and Washington, DC. From 2002 to 2004 he managed the socioeconomic components of a project in the Bolivian Amazon that won a prize from Harvard's JFK School of Government. His essays on global issues have appeared in the *New York Times*, the *Washington Post*, *Slate*, the *Sun*, and the *International Herald Tribune* and have been syndicated to three hundred newspapers around the world. He has appeared on NPR's *Living on Earth*, *The Leonard Lopate Show*, *West Coast Live*, *Left Jab*, and *World Vision Report* as well as on local public television stations and Book TV. Powers is an increasingly active speaker at think tanks, policy gatherings, and writers' conferences. He has worked at the World Bank and Conservation International and holds degrees from Brown and Georgetown. He lives part-time in New York City.

www.williampowersbooks.com.

NEW WORLD LIBRARY is dedicated to publishing books and other media that inspire and challenge us to improve the quality of our lives and the world.

We are a socially and environmentally aware company, and we strive to embody the ideals presented in our publications. We recognize that we have an ethical responsibility to our customers, our staff members, and our planet.

We serve our customers by creating the finest publications possible on personal growth, creativity, spirituality, wellness, and other areas of emerging importance. We serve New World Library employees with generous benefits, significant profit sharing, and constant encouragement to pursue their most expansive dreams.

As a member of the Green Press Initiative, we print an increasing number of books with soy-based ink on 100 percent postconsumer-waste recycled paper. Also, we power our offices with solar energy and contribute to nonprofit organizations working to make the world a better place for us all.

Our products are available
in bookstores everywhere.
For our catalog, please contact:

New World Library
14 Pamaron Way
Novato, California 94949

Phone: 415-884-2100 or 800-972-6657
Catalog requests: Ext. 50
Orders: Ext. 52
Fax: 415-884-2199
Email: escort@newworldlibrary.com

To subscribe to our electronic newsletter, visit
www.newworldlibrary.com